Municipal Management Series

Managing Local Government:
Cases in Decision Making

International
City/County
ICMA
Management
Association

The International City/County Management Association (ICMA) is the professional and educational organization for appointed administrators and assistant administrators in local government. The purposes of ICMA are to enhance the quality of local government and to nurture and assist professional local government administrators in the United States and other countries. To further its mission, ICMA develops and disseminates new approaches to management through training programs, information services, and publications.

Local government managers—carrying a wide range of titles—serve cities, towns, counties, councils of governments, and state/provincial associations of local governments. They serve at the direction of elected councils and governing boards. ICMA serves these managers and local governments through many programs that aim at mproving the manager's professional competence and strengthening the quality of all local governments.

ICMA was founded in 1914, adopted its City Management Code of Ethics in 1924, and established its Institute for Training in Municipal Administration in 1934. The institute, in turn, provided the basis for the Municipal Management Series, generally termed the "ICMA Green Books."

ICMA's interests and activities include public management education; standards of ethics for members; the *Municipal Year Book* and other data services; urban research; newsletters; a monthly magazine, *Public Management*; and other publications. ICMA's efforts toward the improvement of local government management—as represented by this book—are offered for all local governments and educational institutions.

Editorial board

Municipal Management Series

Managing Local Government: Cases in Decision Making

Second Edition

Published by the
International
City/County
Management
Association

Editor
James M. Banovetz
Northern Illinois University

Municipal Management Series

Managing Local Government: Cases in Decision Making

Advanced Supervisory Practices

Effective Communication

The Effective Local Government Manager

Effective Supervisory Practices

Emergency Management

Local Government Police Management

Management of Local Planning

Management of Local Public Works

Management Policies in Local Government Finance

Managing Fire Services

Managing Local Government Finance: Cases in Decision Making

Managing Small Cities and Counties

The Practice of Local Government Planning

The Practice of State and Regional Planning

Service Contracting

Library of Congress Cataloging-in-Publication Data

Managing local government : cases in decision making / editor, James
    M. Banovetz. — 2nd ed.
        p.   cm. — (Municipal management series)
      ISBN 0-87326-157-7 (pbk.)
      1. Local government — Decision-making — Case studies.   I. Banovetz,
    James M.   II. International City/County Management Association.
    III. Series.
    JS78.M27   1998
    352.14 — dc21   98-22838
                                                                CIP

Printed in the United States of America

06 05 04 03 02 01 00 99 98
7 6 5 4 3 2 1

Foreword

Managing Local Government: Cases in Decision Making first appeared in 1990 as part of ICMA's enduring effort to maintain a strong link with the academic programs that educate tomorrow's local government managers. This link has its formal institutional expression in the ICMA/NASPAA Task Force on Local Government Management Education, composed of academic members appointed by the National Association of Schools of Public Affairs and Administration (NASPAA) and practicing local government managers appointed by ICMA. This task force proposed the first edition of this book, which was published in the Municipal Management Series, whose ''Green Books'' are developed with substantial input from those who teach in the various public administration specialties.

This second edition of the book was developed with the same objective as that of the first edition: to give readers and students a taste of the kinds of decision challenges that confront professional administrators working in governments at the community level. The second edition pays special attention to critical contemporary local management policy areas. It provides better and more up-to-date coverage of the personnel and budgeting functions. It includes a separate section on planning and economic development, concerns that are dominating so many local government agendas at the turn of the century. It also focuses more attention on privatization, with three different cases dealing directly with this managerial option and its implications.

The second edition has been expanded to twenty-one cases, including twelve cases unchanged from the first edition. Of the remaining nine cases, seven are entirely new, one

has been previously published in ICMA's *Managing Local Government Finance: Cases in Decision Making* (1996), and one case, ''County Prison Overtime,'' was originally published in the first edition and then revised and published in *Managing Local Government Finance*. It is reprinted here in its revised format.

More of the cases in this book have been written by practitioners—the very people who confronted these problems in their own careers. Fourteen, or two-thirds, of the cases were written solely by practitioners. Scholars wrote four cases and collaborated with practitioners in writing the other three. Thus, seventeen cases, more than 80 percent, contain a practitioner's view of the problems confronting local government administrators.

As in the first edition, all but one of the cases in this book describe situations that actually happened and real problems to which an actual local government administrator had to respond. The single exception, case 11, is based on a composite of similar problems that the author, a practicing local government administrator, confronted or with which he was familiar.

To improve their usefulness for teaching and to protect the parties involved, all cases use fictitious names and have been edited to clarify issues and eliminate extraneous detail. While all of these cases are factually accurate in their critical components, ICMA and the editor do not intend for these cases to be regarded as wholly accurate factual portrayals of the events on which they are based. In two cases, the authors have asked that their studies be published anonymously to protect further the privacy of those involved.

On the recommendation of classroom instructors who have used the first edition of this book, this edition omits the aftermath from the cases; students will thus have to work on these issues without knowing what decisions were actually made or what the consequences of those decisions were. These case studies thus capture the flavor of local management, not by giving readers a formula for problem resolution, but rather by describing the complex legal, environmental, and human considerations that lead up to a managerial decision and then throwing the decision into the reader's lap. As such, the cases provide a basis for both discussions of real-life local government policy and simulated policy deliberations.

The case outcomes and their consequences, or aftermaths, are provided together with final discussion questions in a supplement to this book, *Supplement to Managing Local Government: Cases in Decision Making,* which is available separately from ICMA. Thus, readers and classroom instructors have the option to use these cases either with or without concluding information about how the case was ultimately resolved in real life. The supplement also contains the essay "The Case Approach," by John J. Gargan, which appeared in the first edition, as well as suggestions about how the cases might be used as decision-making simulations.

ICMA is grateful to James M. Banovetz for his diligent work in preparing this second edition. Dr. Banovetz selected the cases for inclusion in the book on the basis of a special editorial board's recommendations. ICMA extends special thanks to the members of the editorial board: Rita Athas, assistant to the mayor, Chicago, Illinois; Alexander E. Briseño, city manager, San Antonio, Texas; George A. Caravalho, city manager, Santa Clarita, California; Eugene H. Denton, county administrator, Johnson County, Olathe, Kansas; Prisilla Hernandez, deputy city manager, Peoria, Arizona; Mary Jane Hirt, assistant professor, Department of Political Science, Indiana University of Pennsylvania, Indiana, Pennsylvania; Roger L. Kemp, city manager, Meriden, Connecticut; J. Thomas Lundy, county manager, Catawba County, Newton, North Carolina; Sylvester Murray, professor, Cleveland State University, Maxine Goodman Levin College of Urban Affairs, Cleveland, Ohio; Charldean Newell, regents professor, Department of Public Administration, University of North Texas, Denton, Texas; Roger Storey, deputy city manager, Stockton, California; and James H. Svara, professor and M.P.A. program director, Department of Political Science and Public Administration, North Carolina State University, Raleigh, North Carolina.

The editor wishes to acknowledge the valuable suggestions for the book made by Mark Levin, city administrator, Maryland Heights, Missouri, and current co-chair of the ICMA-NASPAA joint task force that suggested the development of the first edition of this book; Ruth Hoogland DeHoog, University of North Carolina at Greensboro; Paul Nordin, Fountain Hills, Arizona; and Jeffrey Straussman, the Maxwell School, Syracuse University. A special note of appreciation is owed to June Kubasiak who provided secretarial assistance to the editor and managed all of the communications with the editorial board and case authors. Finally, the editor expresses his special appreciation to his wife, Audrey, who provided multiple kinds of assistance and put up with many hours of loneliness to see this book completed.

Several ICMA staff members contributed to the project: Barbara Moore, director of publishing and data services, provided editorial leadership and guidance; Verity Weston-Truby served as project editor; Jane Gold copyedited the manuscript; Julie Butler provided administrative support; and Dawn Leland supervised production.

William H. Hansell Jr.
Executive Director, ICMA

Contents

Matrix of
coverage

Matrix of coverage

A major advantage of the case approach to teaching is the flexibility it offers the instructor. Following is a matrix listing topics that are typically covered in urban management and other public administration courses, with an indication of the cases that relate to those topics. As the matrix shows, these cases can be used with virtually any course outline and in conjunction with a wide selection of other materials.

Subject	1	2	3	4	5	6	7	8	9	10	11	12	13	14	15	16	17	18	19	20	21
1. Kind and level of government																					
County							7					12				16			19		
Small city	1	2						8		10			13				17	18			
Medium city			3	4		6									15					20	21
Large city					5				9		11			14							
2. The context of local government																					
Governing structure	1			4													17				
Politics	1		3	4	5			8				12	13		15			18	19	20	21
Intergovernmental relations						6	7		9	10		12									
Public/private interface		2					7	8	9	10	11				15	16					
Privatization										10	11				15	16					
3. Professional administration																					
Bureaucracy		2			5		7								15	16	17		19		
Policy making			3					8	9	10	11					16		18			
Administrative leadership	1	2	3		5					10			13	14	15	16	17	18	19		21
Administration in a political setting	1		3				7	8				12		14	15			18	19	20	21
Administrators and policy making			3	4		6		8		10		12				16		18			
Relations: Elected and appointed officials	1	2					7	8				12					17		19	20	21
Relations: Appointed officials and community		2	3	4	5		7														21
Ethics	1					6		8				12	13			16				20	21
4. Management theory																					
Organization theory				4						10				14	15	16	17				
Administrative organization		2		4						10					15		17				
Decision making					5	6			9	10	11					16		18	19		21
Program analysis and evaluation			3				7			10	11	12				16		18	19		
Finance		2	3		5				9	10	11	12			15	16	17	18	19		
Budgeting			3				7									16	17	18	19		
Personnel	1									10			13	14	15	16				20	21
Labor-management relations															15	16					21
Affirmative action														14							
Management of change		2	3	4		6		8	9	10	11					16	17	18			
5. Policy and service functions																					
Planning						6		8	9			12									
Economic development			3			6		8	9							16					
Housing							7	8													
Human services							7					12									
Neighborhood redevelopment								8				12									
Public works											11			14		16					
Environment								8								16					
Land use						6		8	9			12									
Parks and recreation					5			8													
Police	1																				21
Corrections						6													19		
Fire													13		15						
Sanitation											11										
Health										10											

Part one:
Introduction

The nature of local government

James M. Banovetz

Persons born at the turn of the twentieth century experienced what may have been history's most interesting time to be alive. It was a time of radical change. In the space of a single lifespan, society went from the horse-drawn carriage to the horseless carriage, to the automobile, to the airplane, to the spaceship. Labor went from the sweatshop to the assembly line to the robot. Calculation went from the adding machine to the mechanical calculator, to the electronic calculator, to the computer. African Americans went from the farm to jobs in unskilled labor to factories, to colleges, and to positions of leadership in business, industry, and government.

By the turn of the century, local government, too, had come a long way from the days when Tom Lincoln, Abe's dad, had his property taxes reduced if he used his horse and farm implements to maintain the county road that bordered the Lincoln farm in Kentucky. Local government had grown from a self-help, neighborly arrangement to a very large and very corrupt business, especially in urban areas. In fact, the condition of local government was such that James Bryce, in *The American Commonwealth,* wrote: "There is no denying that the government of cities is the one conspicuous failure of the United States."[1]

This condition, too, changed dramatically in the twentieth century. Like every other institution, local government was affected by advances in transportation, changes in industrial methods and technology, and vast sociological transformations. At the same time, local governments moved to reject the characterization given them by Lincoln Steffens when he wrote *The Shame of the Cities.*[2] The operations of local government were significantly altered by the good government movement, with its Australian ballot, nonpartisan elections, use of the referendum and recall, elimination of corruption, and emphasis on merit and the Protestant ethic in public service; by structural reforms that produced at-large elections and the council-manager system; by the invention of the private automobile, federal housing programs, and the resulting emergence of suburban communities and government; by *Baker v. Carr* (which established the one-person, one-vote principle), the reemergence of wards for legislative representation, and decennial reapportionment; and by the Nineteenth Amendment and the civil rights movement, which opened the door to participation in local politics and government for people who had been excluded.

Democracy and local government

Through all these changes, however, the basic nature and function of local government remained the same. Local government has always been the government of the community; it is the social, economic, and political ordering of people's activities where they live and work. It is interaction among neighbors for the common good.

In the earliest American communities, local government was simply the social organization of people who lived in the same frontier community—people who helped each other with barn raising, birthing, and healing; people who farmed, hunted, worshiped, and sometimes fought together for the common defense. As communities grew, the structure of social organization—of government—became more complex with the selection of leaders and the assignment of duties. Even then, however, government retained its essential linkage to the people: it still drew its leadership from the local citizenry and provided the social organization and the physical services needed to support people as they went about their daily tasks.

Local government also was the cornerstone of the governmental system. The New England township, the Atlantic coastal city, and the southern county offered the structure within which colonial citizens met, interacted, and debated the issues of the day, and from which they sent representatives to serve in their legislatures. It was in these local governments that American democracy first emerged. It was to these local governments that Thomas Jefferson referred when he spoke of the "cradle of liberty" and "grass-roots democracy." It was from these local governments west of the Appalachian Mountains that Andrew Jackson brought his concept of "government by the common man" to the nation's political culture. And it was from the small towns of the Midwest—the New Salems, Vandalias, and Springfields—that Abraham Lincoln brought his sense of government "of the people, by the people, for the people."

Local government today

Even today, local government is still the level of government that is closest to the people and that delivers the public services that are a part of people's everyday lives. Henry Churchill best captured the relationship between the people and their local government in the title of his book *The City Is the People*.[3]

National and state governments are housed in distant capitals. Their leaders are persons who make a business of government and politics, and who depart from their home communities to legislate, execute, and adjudicate the laws. National and state governments are responsible for crucial functions—for example, national defense, maintenance of economic stability, protection of civil rights, economic regulation, environmental protection, public health, and interstate highways. They are responsive to citizen action and opinion, but most citizen interaction with these governments is channeled through interest group activity.

Local governments, on the other hand, are close to home. Except in the largest communities, their leaders are friends and neighbors who hold elective office on a part-time, temporary basis, serving out of a sense of civic obligation rather than career ambition. These local governments provide another array of services. They build and maintain streets, parks, and schools; supply clean water and treat sewage; pick up and dispose of the garbage; provide police services, ambulances, and fire protection; offer aid to the impoverished and the handicapped; support mental health services, senior citizens' programs, and youth activities; and are the first source of assistance in emergencies. In short, they provide the direct public services on which people depend every day. They, too, are responsive to citizen action and opinion, and most citizens deal directly and personally with their local officials without the intervention of lobbyists or interest groups. This means that pressures from constituents are more immediate and direct at the local level. As Churchill noted, local government "is the people."

Local government administration

Local governments are served by administrators, who are responsible for the basic public services the governments provide. The way in which these administrators perform this function ultimately affects not only the effectiveness of local government but also the viability of grass-roots democracy. In this sense, local public administrators are custodians of democracy, discharging the "sacred trust" about which Woodrow Wilson wrote in the 1887 essay in which he laid the foundation for professional public administration.[4]

The evolution of professional local government administration was a major plank in the reform platform of the good government movement that emerged late in the nineteenth century. Professionalization evolved during one of those rare times in history when everything came together:

The American middle class . . . was growing as the nation's economy changed from artisanry to industry. Public service professions were forming, beginning with public schools and public health in the mid-19th century and expanding later as associations of public officials were formed in finance, planning, recreation, parks, personnel, and city management.

It was not enough to organize a campaign and elect a reform mayor and council. Local governments had to have accountants, engineers, planners, and park and playground superintendents. From there it was just a short step to the manager.[5]

A strong commitment to professional administrative leadership and the merit concept in employment continues to be a cornerstone of the Model City Charter promulgated and kept up-to-date by the National Civic League.[6]

Despite its efficacy at producing good government in an era of politics and corruption, professional local government administration grew slowly and, initially, only in cities. It was not until after the Second World War, at midcentury, that professional local government administration really took hold. Council-manager government became the most common form of government in the nation in medium-sized and large cities; strong mayor-council governments began to incorporate professional chief administrative officer (CAO) positions; and county governments began adopting county administrator forms. Special districts, municipal leagues, councils of governments, and associations of local government officials also relied with increasing frequency on professional administrators to function as their CAOs.

With such administrators serving as role models and emphasizing professional competence as a standard for performance and promotion, the trend toward professionalism radiated outward and downward in local government organizations. Clerks and treasurers established programs of professional certification for these offices; administrative departments—especially in police, fire, public works, planning, finance, personnel, health, parks and recreation, and social services—were increasingly headed by persons with professional education and experience. Currently, the trend toward professionalization is reaching to such middle-management supervisors as police sergeants, fire lieutenants, and public works division heads, and to such specialists as management analysts, planning aides, health officers, accountants, data management technicians, and social workers.

The difference a professional makes

The presence of professionals in local government does not mean that government is raised above the level of the common citizen. Professionals supplement, rather than replace, the civic-minded community leaders whose assumption of local government office ensures that these governments are run for and by local people. Professionals perform a role quite different from that of the elected leadership. Specifically, they add four values to the operation of local government:

1. Technical competence based on training, experience, and access to information

2. An informed, long-range vision of contemporary trends and their intersection with community needs
3. Political neutrality
4. A principled commitment to serve the public interest.

Ideally, professional administrators should be selected on the basis of their training, experience, and demonstrated competence in both organizational leadership and technical skills. Administrators should know how to acquire the information they need to perform their jobs and to advise on policy matters, and they should be expert in methods of analyzing that information for policy makers. They must be skilled at working with constituents, elected officials, other administrative leaders, subordinates, and representatives of other agencies. They must, in short, be capable of solving a local government's problems, not by reflexively turning to "the way we handled this the last time," but by creatively applying new knowledge and experience.

Such problem-solving technologies should also encompass long-range vision. Democratic notions of responsiveness—calling for official accountability at intervals corresponding to the timing of elections—tend to emphasize short-range, immediate consequences in public sector decision making. Increasingly, however, the public interest requires a longer-term perspective. Although city councils are elected for two- or four-year terms, they are most effective when working to improve the quality of life five to twelve years in the future.[7] To achieve that time perspective, they need the help that professionals, trained to study long-term trends, can give in terms of vision, insights, information, and empirical analysis of the likely consequences of alternative courses of immediate action. They need both encouragement and support from their professional staffs if their work is to venture far into the uncertainties of the future.

The tenets of professional public administration demand nonpartisan official behavior from the local government administrator. Such a position frees the administrator from dependence on electoral time frames as well as from electoral politics, thus facilitating long-range planning and policy making. But the principle of nonpartisanship in administration means much more: it means that professional administrators are committed to "serving equally and impartially all members of the governing body of the (local government) they serve, regardless of party."[8] It means that they leave politics and legislative policy making to elected officials while they concentrate on the delivery of public services to the community.

These objectives of professional public administrators are reinforced and supplemented by the professionals' principled commitment to serve the public interest. That commitment is extended by the codes of ethics adopted by the American Society for Public Administration (ASPA) and the International City/County Management Association (ICMA).[9] As articulated in those codes, professional local government administrators are expected to "demonstrate the highest standards of personal integrity," "serve the public with respect, concern, courtesy, and responsiveness,"[10] "recognize that the chief function of local government at all times is to serve the best interests of all the people," and "be dedicated to the highest ideals of honor and integrity in all public and personal relationships in order that the (administrator) may merit the respect and confidence of the elected officials, of other officials and employees, and of the public."[11]

All these attributes are meaningless, however, if professional administrators are not responsive to the people they serve—the citizens of the local community. In a democracy, the ultimate test of efficacy is less efficiency than it is responsibility, less effectiveness than it is responsiveness. Professional administrative leaders are better than political appointees only if they are equally responsive. To promote such responsiveness, local government practice has been to appoint local CAOs to serve "at the pleasure of the council" instead of for a fixed term. As county and city managers are wont to say, "My term of office lasts until the next council meeting." Since the council can remove them at any time, they trade job security for public responsiveness, thereby achieving this last, and ultimate, value for professional administration.

Professionals, elected officials, and the public

As powerful as it is, the imminent threat of dismissal is not by itself a sufficient base for defining the relationship between professional administrators and the political system they serve. That relationship also encompasses three other considerations: the role of elected officials, professional principles, and public accountability.

Role of elected officials

Of the above considerations, the most functional on a daily basis is the role of the elected officials. They are the central elements in the organizational structure of local government; they are the foundation of the representative system, ensuring that local government remains the government of the common person run by local people. Local elected officials typically are long-time residents who are elected because of the breadth of their personal contacts in the community and the esteem in which they are held locally. Their contribution to local government is based not on their knowledge or experience in dealing with the technical issues of government administration, but rather on their ability to reflect community values in policy discussions and to work with local residents in building support for needed public policy changes.

The rudiments of the relationship between elected officials and professional administrators are typically defined by law—that is, by state statute or local ordinance spelling out the duties of the administrator. The *Model City Charter* articulates a standard format for this relationship: All powers are vested in the council except for those specified elsewhere, an exception that includes the delegation to the manager of specific responsibility to make appointments, direct administrative operations, enforce the laws, prepare and administer the budget, and advise the council on policy matters.[12]

Strict adherence to such a delineation of roles can prove to be more troublesome than helpful, however, and the prudent manager will work out an understanding with the council relative to their respective roles rather than standing inflexibly on statements of principle. In practice, the manager may become involved in some questions that could be construed as policy; similarly, the manager may find it useful to consult the council on key personnel appointments, even though these are technically the manager's responsibility. The local government administrative structure functions best when its participants —selected officials, the CAO, administrative staff, department heads, and employees—work together as a coordinated team, performing mutually understood roles and supporting one another.

The responsibility for defining roles and relationships is best left to negotiation between the administrator and elected officials, not to the language of statutes, ordinances, and codes. Such negotiations should be repeated, at a minimum, whenever new persons assume elective office. Most important, the negotiations must always be based on a mutual recognition that it is the elected officials who most directly represent the citizens, who are the direct link with democratic theory and principles, and thus who must carry the burden of reporting to, and interacting with, the citizenry.

Professional principles

This recognition of the role of elected officials, however, does not reduce the administrator's responsibility. Indeed, the second consideration defining the administrator's relationship with the public in a democratic system—professional principles—demands no less. No fewer than seven of the twelve tenets in the ICMA Code of Ethics refer to the administrator's relationships to elected officials and responsibilities to the public. The code requires dedication to "the concepts of effective and democratic local government by responsible elected officials" and to "the highest ideals of honor and integrity in all public and personal relationships," and it directs administrators to provide elected officials "with facts and advice on matters of policy" and to "keep the community informed on local government affairs."[13]

Public accountability

Keeping the community informed is an important component of public accountability, the third consideration defining the professional administrator's relationship to the political system. Public accountability—the need to operate in the goldfish bowl of public information and to submit to public observation of official behavior, public oversight, and public reaction to administrative activity—is a constant in local government administration. The intensity of such accountability, of having to work within the narrow confines of open meeting laws, freedom of information acts, publication requirements, and neighborhood-level public hearings, serves both to limit the administrator's freedom of action and to ensure direct and immediate responsiveness to the public. Perhaps more than any other administrator in either private or public organizations, the local government administrator must work closely with, and under the direct supervision of, the individual members of the public being served.

What does it all mean?

Local government, and the professional administrator's role in it, is a big job. It is big not just because of the number of people or the volume of resources involved in it on a national scale, but because it is so important to people's everyday lives.

Local government serves the people directly, immediately, daily, and personally. It is the part of government that citizens can best understand and appreciate, to which they can most easily communicate their grievances, from which they are most able to achieve responsiveness, and against which they can most effectively retaliate when they are dissatisfied. It is the cornerstone of their democracy, the base from which their political principles have been derived and from which they will continue to evolve. It is the ultimate manifestation of "government by the people."

Because the professional administrator serves a central role in local government, whether as CAO, department head, or supporting staff member, the challenge of serving at the local level is enormous. It is a challenge that manifests itself in the big issues, such as economic development, neighborhood design, and tax policy, and in the everyday matters of cost containment, humane and fair treatment of citizens and employees, and relationships with the public. The administrator's response to this challenge contributes significantly to the success of local government and, consequently, to the quality of life in the nation's communities and the quality of democracy at its grass roots. In this sense, the responsibility of the task is awesome.

The administrator's success in fulfilling this responsibility is best measured by the aggregation of the decisions—small as well as large—that make up the pattern of daily activity. This book is designed to mirror that aggregation through the presentation of a representative sample of actual cases requiring administrative decisions. By so doing, the book provides a unique insight into the real-life challenge of local government and also offers a vehicle through which practicing and future administrators can develop, test, and evaluate their own decision-making capabilities.

The book is designed to promote a fuller understanding of local government administration. The cases are presented in an order commonly used in local government courses, but the matrix of coverage that precedes this introduction provides a supplement to the table of contents by showing how the cases can be applied to other kinds of courses or educational formats. The matrix shows the range of administrative topics covered by each case, suggesting the various kinds of discussions that can be supported by its use.

By making this collection of cases available, the book seeks to sustain and promote the ultimate goal of professional local government administration: local governments that are both effective and responsive in the service of the people they represent.

1   James Bryce, *The American Commonwealth,* vol. 2 (London: Macmillan and Co., 1988), quoted in *Classics of Urban Politics and Administration*, ed. William J. Murin (Oak Park, Ill.: Moore Publishing Co., 1982), 3.

2   Lincoln Steffens, *The Shame of the Cities* (New York: Hill and Wang, 1904).

3   Henry S. Churchill, *The City Is the People* (New York: Reynal and Hitchcock, 1945).

4   Woodrow Wilson, "The Study of Administration," *Political Science Quarterly* 2 (June 1887).

5   David S. Arnold, "ICMA and the City Manager: The Plan, the Profession, the Association," exhibit at the ICMA Annual Conference, Des Moines, Iowa, 1989.

6   National Civic League, *Model City Charter*, 7th ed. (Denver, Colo.: National Civic League, 1989). See especially Articles III and IV, pp. 33–43. The charter "stresses the basic principle of the council-manager form that the manager is a *qualified, professional administrator*" (p. 37, emphasis added) and "should strongly state the commitment to the merit principle" (p. 42).

7   Laurence Rutter, *The Essential Community: Local Government in the Year 2000* (Washington, D.C.: International City Management Association, 1980), 17.

8   Guideline for tenet 7, the ICMA Code of Ethics, which is reprinted as an appendix to this book.

9   The ICMA Code of Ethics. A convenient reference for the "ASPA Code of Ethics and Implementation Guidelines" is *Ethical Insight, Ethical Action: Perspectives for the Local Government Manager*, ed. Elizabeth K. Kellar (Washington, D.C.: International City Management Association, 1988), 161–6.

10 Excerpts are from the ASPA Code of Ethics.

11 Excerpts are from the ICMA Code of Ethics.

12 National Civic League, *Model City Charter*, Articles II and III.

13 The ICMA Code of Ethics, tenets 1, 3, 5, and 9.

Part two: The role of professional administration

Introduction to part two: The role of professional administration

Future political historians will remember the twentieth century as the one in which professional administration came to local government. Council-manager government was born in the century's first decade; the concept of professional administration quickly took root in school districts and special districts, but it had to prove its value and its compatibility with local politics and grass-roots democracy before becoming widely accepted as the preferred form of municipal administration in the second half of the century. Counties were slower to employ administrative professionals, owing to the closer linkages between their elected leadership and state-level politics. Some states moved to professionalize county government in the middle of the century, and by the last decade of the century, this trend was definitely in full swing.

Part two presents two cases that provide an insight into the difference that a professional administrator can make. The difference is rooted in the values of the twentieth-century local government reform movement. That movement sought to change local government from its nineteenth-century "unreformed" emphasis on politics, special interests, and political influence as key elements in decision making to a "reformed" emphasis on public interest, scientific management, and technical expertise. The adoption of council-manager government and, in many instances, the appointment of a professional city or county administrator, are usually associated with this change in the value structure used to manage local government. The two cases in this section demonstrate the differences between the ways in which reformed and traditional, or unreformed, governments address key local government management functions.

In the first case, a manager is faced with political pressure as he seeks to apply professional values in the recruitment of personnel—specifically, in this case, of a police chief. Few positions in local government are more critical to the delivery of public services than that of police chief. Perhaps more than in the case of any other position, police chief selection is complicated by political pressures as different community groups attempt to protect themselves by ensuring the appointment of someone who, in their opinion, would be "the right kind of person." This case describes the intensity of the politics that can emerge in police chief selection, and it contrasts the recruitment values and approach associated with the kind of leadership brought to local government by a professional administrator in a reformed government with those typically taken in a traditional, nonreformed system, where political considerations or "clout" are the primary selection considerations.

The second case offers insight into the kind of process differences associated with the management of money or, more specifically in this case, the way in which government purchasing is handled. It also portrays some of the difficulties and pressures that can accompany the process of changing from an unreformed to a reformed system of operation. As the case indicates, this process of change is never easy, not even when supported by political leaders, because it involves alterations in time-honored and familiar ways of conducting municipal business. Not only must local officials change the way in which they manage the government, but the citizenry must recognize and accept the changes as well. In this case, those citizens involve many of the city's business leaders long accustomed to casual processes for doing business with the city.

By describing professional administrators at work confronting the differences between reformed and unreformed values and processes, these two cases give a representative picture of the continuing tensions between professional and political approaches to managing city and county government.

1

Replacing the police chief

William R. Bridgeo and Paul M. Plaisted

Editor's introduction

Professional managers are expected to increase the efficiency and economy of local government operations. Even more important, however, they bring to their job a set of values that emphasizes the public interest over private and personal interests, that considers long- as well as short-term consequences, that demands competence and qualifications as well as compatibility from employees, and that places integrity over politics in decision making.

These values are usually endorsed by both the general public and the professional administrator, but that endorsement does not ensure their easy application. No matter how much a person or community espouses good government values in principle, the daily operations of government present frequent temptations to put such values aside in order to solve tough problems, achieve personal goals, or simply acquire more power and influence for the governing challenges that lie ahead. Such temptations are fairly common among elected officials and local influentials, who may seek to use government action to achieve private ends, but the temptations can also afflict professional managers, especially when the manager's job is on the line.

This case describes the dilemma of a manager whose attempt to administer in accordance with the tenets of professionalism runs into strong opposition from a politically influential family. The result is an all-too-common scenario: politics intrudes on the manager's prerogative to appoint department heads, threatening a basic tenet of council-manager government. An important value of good government (i.e., the commitment to merit in personnel recruitment) is challenged; long-term community welfare is pitted against short-term political tranquility; local politics and state legislative politics become intermingled; obvious options are all flawed; and the manager faces conflict between his personal well-being and his commitment to professionalism.

The case shows council-manager government in action, facing one of the most severe tests that can confront this form of government. Situations such as the one described here can quickly lead to a twofold demand—not only to fire the manager, but also to change the form of government to one that will "respond to the wishes of the people" (or at least to those people who want more influence over local affairs). It also describes precisely how council-manager government works at its best, making it the most commonly used form of government in all but the nation's smallest and very largest cities, and in a growing number of counties as well.

For those interested in comparisons, the case shows in stark contrast the difference between a purely political approach and a professional approach to leadership recruitment. Competing head-on in this case are the pre-reform and the reform (professional) approaches to local government. The politicians are determined to have their way even if this means circumventing the authority of the manager.

Unhappily, as long as community leaders and elected officials are tempted to expand their personal influence beyond that prescribed by law, the management decision described in this case will be all too common in cities and counties of all sizes.

Case 1
Replacing the police chief

Background

Will Spanning had been in Dover, in his first city manager's job, for five years. When he took the job, he was as well prepared as most novice city managers, having served for three years in another city as an assistant to a seasoned and well-respected city manager. During those years he completed an M.P.A. degree by attending night classes. Shortly thereafter, he had been urged "out of the nest" by his boss and mentor, had applied for several city manager positions, and was hired in Dover.

A northern New England community of about 5,000 residents, Dover serves as the regional center of urban activity in a sparsely populated section of the state. Getting established in Dover had been a constant professional challenge for Spanning, but after five years of hard work, he found himself happy and well adjusted. By then a board member of the state city managers' association and the state municipal league, he was respected by his professional peers.

During his time in Dover, Spanning had revamped the city's financial structure and taken the community from a serious budget deficit to a healthy surplus. Mending a weak financial structure had meant taking some difficult actions through the years, such as reducing city staffing levels. At times, the staff reductions had led to confrontation with organized labor (Dover's full-time employees—police, fire, and public works—were represented by the International Brotherhood of Teamsters), but in the preceding couple of years, the relations between management and labor had stabilized, new contracts had been negotiated, and life between management and labor was relatively peaceful.

At the time of this case, one of Spanning's priorities was an expansion of the community's economic base to stabilize taxes and to allow both for an increase in municipal services and for capital improvements. A number of positive signs indicated that Spanning's economic development strategies might pay off. The city had received several hefty state and federal grants, its business district was being spruced up, and a new wood products manufacturing plant had announced plans to create 130 new jobs for Dover residents.

The police department

The largest police agency within a seventy-five-mile radius, the ten-officer Dover department was also recognized as the most professional force in the area. However, it had experienced its share of difficulties over the years. For almost a decade before Spanning's arrival, the department had been commanded by a strong-willed and conservative police executive, who had succeeded in shaping the department into an almost autonomous organization, largely exempted from the oversight that local government managers usually exercise over police departments.

Soon after Spanning's appointment as city manager, the chief resigned. After a comprehensive selection process, Spanning appointed the deputy chief to fill the position. This choice soon proved ill-advised, for while the new chief had been an outstanding young police supervisor, he was not prepared to deal with the stress of managing an active department with a strong union presence. After only a year in the position, he, too, resigned, and Spanning again faced the task of selecting a new leader for the department. Confronted with a dismal response to the city's advertisement for the position, Spanning was directed by the assistant district attorney toward Charles Johnson, a young but well-educated and well-trained supervisor with the county sheriff's department. Recognizing the challenge and opportunity presented by the Dover chief's position, Johnson agreed to accept the job.

Over the next four years, the relationship between Spanning and Johnson developed into one of mutual trust and respect. While at first very cautious about granting Johnson the authority to make major decisions, Spanning saw that the young police chief learned quickly to cope with the pressures of the job and displayed a willingness to explore nontraditional approaches to the police department's problems.

In contrast to previous Dover police chiefs, Johnson saw the inevitability of budgetary constraints and implemented required staffing reductions while maintaining the level of services expected by the community. Recognizing that the city had relinquished too many management prerogatives in its first two attempts at collective bargaining with its public safety employees, Spanning and Johnson presented a united front in subsequent contract negotiations and managed to reverse the situation in several key areas.

Finally, the most critical dimension of the relationship between Spanning and Johnson was their firm commitment to work together to prevent other actors within the municipal structure from playing the police chief and the city manager against each other. In the past, Dover police chiefs and managers had developed separate power bases within the city council and had sometimes battled publicly over issues and resources. Spanning and Johnson elected not to operate in this fashion. The Dover city charter contained a specific noninterference clause that prohibited council members from exercising direct control over city departments. Whenever a council member would "stop by" the police station to discuss a matter with the chief, Johnson would invariably begin the conversation by subtly referring to the charter clause. Following the conversation, Johnson would immediately communicate the details to Spanning, ensuring that end-around plays were impossible. Similarly, Spanning communicated to Johnson about all matters, whether of a police nature or not, that might have a bearing on either one's ability to perform as a part of the senior management staff of the city. Communicating completely, Spanning and Johnson presented a strong, unified front to political forces that otherwise might have prospered.

At the time this case begins, in early spring, Dover Police Chief Charles Johnson notified Spanning that he had been accepted into a prestigious M.P.A./M.B.A. program and would be resigning his position in time to enroll as a full-time student in September.

Johnson's resignation left Spanning with the disappointment of losing a trusted department head as well as a confidant and friend. Although happy for Johnson's career advancement, Spanning knew that replacing the police chief would be difficult and would require a careful and thorough approach. He resolved to follow a process that had worked well for him in making other senior-level appointments. Furthermore, he expected to take advantage of Johnson's resignation announcement early to minimize the transition gap.

Dover's city government

Like other city charters in New England, Dover's enabling act contains language that establishes the city council as the body authorized to make policy on every aspect of city affairs. The charter also empowers the council to retain a manager, hired on the basis of education and experience, to serve as the city's chief administrative officer with the authority to carry out the policy directives of the council. That authority includes the power to hire and fire all city employees. In return, the council makes the manager fully accountable for the manner in which city employees implement council policies.

While giving the manager the power to hire and fire city employees, however, the Dover charter reserves to the council the power to confirm, or advise and consent to, the manager's appointment of city department heads.

Under the charter, Dover is governed by a seven-member city council, elected at-large for three-year terms. Each year, two seats become vacant on the council so that, in effect, a new council is organized every January with five continuing members and two reelected incumbents or newcomers, as the case may be. From among themselves, the council members elect a mayor to serve as the council chairperson.

The council in place during the spring of Chief Johnson's resignation was a split group, with two distinctly different philosophies on most issues. One group of three Spanning regarded as personal and less objective in its decision making; a second group of three was readier to decide issues solely on their merits; and the seventh member was unpredictable: he wanted to be perceived as objective but was politically ambitious (then running for a seat in the state legislature) and therefore sensitive to pressure from various local constituencies.

The case

When Chief Johnson's resignation became public, Spanning informed the council that he would forthwith begin advertising the position statewide and place notices in appropriate national police journals. Knowing the temptation of some councils and some individual council members to try to be more "appointers" than "confirmers," Spanning designed the recruitment process carefully, hoping to ensure that politics played no role in this critical appointment.

Spanning set up a four-stage screening process. First, he would screen the respondents and invite the several most promising ones to appear before a specially created five-member professional review board. Second, the review board would conduct in-depth interviews and rank the candidates, by consensus, from best to worst. Third, Spanning would interview the top choice and determine whether he and that individual were compatible and whether the candidate could accept the city's compensation package. If the answers were affirmative, Spanning would authorize a thorough background check of that finalist and, all going well, would offer that person the position. Fourth, he would arrange for the council to meet, interview, and confirm his appointment.

Spanning also let it be known that rejection of a candidate by the council would not mean going down the list until someone the council preferred was chosen. Rather, rejection would trigger a new search, starting the entire process over again.

Finally, and most important, he placed on the five-member review panel well-respected police and management professionals from other similar communities, and he offered the chairmanship of the panel to one of the community's most respected lawyers, C. Abbot White, who had served as part-time city solicitor for thirty years in addition to conducting his private practice. White was noted for his impartiality and good judgment. A lifelong resident of Dover, he ensured high-quality local representation on the panel and added credibility to a process still rather foreign in Dover.

It was at this point that the problems began.

Shortly after Spanning announced his selection process, he was visited in his office by Councilman Arnold Fornby, a member of the group that Spanning felt lacked objectivity. Fornby and the other members of his group on the council shared certain characteristics. None had the advantage of any formal education beyond secondary or trade school, all were lifelong residents of Dover who had had little exposure to the outside world (with the possible exception of military service), and—probably most important—all had, over the years, seen friends and family members leave the area in search of economic opportunity because such opportunity was so limited in Dover. Raised in poverty, scrapping for what status they had achieved in Dover during their lifetimes, their perspective on who should get good local jobs—and on how they should be picked—was certainly different from that of a professional manager. The group's view was supported by many local voters who came from similar backgrounds.

At this meeting with Spanning, Fornby bluntly stated that Spanning's elaborate selection process was unnecessary, and that he and three other members of the council (a majority) had identified a local candidate they liked who they believed should have the job. They felt so strongly about it, Fornby added, that if need be, they would subvert Spanning's selection process to gain their choice. Furthermore, though it was not made openly, Spanning perceived a veiled threat that failure to concede to this pressure would jeopardize his position. (Like most local government managers, Dover's chief executive was subject to removal at any time by a majority vote of the council.)

Spanning knew that some council members supported his use of a professional selection process, and he knew that there was a good deal of respect for him within the community. He recognized, however, that this issue could become the most serious personal crisis he had faced in five years in Dover. He decided to forge ahead with the process.

The candidates

In contrast to the meager fruits of his efforts four years earlier, Spanning was rewarded with several excellent applicants for the upcoming vacancy for police chief. He and Chief Johnson reviewed the applicants' resumes and ranked them on the basis of experience, education, and training. Three candidates emerged clearly from the pack. All had at least a decade of experience, having progressed through supervisory to management positions within law enforcement:

Chip Durning   With twelve years of law enforcement experience, a bachelor's degree in psychology, and extensive training credits, his current position was chief deputy of a large sheriff's department in the state.

Tom Boyd   With eleven years of law enforcement experience in various capacities with the same police department, Boyd had risen to the rank of deputy chief. Along the way, he had obtained a bachelor's degree in criminal justice and attended a large variety of law enforcement training sessions. The similarities between Boyd's current department and Dover's added to his attractiveness.

Sam Warren   Recently retired from the Boston police department, Warren had risen to the rank of lieutenant and had commanded the personnel office of that department. A master's degree in public administration, coupled with high recommendations from the senior management of the Boston police department, enhanced his attractiveness as a candidate for the Dover position.

Councilman Fornby's local candidate was, of course, also an applicant. He was State Police Trooper Jim Waterhouse. Amiable and a passing acquaintance of Spanning, Waterhouse had a variety of social and community connections to several members of the city council. As a rural patrol officer stationed in

Dover for the previous ten years, he also was popular with a number of local residents. His only law enforcement supervisory experience, however, was as a field training officer for new state police recruits, and he had received no supervisory training since becoming a state police officer. Trooper Waterhouse had not chosen to pursue his formal education beyond high school. This lack of supervisory experience and higher education made Waterhouse a weak candidate compared with the other applicants.

Beyond that, Spanning learned through the local grapevine that Trooper Waterhouse had a very special relationship with a powerful local interest—the O'Hara Transport Company.

Big fish, small pond

In the modest-sized working-class community of Dover, there thrived a large, influential company that employed, on the average, 150 area residents. O'Hara Transport Company was owned and controlled by members of a large family, whose personal and corporate interests were intertwined. The corporation had been started by an Irish firebrand named Frank O'Hara, who came to Dover during the depression and gained fame for his ability to get his one truck to its downstate destination—on time and cargo intact—regardless of weather, mechanical difficulties, or personal health.

Through a combination of hard work, six tough and loyal sons, shrewd politics, and a cynicism regarding the law where it hindered business interests, O'Hara Transport was, at the time of Frank's death, the major employer in Dover. Still family run by the six sons and their progeny, the company had grown very large (125 trucks) and diverse, and was tightly controlled by the six brothers. Various spin-off operations, such as O'Hara Sand and Gravel, Erie Land Development Corporation, Dover Cadillac/Olds, and Dover Orchards, were run by various family members and employed numerous area residents. The six brothers met every morning, at the same restaurant in which their mother had waited on tables many years earlier, to coordinate the business of the day.

By and large, the O'Haras lived in an affluent subdivision constructed twenty years earlier by the Erie Land Development Corporation. When the third generation began rearing its own families, the "compound" expanded, but a number of the thirty or so grandchildren of Frank O'Hara also dispersed throughout the residential neighborhoods of the city. Many went away to college (the first O'Haras to do so), but all returned to the financial security of the family business in Dover.

The O'Hara family realized fully the power that comes with maintaining a cohesive family unit, and the six brothers used the leverage of their economic success to command the strict loyalty of family members and employees. They sponsored representatives to the legislature, contributed heavily to both state political parties, held court for state politicians when they came to Dover, and exercised virtually unchallenged control of the local government. This power resulted from the sheer numbers of votes controlled by family and employees, three generations of "favors" to area residents, and a steadfast willingness to coldly punish any individual or local business that might oppose them.

Council politics

Without old Frank's force of will, with waning influence in state government as the rest of the state changed and grew, and with an influx of new residents, Dover's city government had become reasonably independent of the O'Hara family, but not entirely so. Several members of the seven-member city council were "connected." Michael O'Hara, a past mayor, was a grandson of Frank and manager of the Erie Land Development Corporation. Kevin Beal worked for a local auto parts store that valued O'Hara business; he had spent his childhood as a playmate of the O'Hara compound kids. Arnold Fornby, a master mechanic and union shop steward at Brace Machine Corporation, a large independent employer some twenty miles from Dover, had played local politics for forty years, knew where all the skeletons were buried, and regularly joined the O'Haras for breakfast (toward the end of their morning sessions). He bragged about his political independence but belied that brag with an ever-present willingness to cut a deal with the O'Haras if there was something of political value in it for him.

Not surprisingly, these three council members constituted the solid opposition to Spanning's police chief selection process.

Four years after joining the state police, Trooper Waterhouse had transferred to the Dover area. Two years later, after meeting several members of the O'Hara family who were friends of his wife's family, Waterhouse was offered a part-time job as "safety officer" with O'Hara Transport. In accordance with state police policy, Waterhouse applied for and received permission to accept this form of employment with the O'Haras. As safety officer, Waterhouse's responsibilities consisted primarily of ensuring that the company's vehicles were properly equipped for safe highway travel. Depending on perspective, this was a responsibility that either closely paralleled or directly conflicted with his duties as a state police officer and enforcer of highway laws. Like other trusted O'Hara employees, Waterhouse had accepted "special" company benefits—for example, no-interest housing loans and low-cost construction improvements, such as landscaping and driveway paving.

Spanning knew that Waterhouse's mediocre qualifications and dubious connections with the O'Haras dictated against seriously considering him to fill Johnson's job. Seeking a compromise, however, and hoping to allay criticism that city managers "from away" gave no credence to local talent, Spanning opted to include Waterhouse with the three other finalists to be rated by the review panel. This decision had the effect of quieting things temporarily. The Waterhouse group thought perhaps Spanning was capitulating in a face-saving way (by maneuvering Waterhouse through the process), and they ceased to pressure him for the moment. Council members Jim Dixon (a schoolteacher), Marion McQueen (a government accountant), and Jack Redmond (a semiretired manufacturer's representative) strongly supported Spanning and encouraged him to proceed with the recruitment in his own way despite pressure from the others.

Council member Steve Nicholson was the wild card. Young, aggressive, hard working, and politically ambitious, he had long set his sights on high elective office. He was a member of the council that had hired Spanning, and the two had a relationship that ran hot and cold. In years when Nicholson's political ambitions were dormant, Spanning relied on Nicholson's persuasive personality to help carry difficult issues in council. Now, however, Nicholson had a legislative seat within his reach and was devoting more time to politics. As a result, Spanning had increased difficulty working with him. The timing of the police chief selection process brought potential conflict between the two to a head.

Before the review panel met to fulfill its mandate, Nicholson sought a meeting with Spanning and made clear his support of "a local candidate" for the police chief's job because "it's critical that the person understand our community." No mention was made of Waterhouse or of the hundreds of votes the O'Haras could deliver to Nicholson in the fall. No threats were made, but the point was clear: this item was of critical importance to Nicholson.

The selection process

Attorney White convened his panel, and through the course of a beautiful spring day, they thoroughly questioned the four candidates who had emerged from a field of fifty-three applicants. At day's end, as Spanning treated the panel to a good steak for their trouble, they ranked their choices. The panel was unanimous: Boston Police Lieutenant Sam Warren was ranked number one, and Trooper Jim Waterhouse was ranked number four. The panelists even teased Spanning a little at dinner over the obvious differences between Waterhouse and the rest; they suggested that Waterhouse must have been a long-lost relative of Spanning's to have made the final cut.

Meeting Sam Warren, Spanning took to him immediately. Confident, quick-witted, and soft-spoken, Warren soon convinced Spanning that he would adjust easily to Dover. Even though what Dover paid a city manager would have been a significant pay cut for a Boston police lieutenant with twenty-four years of service, the combination of Warren's pension from the Boston police department and the Dover police chief's salary would keep him and his family comfortable. Warren's wife had come from farm country and loved the idea of returning to it, and Warren had spent his nine years of patrol duty with Boston's mounted patrol. The sale of their house in suburban Boston would more than pay for a comfortable country home, complete with barn and pastures, in the Dover area, thus allowing Warren his long-desired dream of raising horses.

Spanning sensed instinctively that Warren would quickly earn the respect of the Dover police department and, probably soon thereafter, the community. His pronounced Boston accent would be a standout in "Yankee Dovah," to be sure, but his sterling record of police work, awards of merit, and recognized leadership abilities with the Boston police department would soon be known in Dover and would clear the way for his acceptance.

On a handshake, Spanning and Warren agreed that Spanning would appoint Warren and seek council confirmation within a few weeks. Spanning explained clearly to Warren the problems he faced regarding confirmation, and Warren, smiling encouragingly, indicated that it was surely worth a try.

Preconfirmation problems

Sensing that most residents were unaware of the dynamics of the selection process and that some counterbalance of political pressure might sway Councilman Nicholson, Spanning crafted a detailed press release that announced his appointment of Warren, elaborated on the review panel and its expertise, and chronicled the superb qualifications of Sam Warren. Spanning counted on an independent press in Dover to report the story accurately, well in advance of the council meeting set to confirm Warren. He judged correctly that council members—including Nicholson—were hard-pressed after its release to find fault with Spanning's appointee. Three council members, locked into their predetermined choice, avoided discussion of the topic except among themselves. Their strategy would still be to vote down Spanning's choice. Nicholson made no public comments prior to the meeting, leaning neither one way nor the other. The remaining three council members supported Spanning whenever their opinions were asked.

And so it came down to the day of the council meeting, and Spanning sat in his office, drinking his morning coffee, contemplating the evening session and his future in Dover. About the last thing in the world he expected was the phone call he received from outgoing Chief Johnson.

"Are you sitting down, Will?" the chief began.

"This is a bad day for that kind of question, Charlie," Spanning responded. "What's up?"

"It's about Councilman Redmond's son, Randy. He's going to be arrested this morning on arson charges."

"Oh, no!"

Spanning had known that young Randy Redmond was a problem for his father. The boy had dropped out of school and had had several minor brushes with the law. The senior Redmond, one of Spanning's supporters on the council, was a proud man who never talked to Spanning about his son's problems. Although Spanning sensed a strength of character in Redmond, he worried about what effect the arrest would have on him at that evening's council meeting. Because the arson arrest was a result of a joint police effort between Dover and state police, Spanning also cynically marveled at the timing. After some thought, he resisted the temptation to seek to have the arrest delayed until the following day.

Things went from bad to worse that afternoon when Redmond's wife, Mary, emotionally distraught over her son's felony arrest, telephoned the state's prime witness against her son, attempting to influence him to alter his version of the circumstance of the crime. To prevent deterioration of the state's case, the arson task force, in consultation with the district attorney, elected to charge Mrs. Redmond with tampering with a witness. Mrs. Redmond was arrested, booked, and released on her own recognizance just hours before the council confirmation hearing. Would Redmond appear in the face of this family scandal? Could he still support Spanning after the day's events? Spanning skipped supper and anxiously waited for the meeting to begin.

The decision problem

Just a few weeks earlier, Spanning had been happy and comfortable in his job. Now he was on the verge of provoking a majority of his city council into firing him as the result of an emotionally charged dispute complicated by intricate power plays. To pursue this issue and lose could very well set the stage for continual conflict that could only lead to Spanning's ultimate departure—voluntary or otherwise. With the severe complication of the arrest of the son of a sympathetic council member, Spanning was forced to take stock quickly of the whole issue and decide how to proceed.

He sat at his desk pondering his problem. As he saw the matter, he had several options:

1. Committed to a course of action that had led to a council meeting scheduled that evening to confirm Sam Warren, Spanning could hold fast, let events take their course, and live with the results. What—if anything— might he do in the few hours before the meeting that would be of help to him?
2. Realizing the critical value of Councilman Redmond's vote, Spanning could attempt to intercede in the Redmond case. The assistant district attorney who was prosecuting the case had, four years before, recommended Johnson and understood the value of obtaining a good police chief and the politics of such a process.
3. To try to defuse the crisis, Spanning could contact the mayor, request a postponement of the confirmation meeting, and regroup to seek a compromise course of action that would somehow result in face-saving for the council members and himself and still lead to the appointment of a qualified police chief.

The council would arrive shortly. Spanning had to make a very quick decision.

Discussion questions

1. What were the advantages and risks involved in pursuing Spanning's recruitment plan?
2. As city manager, Spanning exercised administrative authority over Police Chief Johnson. Would it have been proper for Spanning to seek to delay the arrest of Randy Redmond until after that night's council meeting? What would be the benefits and risks of such a strategy?
3. What, if any, would be the ethical implications of action to defer Redmond's arrest? Given the existing threat to Spanning's effectiveness as city manager, if not to his job, would it be appropriate to put any ethical concerns aside? Given the importance of the appointment to the community's welfare, would it be appropriate to put these ethical considerations aside to secure Warren's appointment?
4. Apart from any action on the arrest, should Spanning have contacted Redmond prior to the meeting to discuss his family's problems?
5. If Spanning decided to delay the council meeting and seek a compromise, what kind of compromise might achieve his purposes and be acceptable to the council?
6. How might a compromise be initiated by Spanning? What would he need to do to execute a compromise without appearing weak or contradictory in the public eye?
7. What would be the long-term effect on Spanning's management ability and his authority if he sought a compromise at this point?
8. What should Spanning do? Why?

2

Developing a purchasing system

Keith A. Schildt

Editor's introduction

Professional local government management not only affects the kinds of people hired to manage city or county business, but also changes the way that business is conducted. It means stricter adherence to financial planning and budgeting, reliance on competitive bidding processes rather than on a "good old boys' system" when purchasing goods and services, and closer scrutiny of the quality of goods and services received. It means that local political pressures and personal interests have to compete more intensively with quality and cost considerations for control of local purchasing processes.

Professionalization of local government management also means changes in the roles played by government leaders—selected officials, chief administrative officers, department heads, and even middle-management personnel. It means, typically, that elected officials are freed from the need to "process paper" and attend to daily management concerns, leaving them more time to devote to making major policy decisions and searching for solutions to community problems.

Such a change is increasingly welcomed by local officials who have limited time and expertise to bring to the process of government leadership. It enables them to focus on the big policy issues and thus affords them a greater opportunity to influence the long-term quality of life in their community. But such a change, even if desired by local leaders, can be painful in the short run. It often means that elected officials must give up their role in routine operations, a role that, while time-consuming, often gives them a major sense of power and renown. Routine work also gives a sense of short-term satisfaction—a decision made today to buy a new police car from a local dealer produces immediate benefits that draw gratitude from the dealer—while policy decisions take longer, are harder to make, and often require more time before their benefits are recognized and acknowledged by the public.

Thus, the process of adopting and then following professional, good management practices finds, at best, ambiguous support from both the public and elected officials. The changes proposed in this case are requested by the elected officials to resolve complaints made by department heads. Yet neither group's support for the changes can be assumed by the professional administrator.

Further, the ambiguity of public values regarding government means that the administrator cannot even count on public support for recommending the changes sought by the city council. While the public clearly wants government business to be conducted at the lowest possible cost and "in a businesslike fashion," that sentiment does not necessarily bring support to a proposal that, while saving taxpayer money, might do so by shifting certain government purchases from local merchants to lower-cost, out-of-town suppliers.

Local officials and the public, in short, can be very ambivalent in their expectations regarding government. The professional administrator must learn to live with that ambiguity even while attempting to promote professional values that emphasize efficiency and effectiveness in the conduct of public business. That is the challenge facing the city administrator in this case.

Case 2
Developing a purchasing system

Background

The village of Lawrenceburg is a small, rural community governed by an elected mayor and eight village board members elected from wards. All terms of elected officers are for four years, with board members serving staggered terms. Historically a farm service community with some light industry, Lawrenceburg has a population of only 3,100 with a service area of 4,500. However, it is located in the path of a wave of urban development sprawling west out of a major metropolitan area. It also lies just east of a smaller metropolitan center that is growing in its direction. Thus, the village's long-term prospects suggest that two separate, growing metropolitan regions will converge on the existing small-town, closely knit community.

Under relatively intense public controversy, the village board of Lawrenceburg recently created the position of village administrator by a 6–2 vote. Proponents of the position argued that an administrator would benefit the village by increasing the level of professionalism and accountability in the government. They further argued that the village needed an administrator to provide expert advice and assistance to the board as it faced mounting pressures for growth and development.

Opponents contended that the position merely added an unnecessary level of bureaucracy, which would make the government less responsive to the citizens. They claimed that there was enough local talent and ability to guide the village through growth, and that an outsider was not needed. Although they never said so publicly, several members of the village board feared that an administrator would erode their own individual power and authority.

Bryan Ferry, a resident of a suburban community approximately twenty miles to the east, was appointed the first village administrator in late January by the same 6–2 vote that created his position. A doctoral student in public administration at a nearby university, he had previously worked for several suburban municipalities, including recent service on a limited, part-time basis for Lawrenceburg, where he helped the village negotiate the annexation agreements for two major subdivision developments. Lawrenceburg was Ferry's first job as village administrator.

Prior to Ferry's appointment, several influential members of the local business community had expressed their preference that a local person be found to serve as the village administrator, but under pressure from four influential board members, Mayor John Fritz chose Ferry. News of the appointment spread quickly throughout the community; reaction to it was mixed. The vote of the village board did not accurately reflect the town's divided opinion on the need for an administrator, and a campaign was initiated to submit the issue to a nonbinding referendum on the ballot in April.

The mixed reaction of the community to the appointment of a professional administrator was mirrored by the reaction of the village's rapidly growing staff, which at the time consisted of thirty-two full-time equivalent positions. On the one hand, Ferry would be one more person telling the staff members what they could and could not do. The heads of the two major operating departments (police and public works) had historically enjoyed relative autonomy over their respective domains.

On the other hand, both department heads had grown fearful that their departments would be micromanaged by village board members who, they felt, did not understand the technical nature of their duties or the changes that would be required to respond to the future growth of the area. Both had also begun independently to establish a professional system of service delivery, and they felt that recent board actions threatened their initiatives. Furthermore, they believed that there was a need to continue the professionalization of the entire government operation. Thus, they greeted the appointment of the administrator with constrained optimism, hoping that the new officer would shield them from excessive board intervention in daily activities.

In considering the mayor's offer of the administrator's position in Lawrenceburg, Byran Ferry had looked long and hard at the situation that would confront him. He accepted the staff's tentative support as reasonable and appropriate, given the circumstances. He knew that he had strong support on the board, especially from Mayor Fritz, but he also knew that, with two opposing board members and a community divided over the need for the position, his support could evaporate in a hurry. His challenge, he reasoned, was to demonstrate to the community the value of having a professional administrator on the payroll. While he was confident of his ability to manage the affairs of the village, he expected that, sooner or later, he would have to face a situation in which the professional values he brought to the position would be directly challenged, even by some of his supporters. Unhappily, that challenge was not long in coming.

The case

Rumors had circulated in the community for years that previous department heads had been abusing their purchasing authority. Allegations of kickbacks, equipment bought for personal use with village funds, and vendors providing gifts to department heads were widespread and generally accepted as true. However, none of the rumors had ever been substantiated, and no misuse of funds had ever been documented.

A failed attempt at change

Shortly after the appointment of two new department heads and approximately a year before Bryan Ferry had been appointed village administrator, the board had responded to the persistent allegations of purchasing abuses by adopting a policy under which each purchase of more than $300 would first require board approval. Prior to this, the departments had been allowed to purchase whatever materials and equipment they needed, provided they stayed within their budgetary constraints. The departments had accepted this revised policy, but not without a good measure of reluctance.

The department heads quickly found that they could easily sidestep the "$300 rule" by making a series of partial purchases through a willing vendor who would submit separate invoices, keeping each below the $300 threshold. Also, instead of buying all the necessary materials for a project at one time, the departments would buy in stages as they needed the materials. Their expressed rationale for such behavior was the arbitrary nature of the $300 limit and the village's limited storage space.

Additionally, the department heads would sometimes request board approval for purchases that had already been ordered and, in some instances, had been received and placed into service. They usually argued that these were emergency purchases. Indeed, the board had agreed that, in emergency situations, the departments had the authority to make purchases above $300 without its prior approval. Since the board had not defined what constituted an emergency, this exception created an easily abused circumvention of the new policy.

By the time Bryan Ferry started his new job as village administrator, the circumventions and inadequacies of the new purchasing policy, when added to the past allegations of purchasing abuses, had fostered a contentious atmosphere between the village board and the operating departments that also affected other aspects of their relationship. The board had become apprehensive about delegating any authority to the departments. Some board members were discussing the formation of new board subcommittees to provide increased oversight and help ensure that the departments were implementing board policies and orders. The departments, in turn, complained that the board was engaging in micromanagement and that such actions diminished the efficiency and effectiveness of their operations.

Barriers to change

Ferry had been on the job less than a week when Mayor Fritz came to his office and ended his honeymoon period in the new job. "Bryan," the mayor said, "the board and I want you, as your first major assignment and top priority, to develop and implement a new procurement policy." Further, he said, board members wanted action immediately or "they would take the matter into their own hands."

Ferry knew that the procedural aspects of a purchasing program were not difficult to develop. However, he also knew that the task would be difficult because of three conflicting forces, forces that he had every reason to suspect could lead to a confrontation between local traditions and sound, professional management practices.

First, the past allegations and current transgressions of policy had undermined the elected officials' trust and confidence in their own staff. A sizable minority of the board already wanted the authority to approve all purchases in advance, regardless of dollar value. This desire was, in varying degrees, the product of two board motivations: (1) to punish the departments for past violations of the spirit and intent of the recent changes in purchasing policies, and (2) to increase the board's effective control over the departments. Some board members, Ferry suspected, were also motivated by a blatant desire to circumvent the administrator's authority over the day-to-day operations of the village. Still others, Ferry knew, had very legitimate reasons for finding common cause on the purchasing issue with their colleagues who distrusted the administrator. They simply wanted to be assured that purchases were necessary and not frivolous. Many of these board members had also expressed concerns about the prices that the village was paying for certain products that they felt could be obtained at less cost.

Second, the department heads had grown accustomed to their autonomy and had proven reluctant to accept policy changes that they perceived would undermine their authority. Then, too, they had both technical expertise and specific knowledge of their procurement needs. All had been hired before the administrator and for the same purpose: to professionalize service delivery. They could reasonably be expected to be suspicious of, and even resistant to, any attempt by Ferry to centralize their authority into his own hands. Some centralization, Ferry realized, was inevitable, but he would rather have had an opportunity to demonstrate the kinds of support he could provide to the department heads before he had to make recommendations that would seem to undercut their authority.

Third, the local business community benefited from the existing purchasing policies of the village. Local businesses perceived the village as a major customer and wanted village supplies bought from local retailers, even when items cost more than when purchased in bulk from larger retailers in adjacent communities. The current department head policies of buying locally in small quantities not only kept the business in town but also discouraged price comparison. Present policies, in short, enabled local businesses to sell the village more goods at higher prices. Ferry knew that any changes he might suggest could well be perceived as a threat to local business interests.

Thus, the task of introducing a new system clearly placed Ferry at a point of friction between the board's desire to have greater management control over the daily operation of the government and the departments' desire to remain relatively autonomous of such control. It also placed him at a point of friction between the village's desire to minimize service delivery costs and the local business community's desire to keep the village spending in local stores. Finally, the board's desire for immediate action gave him no time to work with department heads and business leaders to prepare them for the changes that might come.

The decision problem

As Ferry pondered his assignment, he came to realize that the problem was not simply one of designing and gathering support for a new procurement program. Instead, it involved the deeper ramifications of gaining local acceptance for the values and consequences of professionalism in government. While Ferry knew that many Lawrenceburg residents would, in the abstract, support such practices as competitive bidding and purchasing at the lowest possible cost, he did not delude himself into believing that this abstract support would prevail when time-honored practices—practices that had been used for decades in the small rural community and had provided valued benefits to some residents—were called into question. He knew that any attempt on his part to impose changes that were resisted by long-term members of the community would have an effect on the community's perception of him and of the use of an outside, professional administrator.

Ferry also realized that any recommendation he might make would require a change from the status quo and a sensitivity toward the impact of that change upon the village staff, the board, and the local businesses. The policy would set the stage for his future relations with the board, the departments, and the community—and would have a bearing on the future of his position as well. He certainly did not want his decision to have an adverse effect on the upcoming referendum on the village's need for an administrator.

Finally, Ferry understood that the technical issues surrounding the development of the purchasing system would not pose too much of a problem. The real problem would be identifying and resolving the implementation obstacles prior to the adoption of the system. This would require answers to the following questions:

1. What strategy should he use to sell the new system to the department heads and the board?
2. What could he do to minimize conflict with the department heads and to secure their cooperation?
3. How could the local businesses' perception that any change in policy would negatively impact their sales be minimized? Since he had not yet met the members of the business community, how and when should he approach them?

The board would meet the following week and would expect to hear a report from Ferry on his plans for a new procurement system. That meeting would be held in public, and Ferry knew that both the department heads and local business leaders would be watching. He also knew that he had to make some immediate decisions about the structure of a new system and the process he would use to build support for both the system and his own position. Quick thinking was necessary.

Discussion questions

1. What are the professional values at issue in this case? List those values and prioritize them, indicating which should not be compromised under any circumstances and which might be subject to some compromise.

2. What information should Ferry gather as he begins work on this task? What information does he need about procurement systems? What information about village operations might be essential or useful to him?

3. What kind of strategy should Ferry follow in developing his recommendation? What kinds of changes in the procurement system might he propose that would satisfy the board, improve the system, and win the cooperation of the department heads?

4. With whom should Ferry talk and at what stage of the process? What information should he gather from them? How should he deal with members of the board? How should he handle the department heads? Should he make any effort to meet with business leaders and, if so, with whom? What information, if any, should he disseminate in advance of the board meeting and to whom?

5. What changes in the procurement system would you recommend to the board in this case?

6. How would you present your recommendations to the board in this case (i.e., how would you preface your recommendations; how would you describe them; and what supplementary information would you give to help sell them to the board, the department heads, and the business community)?

7. What principles of good professional practice and leadership would you try to follow in responding to resistance from the department heads? From the business community?

Part three: Community politics

Introduction to part three: Community politics

Community politics—politics at the local government level—is the grass-roots politics that Thomas Jefferson so revered. It is the cradle of American democracy. The average American citizen has more diverse political involvement at the community level—voting, working in political campaigns, communicating with public officials, holding public office, running for election to office, testifying at public hearings—than at any other level of government. It is in local politics that most political leaders get their start; it is in local politics that most citizens have their most personal involvement with government. It is in local politics, where elections are most frequent and referenda are common, that the will of the voters is most evident, most easily measured, and most clearly felt by government decision makers. In short, more than at any other level, local government is the government of the people. Since it is the vehicle through which the people are involved, politics is the warp and woof of local government, the catalyst that makes local government work.

The presence of community politics in local government clearly affects the job of the local government administrator. More than anything else, it is what makes that job different, not just from the job of the administrator in the private sector but also from that of the public administrator in state or national government. Local politics, because it is so close to the voters, is different from state and national politics; the local administrator deals with fewer representatives of large interest groups but has much more contact with voters. Local administrators encounter constituents who wish to "talk business" in the office; at public meetings; in the stores, churches, and parks of the community; and even during the administrator's off hours at home. Local politics permeates all aspects of the local administrator's work and life in the community.

All the cases in this book deal in some measure with community politics. Such politics are a constant theme in local government management and decision making. The cases in part three have been selected to reflect three very different views of local government. The first case looks at the administrator's problem of discovering what the voters want; it demonstrates the difficulty of trying to reconcile the disparate interests articulated forcefully by different groups of voters. The second case examines the difficulty of implementing needed change—change mandated by the common voter's insistence that tax rates not be increased and that services be maintained and improved—in the face of determined opposition from those who see their interests as adversely affected by the change. The third case looks at community politics from the perspective of a citizen trying very hard to secure local government help for his special interest. The three scenarios are all too common to veteran local government administrators.

In the first case, the professional administrator is faced with one of the most common political issues posed in government: the desire of the voters for both lower taxes and increased levels of public spending on desired services. What makes the issue especially difficult at the local government level is the presence of the voters, who express themselves directly through their personal conversations with members of the council and the administrative staff, through their involvement in public hearings, and even through referenda. Local government is easy when the voters agree, but in this case, as in most situations, there is no clear direction of public opinion. It is this diversity of opinion that drags the local government professional administrator into the maelstrom of community politics.

The next case presents a problem with a solution that appears "right" in that it promotes economy and efficiency in government operations; however, it is vigorously opposed by a wide range of community groups. The issue at hand is an effort by the city and the manager to restructure local advisory boards and commissions in a way that would achieve greater administrative centralization and enhance the manager's ability to coordinate their input. The case poses a classic dilemma: the clash between popular control (responsiveness) and administrative effectiveness (efficiency).

The third case looks at political conflict between a constituent group seeking government support and the government's middle-management administrators. The conflict involves fees for the use of park and recreational facilities; the citizens' group questions the government's administrative procedures as well as its fee structure.

All these cases give a sense of the texture as well as the significance of Jefferson's beloved grass-roots democracy in its contemporary manifestations.

3

Unknown taxpayer preferences

Barry M. Feldman

Editor's introduction

Professional public administration places a very high emphasis on government pursuit of the public interest. In their training, public administrators are taught that the task of defining the public interest is, first and foremost, the job of elected officials. They are also taught, however, that it is their responsibility to know and promote the public interest in the recommendations they make to elected officials and in the directions they give to their staffs for implementing the decisions and desires of the legislative body. The fundamental problem, however, is that there is no known method for discovering or defining the public interest.

In reality, there is no such thing as *the* public interest. As political science teaches, each political community is composed of many different citizens with different values, interests, and preferences. There are thus *many* public interests. To make the aggregation problem still more difficult, voters—individually and collectively—hold political preferences that contradict one another. Fulfilling one interest requires that another interest be violated or at least temporarily set aside.

The most difficult task of democratic government is that of aggregating all of these many, contradictory public interests into some kind of clear mandate for government policy and action. The most common and difficult of these contradictory public interest demands in recent years has been the public's strong, unambiguous demand for lower taxes, which has persisted together with the public's continuing demand for more spending for favorite programs (and, when all the public is aggregated, there is no public program that is not *some* interest's favorite program).

This is the conflict discussed in the case at hand. The public clearly wants lower taxes; special interest groups, which together represent a large sector of the community, just as clearly want more community spending for designated programs. Caught in the middle are the elected officials who typically want to satisfy both conflicting demands at the same time. Not knowing what to do, the elected officials turn to the professional administrator for a recommendation.

The administrator has his own preferences and his own uncertainties. Like all professional administrators, the city manager wants to help build a better community. That takes money, more money than the current tax rate will produce. Further, groups on whom the manager depends for the delivery of public services, such as the members of the police force, are in the forefront of those demanding more government spending.

On the other hand, the opponents of tax increases are well organized and vocal in their opposition. The manager, like the members of the council, wants to respond positively and constructively to this important sector of the electorate as well, if for no other reason than that any public leader ignores significant blocks of voters at her or his personal peril.

The city manager and his or her staff certainly have a professional obligation to stay out of local politics, but that option is not available in this case. The politics involved are not the politics of election campaigns; they are the politics of budgeting. Directed by the council to make a recommendation, the manager is thus dragged into the morass of community politics.

While the political issues involved in this case are unusually severe, the manager's involvement in them is very normal: a routine expectation imposed by elected officials and voters alike upon the professional who sits in the chief administrator's office.

Case 3
Unknown taxpayer preferences

Background

Westview is a mature, some say "classy," first-ring suburb of a midsize city in the upper Midwest. Residents—both newcomers and old-timers—call it special because of its tree-lined streets, stately older homes, and a downtown that is the commercial showplace of the metropolitan area. Regional officials call it special because of the enlightened city council members who are always asked to volunteer their time (and knowledge) to one regional board or another. And the professionals of the Westview city administration call it special because city council members have a time-honored commitment to good government.

This commitment to good government has been built over a number of years, partly by the residents who serve on the city council, and partly by a community ethic that values civic involvement by residents. Westview residents, to a larger degree than other area residents, have participated in their city government by serving on the numerous boards, commissions, special study committees, and ever-present "blue-ribbon" task forces. The Westview city council still appoints nine residents to the Fence Appeals Board even though the last documented case of an appeal to the city's six-foot fence height restriction was more than fifteen years ago.

The traditions and values of Westview can be traced to the period immediately following the end of World War I. With the prosperity of the early and mid-1920s fueling the building of larger homes on the inexpensive land west of the urban center, Westview grew quickly. It was incorporated in 1928 with a population of 6,000 residents living within its twenty-two square miles. Over the years, as the local banking and insurance businesses grew, senior management executives built their homes in Westview and built their glass and steel office towers in and near Westview. The region's largest bank, America First, embarked on an aggressive bank-buying and merger spree throughout the 1970s, becoming the upper Midwest's largest and most influential bank and significantly expanding its employment base. Many new senior executives chose Westview for their home.

The decades of the 1970s and 1980s saw strong economic growth, not only in the region but particularly in Westview, where the population more than doubled between 1970 and 1980 to 42,000 residents. Many of the newcomers at that time were insurance and banking executives, who were encouraged by the chief executive officers (CEOs) of America First and Prairie Life, the region's largest insurance company, to become involved in their communities.

The city government

In 1928, Westview became the first jurisdiction in the state to adopt the council-manager form of government. Despite the government's stability, voters did amend the city charter from time to time. In 1965, city council districts were abolished, and a council of seven persons, each elected at-large for a two-year term, was approved by the voters. The charter required that the mayor be elected by the council from among its members. Thus, at the time of this case, the mayor presided over the city council meetings and had the same legislative authority as the other council members. All city council members were part-time officials who served without pay. A standing quip often shared among them, particularly after a long council meeting, was that they were going to get a 10 percent pay raise for all their long hours. In 1975 the charter was again amended to allow the voters the right to petition to have a referendum on the adopted city budget.

The city manager's position in Westview was viewed by government professionals throughout the region as a "plum" job. Westview was a wealthy community with a well-educated, involved citizenry who expected, and for the most part received, excellent municipal services. Its residents paid the highest property taxes in the metropolitan area, but they received services not often found in other municipalities: backdoor garbage pickup, two municipal golf courses, an indoor aquatic facility with three pools, an indoor ice rink, and excellent public safety services. These amenities, the envy of other communities, were standard for Westview residents.

Westview also had a history of stable council-manager relations. The city's first city manager, Dwight Bergstrom, who also served as the city engineer, stayed in office for thirty years. Walter "Skip" Haynes followed Bergstrom and served for fourteen years. Haynes's claim to fame was that he had had the foresight to recommend that the city buy the Jonnsen farm in 1960, which eventually became the Municipal County Club complex; it could boast an eighteen-hole golf course, eight tennis courts, a large pool, and one of the area's best restaurants. Haynes was succeeded by Robert Bartley, who presided over the dynamic growth in Westview until he retired nearly two decades later. When Bartley announced his retirement, the city council embarked on a nationwide search for his replacement.

In true Westview fashion, a citizens' committee of twenty-four residents was appointed to act as an interview panel. With the help of an executive search firm, the panel screened 110 applicants to recommend the best applicants to the council.

Timothy Catler

When Timothy Catler received a call from an executive recruiter, asking if he knew of any qualified candidates who would be interested in receiving the Westview job announcement, Catler was entering his eighth year as assistant city manager in a large southwestern city. After receiving his M.P.A. from a public university in New England, Catler had decided to follow the advice of one of his professors to "head west" and ended up in a small suburban community of 10,000 outside the large southwestern city. Initially hired as the assistant to the city manager, he quickly proved his value to his boss and, after a short while, was promoted to assistant city manager, becoming, in effect, the day-to-day operations manager. When the city manager announced his resignation to accept another position in a nearby city, Catler was first appointed as the acting city manager; ninety days later he was appointed city manager. Tim Catler quickly established himself as one of the region's most capable local government managers.

The region in which Catler worked was dominated by a central city of more than 850,000 residents. With a long tradition of a council-manager government, this city took pride in recruiting nationally the best local government administrators for its senior-level positions. When an assistant city manager position became vacant there, the city manager encouraged Catler to apply and ultimately offered him the post. Thus, almost two years to the day after Timothy Catler was first appointed acting city manager, he became one of three assistant city managers in one of the nation's fastest-growing cities.

Timothy Catler's future was bright. He was credited by staffers, as well as by the city manager and the council, for making city government a showplace of how a large city can use state-of-the-art technology to enhance its public image and improve employee productivity. But after the city manager's untimely death, Catler judged correctly that his age and lack of extensive city manager experience would not get him into the final list of candidates to fill the vacancy. After finishing his telephone call with the recruiter, Catler realized that it might be time to move on, and Westview sounded like too good an opportunity to miss.

The case

Catler began his new job as Westview's fourth city manager on July 1, the start of a new fiscal year and of what he and the Westview city council hoped would be a long and beneficial relationship. With the operating budget already adopted the previous May, Catler knew that he had at least six months before he had to turn his attention to the always challenging process of developing a new spending plan. He also knew that this period would be critical in establishing contacts with numerous external community groups, from senior citizens to neighborhood associations, and with the city employees' labor leaders.

So in his first six months on the job, Catler literally spent every waking moment meeting and talking with taxpayers and employees. He never refused an invitation to attend a civic group or neighborhood association meeting, and he quickly developed a friendship with Joan King, the president of the influential Westview Neighborhood Association. He also decided that he would try to meet as many city employees as possible. He rode with the police officers several times during the day and on evening shifts, and he stayed overnight at one of Westview's two fire stations, even responding with the engine company when it was dispatched to a minor garbage fire. Catler also spent a day with the public works crew cutting grass at one of the city parks in early September.

The city council's feedback from constituents about Catler was, on the whole, positive. Mayor Pam Glassman was particularly pleased because, among all of her colleagues, she had felt the strongest about Westview's need to hire Timothy Catler. While the city council had hired Catler on a 7–0 vote, several council members, and especially Deputy Mayor Ray Nichols, expressed some concern that Catler had spent only two years as a city manager before being hired as a big-city assistant city manager. "An assistant city manager position in a large southwestern city in charge of technology and research may not have provided Catler with the necessary skills and experience needed in Westview," Nichols had argued. Even after he had somewhat reluctantly given his support to Glassman to make Catler's hiring offer unanimous, Nichols had told the other six council members that he was still concerned about Catler's lack of city manager experience and what Nichols termed "Catler's naive answers" to his questions about how best to balance the influence of special interest groups with the interest of the community as a whole. Nichols reminded his colleagues that he believed special interest groups had become too influential, and that several recent council decisions seemed designed to make special interests happy, even at the expense of the whole community.

Unknown Taxpayer Preferences   39

The budget process

The Westview budget had grown by an average of 6 percent per year in the years immediately preceding Catler's arrival in Westview. The former city manager had justified these increases as necessary to service the higher levels of debt incurred to finance the construction of new roads and two new elementary schools, as well as an expansion of the sanitary sewer treatment facility. Increased spending had also been fueled by the employment of additional staff.

During the last several years of his tenure, the former city manager had spent very little time reviewing department budget requests. As a result, the more enterprising department managers, who were always looking for allies to help convince the council of their departmental needs, formed alliances with interest groups that benefited from their departments' services. It was a poorly kept secret in Westview city hall that the way to get a department's budget through the council review process intact—and perhaps even increased—was to have the special interests show up at the budget public hearings to speak in favor of the department's appropriation request.

Early in December of Catler's first year, he asked his assistant city manager, Wanda Epps, to prepare a calendar for the forthcoming Westview budget. Epps's memo noted key dates: February 15, when department budget requests were due in the manager's office; March 1, when the manager's review was to be completed; April 1, when the budget, together with any needed tax increases, had to be submitted to the council; April 7 and 15, when two public hearings would be held to obtain public feedback; and May 1, when the council would act on the budget. Epps concluded her memo by describing the budget referendum option contained in the city's charter and observing that "while the taxpayers of Westview had never petitioned to have a referendum on the city council–adopted budget, it is always a possibility."

Catler's first budget

Timothy Catler's introduction to the Westview budget process that first year came in the form of a telephone call from Benjamin Maxwell, a retired business executive who was the president of the recently formed Westview Taxpayers Association (WTA).

Maxwell's call on that cold March morning caught Catler off-guard. Maxwell did not beat around the bush making small talk; the gist of his call was that he and his WTA would begin to monitor the budget preparation process and attend all the public hearings. Maxwell told Catler that more people than Catler or the city council would ever realize were getting angrier by the day at the high property taxes being paid by Westview residents and businesses. His parting comment, which Catler played back in his mind for several days after their telephone conversation, was not so much a boast as it was a declaration: "How do you and the city council members really know how Westview taxpayers feel about the local taxes they have to pay to support 'city hall.' You don't know. That's why the city government and the taxpayers of this city are on a collision course. It's not a question of *if* there will be a collision, but only *when* it will take place."

Interestingly enough, despite Maxwell's prediction of an impending collision, the development and adoption of Catler's first city budget went smoothly. The usual interest groups appeared at the public hearings to lobby the council to get the funding they believed they needed for their special program or service. Catler, being a newcomer, was not directly lobbied by any special interest, but Mayor Glassman kept him up-to-date on the various calls or visits she had during the city council review of his proposed spending plan.

When the budget came before the council on the first Tuesday of May that year, the council meeting was not well attended. Budget decisions had already been made by three subcommittees of the city council: public safety, public works, and general government. Although council committees had asked probing questions, reports of their inquiries had not circulated in the community. The weekly Westview newspaper viewed its role more as a community booster and advertiser than as a news outlet to inform Westview taxpayers about the complex issues of adopting a budget.

At the council meeting, Benjamin Maxwell stood up and asked Mayor Glassman to recognize him. His comments were to the point. He said that he knew that the council would adopt the proposed budget, which called for a 6 percent spending increase, and that the property tax increase needed to support the budget was above the consumer price index. He wanted the city council and the city manager to know that this was the last year the WTA would suffer in silence. His parting comment was that the city council and the city manager had an obligation to do more to seek out the opinions of the thousands of Westview residents who didn't belong to a special interest or have a favorite city service for which they wanted the council to spend more money. He challenged the council and city manager to find out the true preferences of the Westview taxpayer.

In response, council members were quick to point out to each other, and hopefully to residents watching the televised proceedings, that the forthcoming Westview budget would include money to hire more police and firefighters and to expand recreational programs with the help of two new positions to work directly with the All-Sports Council, a group of volunteer parents who helped coordinate the youth athletic activities in Westview. Mayor Glassman called the city council a group of "visionaries" who did understand what their constituents wanted. Her comments were a direct rebuttal to Maxwell's comments a few moments earlier.

Deputy Mayor Nichols was more reserved. He thanked his colleagues for all the hard work and extra hours they had invested in reviewing and modifying the budget. He wondered out loud if the additional positions were really necessary, but he answered his own question by saying that he had heard from Joan King of the Westview Neighborhood Association, which strongly supported the proposed budget, particularly the addition of more police and firefighters. With few additional comments from the other members, the Westview city council unanimously adopted the budget for the forthcoming fiscal year.

Westview's changing economy

During Catler's first week on the job, Mayor Glassman had introduced him to the two most influential business leaders in the region, Harvey Kuhner, the CEO of America First Bank, and Clayton Ingraham III, the CEO of Prairie Life Insurance. Catler's introduction to the upper Midwest's corporate boardrooms was smooth and friendly. With Westview's economy and that of the region directly influenced by the success of the two companies, Glassman and Catler wanted to maintain nothing but the best of relations with Kuhner and Ingraham.

Unfortunately, the trends that would affect banking and insurance companies nationally were already developing. At the time they met with Ingraham, Glassman and Catler were unaware that a larger insurance company had made an offer to purchase the highly successful Prairie Life Insurance company. When approved by the boards of directors of both companies a year later, the buyout meant that the corporate headquarters of Prairie Life would move some 1,500 miles east, effectively wiping out the company's corporate presence in Westview except for a small regional sales office.

When the buyout was announced by Prairie Life and its new corporate owner in early July, just one year after Catler became city manager and just one week into the new fiscal year, it hit the region—particularly Westview residents—very hard. Most of the six hundred headquarters employees, of whom 75 percent lived in Westview, were offered severance packages. By Thanksgiving of that year, "For Sale" signs were sprouting up all over Westview. While Catler had only anecdotal evidence from the city assessor, real estate values were dropping for what appeared to be the first time in the city's history. A sense of unease was palpable in the region as residents and businesses attempted to come to grips with the loss of one of its biggest and most highly regarded corporations.

Unfortunately, the economic bad news did not stop with the announcement of Prairie Life's purchase by another insurance company. The federal government had just released its report of economic indicators, which showed that a national recession was beginning. Concurrent with this recession was the lackluster performance of banks, particularly the region's leading bank, America First.

When Prairie Life announced that it had been purchased, it also announced that its ten-story corporate headquarters in downtown Westview would be put up for sale. The announcement that more than 150,000 square feet of class-A office space would be put on the market caused a number of real estate problems. Among them was the chilling of the commercial real estate market in the region. America First, a heavy investor in commercial real estate, felt the market downturn quickly. The worsening economy, coupled with a soft real estate market, further depressed earnings at the bank. Harvey Kuhner, in an effort to stem the red ink, announced that America First would undergo a reorganization throughout its retail and business banking divisions. In all, twenty underperforming branches would be closed in the tristate region, and 750 employees from top-level executives to junior tellers would be laid off.

The America First announcement, on top of the Prairie Life announcement, was devastating. Not only would Westview residents again be affected by corporate changes, but the future of the region, which relied on these two corporations, was called into question. With one company leaving and the other significantly downsizing, the region's economy was shaken.

Catler's second budget

Six months after the economic bad news of Prairie Life's departure from the community and America First's downsizing, Timothy Catler started to prepare for the forthcoming fiscal year's budget. He had been more of an observer than a leader during the development of the current (his first) year's budget. He was now determined to make some changes in the way the management team developed the new budget.

In early January Catler developed a budget process that was far more rigorous than anything his senior management team had seen. He wanted to develop a more rational way to make budget decisions, using historical information to put increased spending into proper perspective. He urged his management team to focus on explaining what had caused the Westview budget to grow so dramatically over the past ten years, and to use the continuing demand for city services as the context to explain the additional spending.

When Catler completed his first cursory review of the department managers' proposed spending plans, he realized that there were going to be tough decisions to make. Many of the requests for new positions, equipment, and supplies seemed well justified. For example, he was impressed with the police bicycle squad that Police Chief Brent Oslander had proposed. But to approve the request to fund a bicycle squad would mean four new police positions, plus related equipment and training. Also appealing to Catler were the proposed Sunday openings for the main library and two branch libraries, which would require three additional full-time and three part-time librarians. With this additional funding, the three libraries would be open from noon until 5:00 p.m. on Sundays.

When totaled, the proposed spending plans had twenty-five new full-time positions, as well as ten new police cruisers needed to begin a program Chief Oslander was promoting. This program assigned a police cruiser to one officer who could then drive it to and from work; Oslander's justification was that it would place that many more police cruisers on Westview's streets and provide the benefit of having just one police officer driving each vehicle. In addition, the public works director was requesting a new street sweeper, estimated to cost more than $100,000, and two large dump trucks, estimated to cost $60,000 a piece, that would be used for snow plowing. The new equipment requests exceeded $1,000,000 in additional spending. When combined with a cost-of-living wage increase; normal increases in utilities, supplies, and materials; and a 6 percent health care premium increase, the total spending would increase by 10 percent, a figure Catler knew would be hard to justify in light of the historical average spending increases of 6 percent. The budget increase would also require a significant jump in property taxes.

Catler was torn. On one hand, he could well understand and justify the increased spending. The new services, such as the police bicycle squad and the Sunday library openings, while expensive to provide, were real "quality-of-life" programs that gave Westview that little extra something that made it special. Also, Catler could sense from Mayor Glassman and her political supporters, such as Joan King of the Westview Neighborhood Association, that the city council wanted to keep Westview in the vanguard of providing the best municipal services in the area.

On the other hand, he knew that the Prairie Life and America First business problems were having an effect in Westview. To what degree they were affecting Westview taxpayers, however, Catler was not sure. All he had was anecdotal information about some Westview families who were moving because of those companies' reversals of fortune; this was confirmed by the number of "For Sale" signs. He was very uncomfortable asking about the taxpayers to pay more in taxes, particularly in light of the troubled economic times Westview and the entire region were beginning to go through. Also, Catler had not forgotten Benjamin Maxwell's comments to the city council some nine months ago about the obligation that he and the council members had to determine the true preferences of Westview taxpayers.

Catler submitted his second operating budget, with its proposed 10 percent increase, to the Westview city council on April 2. The council meeting was better attended than most others because the special interest groups wanted to show their support for the additional funding proposed for particular services. In the audience were the president of the Friends of the Westview Library; Joan King, president of the Westview Neighborhood Association; and Paul Martin, president of the Westview police union. Also present were Benjamin Maxwell and six members of the WTA.

Catler described the new municipal services contained in the spending plan and showed a bar chart that compared the proposed budget with previous budgets. He finished to polite applause. Mayor Glassman thanked the manager and his management team for their hard work and reminded everyone that the council would hold two citywide public hearings on the budget to receive citizen comments.

The public hearings

Forty people attended the first public hearing, but only twelve made a presentation to the council. The first speaker was Joan King, who briefly alluded to the unsettled economic times the community and region were experiencing and then urged the city council not to change the city manager's proposed budget. The second speaker was Paul Martin, who urged the council to support the budget and particularly the increased funding for the expanded police department programs. The public hearing lasted one hour, with all twelve speakers supporting one aspect or another of the budget. Catler was surprised that more people did not address the city council, and he wondered why citizens would just sit through a rather dry hearing without taking a few moments to tell the council how they felt about the budget.

As Catler left the auditorium, Martin and King approached him. Both repeated their support for the proposed budget. The question that Catler mulled over in his mind later that night was how strong King's support was in Westview's neighborhoods. While he knew that the Police Officers' Association supported the budget because of the expanded police programs, particularly the take-home police cruiser program, he knew that King's support was based on wanting Westview to stay the way it was, regardless of the national recession or the local economic problems. He only hoped that King truly represented the feelings not just of her association, but also of the many families who paid five dollars for membership to support it.

As Catler arrived about thirty minutes early for the second public hearing, he noticed that Deputy Mayor Nichols and Dr. Patricia Brooks, the newest city council member, were seated at the head table reviewing some papers. Brooks, a professor of public administration and director of the Municipal Research Institute at the state university in nearby Granville, showed Catler what she and Nichols were reading. It was the most recent regional survey data from the institute's semiannual citizens' survey. The results indicated a noticeable drop in citizen confidence and a decline in how citizens viewed the region's future economic prospects. While Brooks cautioned Catler that the survey was conducted right after the news from Prairie Life and America First and that the responses would reflect that bad economic news, Brooks did point out some other disturbing findings. Among the questions asked was whether citizens believed they were getting good value for the taxes they paid in their respective municipalities. The most recent results showed a drop in the percentage of citizens who felt that they were receiving excellent to good value for their property taxes—from 53 percent to 46 percent.

As in the first public hearing, approximately forty citizens were in attendance. In addition to several off-duty police officers and the entire fifteen-member executive board of the Westview Neighborhood Association, the audience included Benjamin Maxwell and members of the WTA. The speakers that night all urged the city council members to support the budget as submitted by the city manager. Their comments ranged from the threatening—"if you don't approve this budget as submitted, the quality of life in Westview will be seriously jeopardized"—to the gratuitous—"you have always done what's right for Westview; please don't fail us now."

Timothy Catler half-listened to the speakers as he thought about the most recent citizen survey data Dr. Brooks had shown him earlier. He had used survey research data when preparing the budget in his former city and had thus gained enough experience with the methodology of survey research to know that it was reliable and provided insight into how citizens felt about a variety of municipal issues. While not inexpensive to do, citizen surveys, done once a year around budget time, were valued by his former city manager and the city council as they wrestled with the far more dramatic questions that occurred in an urban area of 850,000 citizens.

As the last speaker sat down, Deputy Mayor Nichols asked his fellow council members if they had had a chance to review the summary sheet of the regional citizen survey that he had placed on their seats. Nichols asked Dr. Brooks to take a few minutes to explain the survey and what, if any, implications the results might have for the Westview city council. Brooks reiterated what she had told Catler earlier that evening: that the data could be interpreted as warning sign for public officials that citizens throughout the region were concerned about their future and that of the entire metropolitan area. Since the survey data did not separate responses from any of the eighteen cities that made up the region, she could not be certain if Westview citizens felt any differently than citizens in other parts of the region.

After Brooks finished, Nichols picked up the discussion by half asking and half stating that he was not sure if this was the year to expand city services and to increase the tax bill to Westview citizens. His comments caused several icy glares from audience members, but Mayor Glassman was quick to respond. She believed that Westview citizens still strongly supported the high level of city services and that they would be willing to support the new services proposed in the city manager's budget. Glassman looked directly at the audience and said that these residents, as both community leaders and taxpayers, should be sufficient proof to the city council members that Westview citizens did not feel as negative about the future as their regional neighbors. The mayor urged her colleagues to show leadership and to keep Westview as the number one community in the region.

The budget's adoption

At the Westview city council meeting on the budget, Ray Nichols and Patricia Brooks argued for a reduced level of spending from the city manager's proposed 10 percent increase. In an effort to have unanimous support for the budget, Mayor Glassman suggested reductions in equipment and supplies, which lowered the spending increase to 9.25 percent, but Nichols and Brooks argued that the proposed spending increase should be no more than 6 percent.

During the discussion, both Glassman and Nichols expressed concern for Westview citizens and what the future would hold for them, but their positions were quite different. Glassman argued that to keep Westview an attractive community in which to live and work, the city council had an obligation to provide the best municipal services possible. She said that introducing Sunday library hours and adding a police bicycle squad epitomized the type of service that would keep Westview the premier community in the region. She pointed to residents such as Joan King, who represented many Westview families, and said that she relied heavily on King's comments about maintaining the high level of service.

Nichols's argument was the direct opposite of Glassman's. He believed that the city council needed to trim spending, even if that meant not funding these important new services. He lamented that he could not point to any information that would tell him how Westview taxpayers really felt, but he could not vote to support this spending increase, regardless of what the Westview Neighborhood Association, the Friends of the Library, or any other interest group stated about the budget.

Unwilling to reduce any of the new services contained in the budget plan, the five-member majority on the council, led by Glassman, realized that the new budget plan would not have the support of all seven council members and adopted it on a 5–2 vote. As Catler walked to his car after the council meeting, he met Glassman and Nichols, who were still discussing the pros and cons of the just-approved budget. Mayor Glassman, looking for support from the city manager, asked Catler if he believed that the taxpayers from whom the council never heard supported the budget. How, Glassman asked, can we ever really know?

The referendum on the budget

In part, the mayor's question was answered by Benjamin Maxwell and his small but active taxpayers group. Maxwell was in the city clerk's office the following morning to have language approved on the petition calling for a public referendum on the just-adopted budget. If the necessary signatures, 1,200, were secured, Westview citizens would be asked to go to the polls to vote on whether they supported the new budget.

Although they had just three weeks to collect the 1,200 signatures, it took Maxwell and his group of petition circulators only two weeks to turn in the required number, which the city clerk certified on May 17. The charter required that the city council set the vote on the budget within thirty days of petition certification. In a special city council meeting held later that week, the council set Tuesday, June 16, for the referendum vote.

There was no precedent for a referendum on the municipal budget. And during the four weeks between the petitions' certification and the referendum, there was no organized effort within the city to either support or defeat the adopted budget. Even though Maxwell and the WTA worked hard to get the required signatures, the taxpayers chose not to continue their efforts to defeat the budget. In an interview in the *Westview Weekly,* Maxwell said that the citizens could make up their own minds as to whether they supported the budget. He was satisfied that the city council would finally hear from the "real" taxpayers.

Joan King, interviewed in the same edition, said that she felt very positive about the election. She believed that the Westview voters would support the city council's adopted budget and confirm in everyone's mind how the citizens really felt about it. She did express concern about a light turnout since this special election was an unusual event in Westview; she said that the worst outcome in the election would be a low voter turnout because it would then be difficult for the city council to determine the extent of taxpayer support for the budget.

As it turned out, June 16 was a perfect spring day—warm weather and blue skies. The polls opened at 6:00 a.m. By the time they closed thirteen hours later, barely 28 percent of the Westview voters had exercised their right to vote on the city budget. Of those who voted, those who elected not to support the budget outnumbered those who elected to support it by 167 votes. The adopted Westview city budget was defeated.

The city charter required that, "in the event that the Westview electors defeat the adopted city council budget, the city council must adopt a new budget within 14 days that has a total spending aggregate less than the rejected budget." Unfortunately, the Westview charter did not stipulate whether a specific amount had to be cut, leaving that decision in the council's hands.

The decision problem

The day following the budget's defeat, Mayor Glassman called Timothy Catler to let him know that the city council was planning to meet within forty-eight hours to begin reducing the budget. She asked him to be ready to discuss two key questions with the city council: first, what his recommended budget changes were, and second, and most important, what, if anything, Catler and the council could have done differently during the budget process to understand better the taxpayers' preferences. As if Glassman were reading Catler's mind, she said that, given the light turnout and the almost even vote, the city council had no more insight into the real preferences of Westview taxpayers after the referendum than it had before.

As Catler hung up the phone, he knew he now faced the biggest challenge of his career to date: how to respond to the two questions posed to him by the mayor. He knew that the council had a mandate from the voters to cut the budget. Yet he also knew that the Westview Neighborhood Association, the Friends of the Library, the police union, and other groups would want the smallest possible cuts. He knew, too, that his staff would be watching to see how well he defended their requests. And finally, he knew that Maxwell and the WTA would have their predicted "collision." Perhaps worst of all, Mayor Glassman had made it clear that he was expected to make the first recommendation. Catler's anxiety only grew in the following days. Word came to him that the Channel 46 "Action Van" was going to do a live telecast of the council meeting. Maxwell made it publicly known, well in advance of the meeting, that his group expected that the manager would recommend a "no tax increase budget." Joan King called to remind him that her organization would be out in force with nearly all of her members in attendance, calling for the most minimal budget cuts allowed under the charter. The policemen's union was encouraging its off-duty officers to attend the meeting; the Friends of the Library were organizing to appear in strength. Maxwell, too, he learned, was gathering new recruits to the WTA by circulating reports that the council and manager were not taking the election outcome seriously.

Catler ordered his city hall custodians to set up chairs to seat an overflow crowd in the council chambers and then gathered together his management team and posed the question, "What should I recommend to the council?"

Discussion questions

1. How should Catler go about formulating his recommendations? With whom should he consult? What role should be given to his staff? Ultimately, should he rely primarily on his own management instincts, on the recommendations of his staff, or on the informal advice he might gather from members of the council?
2. As city manager, Catler must produce a list of recommended cuts to the budget. Given that the Westview city charter does not stipulate a specific amount, how should Catler determine how much to cut from the budget? What strategy would you recommend that he follow on this matter?
3. From the information given in the case, set up a priority list of the budget cuts that Catler should recommend to the council.
4. Should Catler communicate with King, Maxwell, and other interest group leaders in advance of the meeting? If so, how should he handle the communications?
5. Obviously, the mayor and the deputy mayor are deeply divided over this issue, and Catler knows he could easily be caught in the middle. How should he handle his relationship with the two council leaders?
6. What changes should Catler propose to make in the budget process to avoid similar situations in the future?
7. Should Catler develop a strategy for crowd control on the night of the council meeting? If so, what should it be?
8. Should Catler develop an overall strategy for addressing the divisions within the community? If so, what should it be?
9. In retrospect, should Catler, after seeing the citizens' survey at the second public hearing, have reacted differently to the data? Should he have used this input as a basis for encouraging the council to delay implementation some of his budget proposals?

Efficiency, effectiveness, and patronage

Joe P. Pisciotte

Editor's introduction

Few themes are more commonly articulated in local political campaigns than the need for economy and efficiency in government operations. Presumably, the public is committed to these values and expects both the structure and the processes of government to promote them.

As with other values, however, the public's concern for economy and efficiency must be reconciled with other, sometimes competing, priorities. As a result, what the public wants, and consequently what the public gets, is not always so clear and unambiguous.

This case shows the impact of competing values on one community's attempt to modernize its governmental structure so that its operations can be made more efficient, with immediate budgetary savings. As the case unfolds and reaches a decision point, a classic contemporary political paradox emerges: every citizen wants reductions in government expenditures; yet no citizen wants cuts that are likely to affect his or her political influence or material well-being. The case also highlights another reality of contemporary politics: the citizens who take an active role in a political issue are those with a personal stake in the outcome. Citizens who will benefit only from better and more efficient government seldom make their voices heard, with the result that political pressures, and ultimately political decisions, tend to be self-serving for those personally affected and involved.

In such an environment, the manager in this case is faced with a dual task —first to frame a set of recommendations to solve a budgetary crisis and then to determine how to sell them politically to the community. The political salesmanship is not made easier by the fact that the recommended changes are intended to promote efficiency by consolidating public functions under the council and manager, thereby increasing the administrative influence of the manager's office.

Finally, the case highlights questions of strategy. It poses directly to the manager the task of formulating a strategy that will result in the desired change. Of greater importance, it poses the question of whether the manager could have achieved better results by pursuing a more politically sophisticated strategy from the beginning. Is it really the responsibility of the manager to be so politically sophisticated? Is this what the public expects of its professional administrator?

Case 4
Efficiency, effectiveness, and patronage

Background

River City could be viewed as a textbook model of council-manager government. A historically conservative, midsize, midwestern community, River City
has operated under the council-manager form of government for more than
seventy years. The community values highly the "reform" elements of its
government—that is, a part-time, nonpartisan elected city council that appoints
the city manager as chief administrative officer. The mayor is selected from
among the city council members on a one-year rotating basis; the council rarely
wanders from its broad policy-making functions, leaving daily operations to
the manager. The manager hires and fires all employees under his jurisdiction
on a merit basis.

There are no patronage employees in River City; appointments by city council members are limited to nonpaying positions on the city's many citizen
boards and commissions. These appointments, however, have assumed the air
of patronage. Although council members often have difficulty filling some of
the less prestigious positions, they frequently award highly desired positions to
persons who have helped them at election time.

The proliferation of boards and commissions reflects River City's efforts to
respond to the citizens and their diverse needs. In the years preceding this case,
the city made adjustments in housing, health and social services, and neighborhood integration. It adopted policies on civil rights, affirmative action, economic opportunity, fair housing, employment, gay rights, and open meetings.
A citizen participation organization was created: River City was divided into
sixteen districts from which citizens were popularly elected to serve the city
council in an advisory capacity. Numerous additional citizen boards and commissions were created—for example, commissions on women, handicapped
people, aging, crime and corrections, alcohol and drug abuse, and human
resources.

River City government clearly has been capable of responding to the long-
term but often fluctuating values and political interests that make up the community. At the time of this case, however, the city was faced with a new
challenge—perhaps its greatest challenge of the twentieth century.

Fiscal problems

Changes in federal policy, particularly the loss of federal revenue sharing combined with federal policies designed to shift more responsibility for social service programs to local governments, had severely stressed River City's ability
to sustain its social policy initiatives. "Cutback management," "doing more
with less," and "fiscal stress" had become parts of the daily River City
vocabulary.

The changes in federal policy could not have come at a worse time. River
City was experiencing economic downturns exacerbated by significant short-
falls in tax-generated revenues. Favorable cash balances had kept the city from
actually running a deficit, but a revenue expenditure gap of some $16 million
was forecast for the next three years if past trends continued and there were
no major policy changes.

A controversial one-cent sales tax had been adopted by referendum, but only
after bitter public debate involving the community's many business, labor, and
neighborhood groups. However, the tax offered little immediate relief from the

city's financial difficulties because half of the proceeds were pledged to road and bridge improvements and the other half to property tax relief. No proceeds were earmarked for deficits in operating funds.

The twin specters of an increase in the city's property tax and severe cuts in programs loomed large; they led to open controversy between the city manager, Herb Upton, and council member Roy Tanner. Their disagreement over the causes of and solutions to the city's budget crisis became almost daily copy for the news media. Upton, a professional manager, had served the city for nine years; Tanner, an investment counselor, was a veteran council member in the middle of his second term who had well-recognized ambitions for higher office. Upton, who operated on the principle of deference to the elected body, resigned to accept a manager position in another community.

Thus, newly appointed city manager Mike Christian arrived in River City with a crisis confronting him. A career manager, Christian had systematically and successfully come up through the ranks of progressively larger cities. Like many other managers, he hoped to continue on this track. He had a reputation as a tough, no-nonsense budget and finance man; he was known for his penchant for detail when it came to city expenditures.

The city council was not necessarily seeking a change agent when it appointed Christian after a national search, but it was looking for someone with the skills needed to prepare the city for the tough financial times ahead. Nor was the new manager brought in as a hired gun expected to make a quick entrance and exit after implementing tough decisions. But from Christian's career perspective, River City was an important step up the career ladder. The need to succeed by solving the city's financial problems was high on his personal and professional agendas.

Political change

One opportunity for change came sooner than expected. River City voters approved a proposal to change the way citizens would be elected to the council. Departing from the tradition of at-large elections, the voters adopted a modified district plan: in the primary, two candidates would be nominated from each of five districts, and in the subsequent general election, city voters would elect one from each district on an at-large basis. The enabling ordinance for the new district system provided for four-year, staggered terms; under the provisions for the first election, all five council seats were to be filled at one time. The three candidates with the highest vote totals would receive four-year terms while the remaining two successful candidates would win two-year terms.

Two members of the outgoing council, Tanner and Hiram Foley, were re-elected to four-year terms after tough battles against other incumbent council members who had ended up in their respective districts when the boundaries were drawn. Foley, a prominent businessman, had completed one term on the council and had served previously on the school board. The third four-year term was won by Duane Baker, a political newcomer elected from a blue-collar neighborhood that previously had had little direct representation on the council.

Elected to serve two-year terms were Rebecca Nichols and Susan Lancaster. Newcomers to elected office, both had previously been involved with River City government through participation in interest groups and service on citizen boards and commissions. Each had run second in her district primary but had defeated the front runner in the at-large general election by a small margin.

Lancaster's district contained the city's largest African-American population, and she had defeated an African-American candidate in the general election. Nichols had been able to win only with last-minute support from the chamber of commerce.

Growing public support for another referendum on election procedures raised the possibility that in the next election, candidates would be elected by district in both the primary and the general elections. It was also expected that, for the first time, the mayor would be elected directly by the people rather than chosen by the council members. It was more than speculation that each of the five council members would like to be the first elected mayor.

The case

When the new council convened for its first meeting, it faced a unique opportunity to affect economies through organizational change. In anticipation of the new district plan, the terms of all board and commission appointments had been scheduled to expire during the forthcoming year. The new council had to appoint people to all of the several hundred positions that made up the city's board and commission system. The council members could use the opportunity to either build political support for future campaigns or reduce the number of boards and commissions, which would result in substantial cost savings. (Board and commission operations cost nearly $500,000 plus hundreds of hours of staff time annually.)

City Manager Christian recommended to the new council that it undertake a study of board and commission operations with the aim of streamlining the system and gaining economies. The council members were enthusiastic about the study even though the timing was earlier than they had anticipated, given the number of other questions on the public agenda. The council voted unanimously to ask the public affairs center at the local university to undertake the study and report the findings and recommendations back to the council for action.

Christian and the university negotiated an agreement that the study be broad in scope and emphasize the need for (1) full, positive public participation in the city's policy-making process; (2) the best use of city revenue and staff resources; and (3) organizational arrangements that would allow the boards and commissions to operate effectively and be fully accountable to the city and its voters. The council agreed to place a moratorium on all appointments to boards and commissions pending the findings and recommendations of the report, scheduled to be completed in late summer.

The study

The study staff obtained comprehensive information from each board and commission and interviewed the mayor and individual council members, the city manager and his assistants, department heads, and board staffs. In addition, the study group obtained testimony from about thirty board members at a public hearing. Finally, the study obtained, for comparison, information about boards from fourteen other cities comparable in size to River City.

The study staff identified for examination thirty-five boards and commissions, to which the council was to appoint 270 members. The boards and commissions were classified into six categories.

1. The five *administrative boards* generated the most interest and debate during the study. They were the most prestigious boards, and each had the authority to appoint a director and staff, set salaries, purchase materials, let contracts, and establish policies and procedures to implement their programs. The administrative boards identified for study were the Art Museum Board, the Board of Park Commissioners, the Library Board, the Metropolitan Transit Authority, and the River City Airport Authority.
2. *Quasi-administrative boards* had authority over contracts, grants, poli-

cies, programs, and receipt and expenditure of public funds. They were the Metropolitan Planning Commission, the Board of Housing Commissioners, the Board of Health, the Alcohol and Drug Abuse Advisory Board, the Historic Preservation Board, and the Public Building Commission.

3. *Advisory boards* advised the council on programs, policies, litigation, and expenditure of funds within their specified policy areas. They were the Alarm Regulation Advisory Board, the Bicycle Committee, the Citizen Rights and Services Board, the Community Corrections Advisory Board, the Convention and Tourism Committee, the Economic Development Commission, the Historic Landmark Preservation Committee, the Human Resources Board, the Sister Cities Advisory Board, the Commission on the Status of Handicapped People, the Commission on the Status of Women, and the Traffic Commission.

4. *Regulatory boards* had a regulatory, examining, and licensing function related mostly to the building trades. They were the Board of Electrical Examiners; the Board of Building Code Examiners and Appeals; the Board of Examiners of Air Conditioning, Refrigeration, Warm Air Heating, and Boilers; the Board of Examiners of Plumbers and Gas Fitters; the Board of Housing Standards and Appeals; the Pest Control Regulating and Examining Board; and the River City Athletic Commission

5. *Quasi-judicial boards* was a category that contained only one board: the Board of Zoning Appeals.

6. *International administrative boards* developed, administered, and implemented policies related to River City personnel and personnel benefits. They were the Group Life Insurance Board of Trustees, the Personnel Advisory Board, the Police and Fire Retirement Board of Trustees, and the River City Employees' Retirement Board of Trustees.

In River City, as in other communities, the extensive use of boards and commissions originated after citizen involvement had become a requirement of many federal grant programs. Citizen advisory groups flourished in River City even during the Reagan presidency, when the federal role in local government affairs diminished.

Study results

Despite the city's intensive use of citizen boards, the university study found little evidence that the boards and commissions affected decisions made by the council. The study raised the question of whether citizen boards made any real policy difference or were merely political symbols. The study found that the trend in River City toward decentralized policy making with strong citizen involvement contrasted sharply with the city's reform type of government, which espoused the values of economy; efficiency; professionalism; and a centralized, responsive, and accountable organizational structure.

The study presented thirty-five recommendations of two basic types. The first set of fifteen recommendations addressed general policies and operating procedures for all of the city's boards and commissions. The main focus of these recommendations was to correct demographic imbalances on the boards and commissions through improved recruitment, appointment, communication, and training procedures. White males from the business, real estate, banking, and investment communities made up the largest category of those serving on citizen boards. Women and African Americans tended to be appointed to the less prestigious boards—for example, those addressing the status of women, handicapped people, and citizens' rights. More than two-thirds of the appointees came from the two districts that made up the east and northwest sections of

River City. One district elsewhere in the city had only 4 percent of the appointments and another had only 6 percent. Although turnover was high on some of the less visible boards, the average tenure of a board member was long; thus, the number of citizens who could serve was limited.

The second set of twenty recommendations focused on duplication and accountability. These recommendations dealt with reorganization and elimination of individual boards and commissions. Numerous overlapping functions were identified among the boards and commissions and, in some instances, between a particular body and the city council. Two of these recommendations became the most controversial and generated the most pressure on the council to ignore the report and retain the status quo.

The first controversial recommendation, which became known as number 16, was that the Airport Authority, the Art Museum Board, the Library Board, and the Metropolitan Transit Authority remain as administrative boards but that the directors of these boards be appointed by, and responsible to, the city manager. The purpose of the recommendation was to make administrative operations more accountable to the city manager. The existing procedure was that the city council made appointments to the boards, and that each board in turn appointed its administrative director without input from the council or the city manager. The director served at the pleasure of the board as its chief operating officer, responsible for the board's budget, personnel matters, and policy recommendations and implementation. The council and the manager, ultimately responsible for all city policies, revenues, and expenditures, often found it difficult to exercise their responsibility because of the organizational arrangement with the administrative boards.

The other controversial recommendation, number 17, also tried to increase the accountability of administrative operations to the city manager. The recommendation was twofold: (1) that the city's parks and recreation function become a city department, with the director appointed by the city manager; and (2) that the Board of Park Commissioners be recreated as an advisory rather than an administrative board.

The study also recommended the following actions:

- Consolidate the Historic Preservation Board and the Historic Landmark Preservation Committee.

- Expand the Alarm Regulation Advisory Board into a city/county board with a one-year sunset provision.

- Eliminate the Bicycle Committee and place bicycling and bicycling safety under the director of parks and recreation.

- Merge the commissions on the Status of Handicapped People and the Status of Women with the Citizen Rights and Services Board, develop a mission for the new structure, and allocate resources to support its combined purposes.

- Eliminate the Traffic Commission and assign its duties to the Department of Public Works.

- Reorganize into a less complex arrangement the six separate boards involved in licensing or regulating eighteen activities related to housing and building codes.

- Eliminate the River City Athletic Commission and transfer its duties and responsibilities to the director of community facilities.

- Eliminate the Personnel Advisory Board and replace it with a procedure for appointing an ad hoc citizens committee to review employee grievances as the need arises.

- Merge the city's two employee retirement boards to reduce the cost of money management, increase the return on investments, and correspondingly reduce the city's retirement liability. Retain the two existing retirement funds as separate funds to be administered by the consolidated board.

Public reaction

The dialogue following the study's release was far more spirited—and antagonistic—than the council members had anticipated when they commissioned it. The first set of fifteen recommendations was received relatively calmly by the public and by affected groups, but all of the second set of recommendations met opposition from interest groups in the community or from segments of the city hall bureaucracy.

The report immediately became the most visible and controversial topic on the local public agenda. The major daily newspaper lauded it and editorially endorsed the recommendations as well reasoned, well documented, and worthy of implementation. But there was little, if any, support from members of the boards and commissions or their constituent groups. In fact, the collective outcry of these groups far exceeded what even the closest political observers would have expected. Together, they constituted a formidable lobby group.

The first indication of opposition came before the report had been completed, when speculation about the recommendations on the administrative and retirement boards began to float through city hall and around the community. An informal, friendly, but organized telephone campaign was launched to convince the authors of the report that "if it ain't broke, don't fix it." Police and fire employees let it be known that they would oppose any recommendation to consolidate their retirement system with that of the other city employees. A group known as Friends of the Library began their own effort to ensure that the library director would not become answerable to the city manager. One caller argued that supporters and library benefactors would no longer give to the libraries if the libraries became part of city government. Another, echoing the calls of many, pleaded that the authors "safeguard the intellectual freedom of the libraries, which might be threatened if libraries were subjected to the politics of the city manager and the city council."

After the report had been submitted, letters to the editor began to appear and phone calls—sometimes threatening the withdrawal of reelection campaign support—were made to city hall and to council members' homes. Council members' calendars were filled with names of those wanting to plead their cases.

No council member wanted to reject the report in its entirety; and most numbers were supportive, at least in principle, of the need to "reorganize to economize." However, every member was opposed to one or more of the recommendations that affected his or her particular interest. The campaign against the recommendations reached its peak on August 25, when the council held a public hearing on the report.

The decision problem

The council chamber was packed with people waiting to either testify in support of the status quo or oppose the report; few, if any, were there to endorse the report. Included among the opposition speakers were two former mayors, one former city manager, and dozens of board and commission members. Most visible were the directors of the Art Museum Board and the Board of Park Commissioners. Both were openly leading and orchestrating the opposition to recommendations 16 and 17. Arnold Benjamin, the Art Museum Board director, threatened to resign if his position were placed under the manager's control.

In open defiance of the council and the manager, he led the cheers each time a speaker criticized the report or expressed dissatisfaction with the council if it were to adopt recommendation 16.

Dozens of citizens paraded to the microphone, each underscoring how the interests of the board or commission he or she supported would be threatened by the recommendations; all implied that they were speaking for a broad segment of the community. Lost throughout the testimony was the driving force behind the study—the savings of critical tax dollars through organizational change. Typical were the comments of these citizens:

Humphrey Bonner, member of the Art Museum Board: "The museum will lose its attributes and assets if the position of director is placed under the manager's control."

Richard Green, president of the River City Golf Association: "The growth of the golf courses is due to the autonomous nature of the Board of Park Commissioners."

Former mayor Ralph Wheeler: "The city manager should have a voice in the hiring of the park board director, but not the sole hiring and firing capability."

Former city manager Walter Woolf: "Cities with park boards have better parks than cities whose parks are under the city manager's jurisdiction."

Francis Carson, president of the River City Open Space Committee: "If the park board is eliminated, it will leave our committee dangling and unable to raise money for the botanical gardens and other civic needs."

Ronald Meeker, Metropolitan Transit Authority member: "Retain the transit authority but appoint people with dedication and expertise."

Jane Lawrence, member of the Commission on the Status of Women: "Merger with other boards will dilute the strength of women's input in city government. We need continued commitment and more resources from the council."

The comments, sometimes respectful but often not, continued from representatives of most of the boards and commissions. All sounded the same theme: "Don't change our status; leave us alone to continue to operate as we have been operating."

In the aftermath of the public hearing, the city council members—particularly those newly elected—were stunned by the force of the combined opposition to their attempt at effecting organizational change and cost savings. They pondered the position they were in and wondered about the political perils of implementing any of the changes recommended in the report. They could not adjourn into executive session because of open meetings requirements. Nor would the open meetings law allow them to seek each other's counsel, one on one, regarding the complexities of the tough decision they were facing. The dilemma was clear: reorganization was needed to trim costs in the operating budget and to streamline accountability, but adoption of the report would carry with it the threat of political opposition within the community.

The council side-stepped the decision, at least for a short cooling-off period. Immediately following the August 25 hearing, it voted unanimously to direct the city manager to prepare a staff report on implementation of the study's recommendations, including which, if any, of the recommendations should be adopted. The manager's report was due in two weeks and was to be put on the agenda for discussion and final vote at the September 8 council meeting.

The council then adjourned its August 25 meeting. City Manager Christian laboriously gathered his papers and headed for the privacy and temporary comfort of his office, pondering the difficulty of his situation. He was having second thoughts about his endorsement of what had appeared initially to be a straightforward attempt at reorganizing city functions, an activity that usually received little or no public attention. His conclusion as he arrived at his desk was that "everyone likes progress but no one likes change." How would he prepare a report that would balance the city's administrative needs against the council's political concerns?

Discussion questions

1. What political considerations will affect the council's decision? What degree of importance should be attached to each?
2. Is there a strategy that would build political support for a council decision to adopt all or most of the recommendations in the report? If so, what is it? Evaluate it.
3. Is there a "minimax strategy"—one that would maximize cost savings and minimize political opposition? If so, what is it? What are its advantages and disadvantages?
4. What alternatives should Christian consider as he decides on his course of action?
5. What should Christian recommend to the council?
6. Since the prerogatives of the manager's office are involved and the city's fiscal health is affected, Christian might use the prestige of his office to promote his recommendation publicly. Should he do so? Summarize the arguments for and against his becoming publicly involved.
7. What, if anything, can Christian do to "sell" his proposal to the individual members of the council? To the council as a whole? What should he do?

5

Politics, user fees, and Barracudas

John Doe

Editor's introduction

Politics is a problem not only for local administrators but equally so—and equally frustrating—for citizens. This case looks at local politics from the perspective of a citizen who, in his capacity as an officer of a local swim team, attempts to negotiate a fee agreement with the city that will enable the team to use a city swimming pool for its practice sessions.

The city's park and recreation administrators proceed to propose a fee structure, seeking to negotiate an agreement that will provide adequate city revenues and be fair to other groups that contract to use the city's pool. The swim team, on the other hand, clearly wants to keep its costs down and believes the city's proposed fee is too high.

The request quickly becomes political. If the swim team were negotiating with a privately owned swimming pool, it would be just another potential pool customer. In this case, however, the team members and leaders are also citizens and voters who can, and do, seek to gain their ends by appealing to the city council. Political pressure is added to economic pressure, and the problem only becomes more difficult and more intense for the administrator.

Adding to the complexity in this case are differences in perspective between the city manager's staff and the park and recreation department staff. Each seeks different goals; each has its own public interests to protect. At its climax, the case revolves around differences of opinion among the swim team, the manager's staff, and the park and recreation staff, while the city council is demanding that the issue be resolved, and resolved immediately.

Still another dimension that complicates decision making is the way in which the conflict escalates as the case proceeds. What starts as a disagreement over fees becomes a disagreement over administrative methods as well. What starts as a problem in parks and recreation becomes a problem for the manager and, ultimately, for the city council.

Finally, the case provides an instructive look at government administration from the perspective of the citizen. The reasons for administrative actions are not always apparent to citizens, and in this case, failure to communicate fully and adequately becomes an administrative mistake that only exacerbates the administrator's political problems.

Case 5
Politics, user fees, and Barracudas

Background

The Uptown Skating and Aquatic Center (USAC) in Western City was to be the first indoor ice rink in that part of the state. Both the Olympic-sized pool and the rink were to be the premier facilities of their types in the region. City voters had approved a quarter-cent sales tax to finance it, construction had run ahead of schedule, and the final preparations were being made for the grand opening a few months hence.

Administrators in the Western City Department of Recreation were simultaneously proud of and nervous about USAC. On the one hand, it would add luster to the department's award-winning facilities and programs. On the other hand, the Western City Council had become increasingly concerned about the department's operating budget; recreation administrators were anticipating considerable pressure from the council and from certain sectors of the community regarding recovery of USAC operating costs. However, operating costs and revenues were impossible to project with confidence; technological and design innovations had been incorporated into USAC, and no data were available from comparable facilities because there were no comparable facilities. Moreover, user demand—particularly for the ice arena—was also an unknown.

Chuck Morgan, the newly hired manager of USAC, felt the pressure more intensely than anyone. Although young, Morgan had several years' experience as manager of a public ice arena in another state. That experience was invaluable because no other administrator in the Department of Recreation had any firsthand knowledge of ice rink operations. Morgan's relative inexperience in pool management was not considered critical when he was hired because the department had several experienced pool managers on its staff. Moreover, Morgan had hired an assistant manager whose background had been primarily in pool programming and management.

During his relatively brief time in Western City, Morgan had tried to identify the community groups that were likely to become regular users of USAC. Anticipating a February 1 opening for the new facility, he spent a good deal of time during the preceding summer getting acquainted with the leaders of these organizations and with their plans and preferences for using USAC.

Morgan had met on several occasions with David Arnott and Grant Winger, president and vice president, respectively, of the Western City Barracuda Swim Team, the only year-round competitive swim team for youngsters in Western City. The team relied almost exclusively on public pool facilities for its practice sessions and home meets. Although it was a private association, its membership was not exclusive, and it had developed a good working relationship with the existing aquatics staff in the Department of Recreation. As is typical of such volunteer youth organizations, the leadership was composed of a relatively small number of enthusiastic parents—in this case that number was especially small because in recent years, a series of problems had reduced the swim team's membership to approximately forty swimmers.

In their meetings with Morgan, Arnott and Winger repeatedly stressed their hope that the team would increase significantly in size in the near future. They emphasized that the availability of pool time at reasonable hours and at reasonable cost would be an important factor affecting their plans for growth. All three understood that a thriving swim team would help alleviate some of the performance pressures felt by Morgan. Morgan was careful in these conversations not to commit himself prematurely to any time or cost figures; however, he did let the team leaders know that he was sympathetic to their goals. On at least one occasion he indicated that charges at USAC would have to be somewhat higher than the $2.50 per lane-hour that the Barracudas had been paying to swim in the existing city pool. Arnott and Winger understood him to imply, however, that lane fees at USAC were unlikely to exceed $3.00 per hour.

As the summer waned, so did the interaction between Morgan and the Barracudas. Morgan's time was devoted increasingly to supervising the final details of constructing, equipping, and staffing USAC and of putting together the first year's operating budget, which the council was scheduled to adopt in October. He did try to keep Arnott informed of budgetary items of interest to the Barracudas, including the fact that lane charges were likely to exceed $3.00 per hour. However, Arnott did not share that information with Winger or the other members of the Barracuda board.

The case

On October 9 the Barracuda board was told of the USAC fee schedule. Invited by Arnott to attend the October meeting of the board, Morgan and his newly hired assistant manager, Jack Scott, announced that hourly lane charges were to increase 60 percent, from $2.50 to $4.00. Furthermore, the new fees were to be uniform at the existing Western City pool and USAC, so there would be no less-expensive alternative. Prepared to hear a worst-case charge of $3.00 per lane-hour, the board members expressed shock and outrage at the $4.00 figure. To make matters worse, Arnott's failure to inform the board earlier of the fee hike had permitted the figure to go unchallenged during critical stages of the city's budget process. Only two days before, the Western City Council had approved the $4.00 fee along with all other recreation department fees and charges.

Scott tried to calm the board members by offering to help them develop fund-raising ventures so that the club could pay the new fees without raising its membership dues excessively. However, the board showed no interest in Scott's offer. They feared that a fee increase would have a chilling effect on the growth of the club at precisely the time when other aspects of their membership drive were falling into place.

During the first week in November, the Barracudas held their annual membership meeting and election of officers. Arnott had arranged with Morgan for the members to have an advance tour of the USAC complex and for Morgan and Scott to address the full group of Barracuda parents. Morgan and Scott hoped to gain acceptance of the fee increase by appealing directly to the membership.

Morgan and Scott explained the rate increase by citing projected operating costs of USAC and the need for users of city facilities to pay a higher percentage of operating costs. Scott also repeated the suggestion he had made earlier to the board that the club become more assertive in outside fund-raising activities. He also presented some figures showing that the new fees were in line with those paid by other swim clubs in the state and that the Barracudas had been subsidized by the city in the past and had an artificially low dues structure as a result. Despite this hard line, Morgan and Scott could tell from the questions and comments from the audience that they had not succeeded in winning acceptance for the new fees.

New leadership

Following the pool fee discussion, Winger was elected president of the Barracuda organization. During the month since he had first learned of the new fees, Winger had become convinced that, in the short run, the only way the club could afford to pay the new rates would be to raise membership dues to levels that would discourage growth and confine membership to the relatively affluent. Such a prospect was unacceptable. He privately vowed that fighting the fee increase would be his top priority as president.

One of Winger's first acts after taking office was to schedule an appearance at the December meeting of the Western City Recreation Advisory Board (Rec Board), a panel of citizens appointed by the city council to review recreation department plans, programs, and policies and recommend appropriate action to the council. Winger came before them to request a recommendation from the Rec Board to lower the proposed pool fees for the Barracudas.

Before the Rec Board meeting, Winger had the first of numerous sessions with Morgan to discuss fees, scheduling, and other aspects of Barracuda–Western City relations. At their initial meeting, Winger had two objectives: (1) to make Morgan aware of the magnitude of the adverse effects that he believed the new fees would have on the swim club, and (2) to explore alternative fee structures so that he could develop a sense of how flexible the recreation department might be.

Morgan and Scott (who sat in on this meeting) were willing to consider any formal alternative fee proposal that the Barracudas might offer. For their part, Morgan and Scott were under pressure to see that users of the new USAC facility paid a reasonable proportion of the costs of its services. They couldn't understand why the Barracudas had rejected their offer to help the club organize additional fund-raising efforts since the youth hockey club, which they were helping to organize, had been successful in soliciting business sponsorship. Winger, however, was disappointed. He concluded that neither Morgan nor Scott understood the operations or financing of competitive swim teams and that they were less interested in providing youth sports programs than in generating revenue at USAC.

On the evening of December 10, Winger arrived at the Rec Board meeting accompanied by the Barracuda coach and one other member of the Barracuda board of directors. One of the nine Rec Board members was absent, but Winger noted that Elizabeth Conant, with whom he had a passing acquaintance, was present. He knew Elizabeth to be an open-minded person who would listen to the argument he had prepared and judge it on its merits. He did not know the other members but noted that several, including the board chairman, appeared to be highly deferential to Jake Willoughby, the long-time director of the Western City Department of Recreation. When the time came to take up the Barracudas' request, Willoughby took control of the meeting.

He introduced the Barracuda representatives and briefly outlined the issue, emphasizing the pressure on the department to generate revenue. He then called on Morgan to address the Barracudas' pool fees directly.

Morgan began his presentation by distributing a data sheet that compared projected USAC operating costs with projected revenues from the Barracudas and the youth hockey club. The figures indicated that even with the fee increase, the swim team was being asked to pay a smaller percentage of its costs than was the hockey club. He pointed out that the pool fees paid by the Barracudas at the old pool had not increased in more than two years and were artificially low as a result. It actually cost the city $5.20 to provide one lane to the team for one hour. Morgan concluded by noting that Barracuda membership fees were "the least expensive in our area" and that the club could and should do more outside fund-raising if it found itself in financial difficulty.

Throughout Morgan's presentation, Winger found himself growing increasingly angry at what he perceived to be factual distortions and unverified assertions. He felt that Willoughby and Morgan had prejudiced his case before he even had a chance to state it.

When Winger's turn came to speak, he began by pointing out the various ways in which the Barracudas contributed to the quality of life in the community and suggested that the club's social and economic contributions would be considerably greater if its plans for growth could be realized. He then described the negative impact the new fees would have if they were implemented in February as planned. He requested that the increase be delayed for six months to permit the club to grow to a size at which it could more easily absorb the additional costs. Winger concluded by questioning Morgan's claim that the club's membership dues and pool charges were low compared with those of other swim teams in the area. However, there was no way he could counter the comparison because, until that evening, he had never seen any of the figures that Morgan had cited.

From the questions and discussion that ensued, it was clear that the Rec Board was divided. Finally, Elizabeth Conant offered a compromise motion: that the Barracuda pool fees be set at $3.25 per lane-hour throughout the first year in the new facility, exactly halfway between the continuation of the current $2.50 charge requested by Winger and the staff's figure of $4.00. Although the compromise provided for a higher pool fee than Winger had requested, it had the advantage of extending the duration of the fee reduction to one full year. Winger and the other Barracuda representatives indicated that the compromise motion was acceptable to them.

An animated discussion followed, during which Willoughby and Morgan vigorously opposed the compromise. When the dust settled and the vote was taken, the compromise failed to carry by a vote of 4–4.

The search for alternatives

Winger and his colleagues were disappointed at the loss, but they took some comfort in the fact that the Barracudas had received enough support to permit them credibly to continue the fight. As Winger was preparing to leave the room, Willoughby approached him and congratulated him on his near success. He added that his opposition to the fee reduction did not reflect his personal preference but rather the cost recovery requirements imposed on the department by the city council. He also expressed the hope that the swim team and the recreation department would maintain the cooperative relationship that they had developed over the past several years. Winger took this as a sign that Willoughby realized that he had only narrowly escaped defeat and that he would like to avoid further conflict with the swim team.

The Barracuda board met the following evening. They concluded that their position was stronger than it had been before the Rec Board meeting. They clearly would have preferred a positive vote on Elizabeth Conant's motion, but even then the issue would not have been settled. They would still have had to carry the battle to the city council, where they could expect strong staff opposition. A Rec Board recommendation would have helped, but a tie vote was almost as good as a narrow victory.

Over the weekend, Barracuda board members systematically contacted a number of swim teams in the state, including all of those that Scott had cited as having significantly higher dues and higher pool fees than the Barracudas. They gathered enough data to demonstrate that neither claim was warranted once adjustments were made for the greater amount of pool time the other clubs were using. Armed with this information, Winger wrote a memo to Morgan in which he challenged the accuracy of Scott's research and the comparative cost data that Morgan had distributed at the Rec Board meeting. His plan was to establish a written record that showed the Barracudas to be a responsible community organization that did its homework with care. He hoped to show by contrast that the data analyses produced by the recreation department staff were haphazard and superficial. Such a record, he reasoned, would be valuable when the time came to appeal to city council for relief.

On Monday, before he had received Winger's memo, Morgan phoned Winger to tell him that Willoughby had been impressed with the support the Barracudas had received at the Rec Board meeting and that Willoughby was prepared to listen to any reasonable proposal the club might offer for an alternative fee structure. They agreed to meet on Thursday, December 18, to discuss the matter further.

The Barracuda board met again on December 17 and discussed several alternative approaches for developing a pool fee proposal. They decided to propose that the Barracudas be charged on the basis of swimmer admissions rather than lane-hour rental. This approach had the virtue of placing the Barracuda youngsters on the same footing as other pool users so that their charges could be compared directly. No other community users of the city's pool facilities paid lane-hour charges, so meaningful comparisons were difficult. The board authorized Winger to submit such a proposal if, after working out the details, it appeared to offer reasonable relief for the team.

Winger and Morgan met on December 18 as planned. Morgan had received Winger's earlier memo and responded orally to some of its inquiries. Winger had difficulty understanding the method by which Morgan calculated the costs attributed to the Barracudas, but he did not press the matter. He wanted to move on to discuss the admission charge approach to pool fees. In the absence of a formal proposal, Morgan was unable to make any commitments, but he did not try to dissuade Winger from using swimmer admissions as the basis for his proposal.

On January 2 Winger mailed a formal fee proposal to Morgan. It called for the club to pay on behalf of its swimmers the same pool admission per practice session that other youngsters paid for a recreational swimming session if they purchased a multiple-admission pass. Under reasonable expectations regarding membership growth and frequency of practices, Winger reasoned that the proposal would generate a considerable increase in revenues to the city while permitting the Barracudas to maintain a reasonable schedule of membership dues. Two additional financial sweeteners were built into the proposal: (1) a demonstration that the city would receive more than $4.00 per lane-hour whenever the team practiced in the full fifty-meter lanes at USAC, and (2) an offer to pay more than $4.00 per lane-hour to hold swim meets with other teams. The rental figure in such cases was to increase as the team's membership grew.

In January the Barracuda board announced an increase in membership dues, to be effective February 1. The board reasoned that an increase would be necessary in any event and that the club did not have the luxury, financially, of waiting until the fee issue was settled. The increase was predicated on the optimistic assumption that the club's proposal or something similar would be accepted and, although more than some members wished, was less than would be required if the club ended up having to pay $4.00 per lane-hour.

When Morgan received Winger's proposal and calculated its probable impact on recreation department revenues, he knew that it would not be acceptable. On January 29, he met with Winger in his office. Barbara Matlock, one of Willoughby's chief assistants, was there to represent the department's administrative staff. Winger was told that the proposal had been rejected. Matlock added, however, that Willoughby was prepared to lower the Barracuda charges to $3.50 per lane-hour for the first year but that the fees would revert to $4.00 thereafter. Winger told them that he would relay Willoughby's response to his board at a meeting the following week and give Morgan a reply shortly thereafter.

The Barracuda board received the news with indignation. Several of the members were in favor of taking their case immediately to the city council. Winger counseled against this course because Willoughby would have the advantage in such a confrontation—particularly now that he was on record as having offered a reduction. To reject it out of hand and to go before the council prematurely would be to court disaster. Winger felt that when Willoughby had gone before the Rec Board, he had subtly portrayed the Barracuda parents as an ill-informed special interest group seeking to indulge their children at public expense. He did not want the same scene replayed before the council. He had come to believe that a strong case could be made for the Barracudas but that time and considerable work were needed to do so. So long as Morgan's claim that it cost the city $5.20 to provide one lane of water to the team for one hour remained unchallenged, it was doubtful that the council could be persuaded that a lane charge of $3.50 was unfair. But to offer a credible challenge to Morgan's cost projections, the club would need more information. Winger succeeded in convincing the board to exercise patience. Winger drafted a response and posted it to Morgan on February 8. He challenged the fairness of the $3.50 lane-hour charge and again questioned, for the record, the validity of Morgan's cost projections. However, he declared that the Barracudas would accept lane charges of $3.50 through May while monitoring the actual operating costs and revenues at USAC, and he indicated that a new pool fee proposal would be forthcoming from the swim club once actual cost data became available.

An accounting problem

During the next three months, Winger met periodically with Morgan, who shared USAC financial data with him. Morgan explained the cost-accounting system that he was using, which was based on the concept of a program-hour. Since the bulk of USAC operating costs could not be traced directly to specific programs, all the operating costs were apportioned to the various users in proportion to their shares of the total program-hours generated by all user programs. To arrive at a lane-hour cost for the swim team, Morgan simply divided one program-hour by ten, the number of lanes in the pool.

When Winger first encountered the program-hour concept, he understood it to mean the equivalent of one hour during which time the Barracudas rented the entire USAC pool—ten fifty-meter lanes. Thus, two clock-hours during which only five lanes were rented would amount to one program-hour, or so he thought. As Winger began to understand the concept and the role it played in Morgan's accounting, however, his suspicion increased that it was the cause of what he still believed was the attribution of excessively high costs to the Barracudas' pool use. At first his misgivings focused on the possibility that ice rink costs were being shifted to pool users. To document such an effect, however, would require that separate accounts be kept for each area. Since utilities, maintenance, and other accounts were not broken down by functional area, it was impossible for him to confirm this suspicion.

In the course of exploring this issue with Morgan, Winger unearthed two additional problems deriving from the program-hour concept. The first problem was that the overhead costs associated with several user locations in USAC were included in the aggregate cost figures, but no recreational programs conducted in those areas were assigned a share of those costs. Thus, the overhead costs were hidden in the operating costs charged to pool and rink users. The second problem stemmed from the fact that the USAC pool, which by this time was in use, had movable bulkheads so that it could be configured alternatively as either a single pool having ten fifty-meter lanes or three separate pools—a deep pool for diving at one end, a shallow pool at the opposite end, and a middle section containing ten twenty-five-yard lanes. The Barracudas most often practiced in the latter configuration, renting from three to seven of the twenty-five-yard lanes at a time.

Winger was troubled by the suspicion that Morgan's accounting system attributed costs to the Barracudas as if they were renting fifty-meter lanes even when they were swimming in the twenty-five-yard configuration. When he raised this concern, Morgan assured him that the accounting system was fair and that it conformed to accepted public cost-accounting principles. Nevertheless, Winger remained skeptical.

By June the Barracuda membership had grown fourfold to more than 150 swimmers. Consequently, the club had become a heavier user of the city's aquatic facilities than anyone had predicted. Moreover, all types of user demand and revenues at USAC had exceeded even the most optimistic projections. Therefore, the Barracuda board decided that the time had come to reopen fee negotiations.

Winger sent a second formal fee proposal to Morgan on June 14. He also proposed an alternative method of calculating the actual costs of providing practice lanes for the swim team. In contrast to the program-hour concept, Winger's method took into account the length of the lanes in which the Barracudas swam. His figures also differed from Morgan's earlier projected costs in that they were based on the actual costs of operating USAC during its first three months of operation. The new figures corresponded very closely to Morgan's projected costs as long as the team swam in fifty-meter lanes, but they were only about half that amount when twenty-five-yard lanes were used. According to Winger's calculations, the flat $3.50 lane-hour charge the Barracudas had been paying represented 67 percent cost recovery for long lanes and 134 percent cost recovery for short lanes. Both cost recovery percentages were higher than what he knew that other youth sports groups paid for the use of public facilities. Nevertheless, he proposed a new fee structure that would yield approximately 90 percent cost recovery to the city on the basis of his cost calculations. The proposal called for rates of $4.75 per hour for fifty-meter lanes and $2.50 per hour for twenty-five-yard lanes.

More than a month passed before the city responded. On July 31 Morgan wrote to Winger and again rejected his proposal. Morgan explained that the city was placing a "greater emphasis on recovering a higher percentage of operating expenses" and noted that the proposed fees would reduce revenues "above and beyond the reduction in revenue the city is already absorbing from the adjustments of $4.00 per lane-hour to $3.50 per lane-hour." He affirmed the staff's intention to revert to the $4.00 figure in the second year.

Winger and the Barracuda board were incensed. They had taken Willoughby's invitation to submit a proposal at face value and had submitted not one but two proposals. Each had been well reasoned, temperate, and offered in good faith. Now each had been summarily rejected, leaving no apparent room for further discussion. They now questioned whether the original invitation had been genuine or merely a tactic by Willoughby and Morgan to buy time. They believed that the swim team was being victimized and agreed that the time had come to shift the battle to a more political arena. They decided that the best strategy would be to emphasize the flaws in the program-hour cost-accounting system and to frame their position as a request for a fair cost recovery rate applied to accurately determined costs.

Politics and the budget

The timing coincided with the city budget process, as the recreation department was to submit its proposed budget for the next fiscal year to the Rec Board in August. That board, in turn, was to send its recommendation to the city council in September, and the council was to adopt the budget in October. Winger requested and was granted a slot on the Rec Board's agenda for its August meeting. Prior to the meeting, he sent a letter to all members of that board in which he reiterated his analysis of USAC operating costs, challenged the program-hour concept, and questioned the appropriateness of the cost recovery percentage that the Barracudas were being asked to pay. He also pointed out other aspects of administrative policy that the Barracudas believed were unfair. He requested that the board recommend lane fees of $2.50 and $4.75, the same figures that he had requested in the second proposal to Morgan and Willoughby.

Winger sent a copy of the letter to Blaine Perry, a member of the city council who he believed would be sympathetic to the Barracuda cause, and he enlisted several other Barracuda parents to lobby their council contacts on behalf of the Barracuda position.

The Recreation Advisory Board met on August 26. At the beginning of the meeting, Winger was given a copy of a three-page memo dated August 24 from Morgan to the board, which addressed several points made in Winger's letter. Winger read it hastily, and his first impression was that it contained incomplete information and appeared to discredit the Barracudas. The concluding paragraph contained an additional surprise. The department was requesting lane fees of $4.00 for twenty-five-yard lanes and $6.50 for fifty-meter lanes for the coming year. The principal justification offered for the increase was that the department needed additional revenue. After lengthy and at times heated discussion, the board deferred a decision until its September meeting and asked that the administration prepare an analysis of the implications of Winger's proposed cost-accounting methodology.

Morgan caught up with Winger after the meeting and apologized for the lack of warning about the proposed increase in fifty-meter-lane fees. Morgan was embarrassed by the move and explained that it was a last-minute decision by his administrative superiors.

During the following week, Winger obtained additional USAC operating cost data from Morgan, covering the first six months of USAC operations. These data indicated somewhat higher operating costs than had the earlier figures. Winger revised his cost calculations, which now showed that it cost the city approximately $3.05 to provide one twenty-five-yard lane to the Barracudas for one hour and approximately $6.65 for a fifty-meter lane. Even so, he believed that the Barracudas' requested lane fees were reasonable, for they represented cost recovery rates of 82 percent and 71 percent, respectively. Both figures were above the 70 percent rate that was ostensibly the overall cost recovery goal of the recreation department.

On September 10 several Barracuda parents attended an informal community meeting conducted by the city council to hear citizen comments regarding the budget. They requested that the council issue clear and unambiguous guidelines to the recreation department regarding appropriate cost recovery rates. They were careful to avoid suggesting any particular percentage or to appear as special pleaders for the swim team. Instead, they tried to convey the idea that Willoughby's department was confused regarding the council's cost recovery expectations and, as a protective measure, had proposed excessive fee increases for many users of the city's recreation facilities.

At the September 23 Rec Board meeting, the recreation department administration once again produced an eleventh-hour memorandum that contained assertions and implications that the Barracudas found questionable. Winger tried to keep the discussion focused on the technical flaws in the program-hour accounting system, but Morgan told the board that he had used the same system elsewhere without criticism and that the Western City Office of Finance had approved it. The vote was 4–3 against a favorable recommendation of the Barracuda proposal; a divided Rec Board once again failed to support a Barracuda request.

Over the next two days, Winger spoke to several experts in public finance and accounting. From each of them he received confirmation that his suspicions about Morgan's cost-accounting method were valid. Thus reassured, he scheduled a meeting with the Western City director of finance and Morgan for Tuesday, September 29. He invited one of the Rec Board members who had voted against the Barracudas to attend as an observer.

Over the weekend, Winger studied the complete recreation department budget proposal that was pending before the city council. He found several discrepancies between data reported in the budget document and figures the staff had cited on previous occasions to support its position. He summarized these inconsistencies and pointed out their implications for assessing pool charges and calculating cost recovery percentages in a three-page document that also outlined the club's objections to the program-hour accounting system. It was a technical document, but he believed it would demonstrate to the city's chief finance officer that the Barracudas had stumbled onto some potentially embarrassing information that cast serious doubt on the care with which the recreation department produced its financial and accounting figures. On Monday Winger made a courtesy call to Morgan to inform him of his findings and to offer him an advance copy of the document, which he planned to distribute at the meeting on Tuesday. Morgan said that he considered the program-hour accounting system to be a "non-issue" and that he was too busy to review any new material prior to the meeting. If Winger had harbored any reservations about embarrassing Morgan before his administrative superiors, they were dispelled with that phone call.

An appeal on accounting methods

The meeting on Tuesday, September 29, was held in the office of David Komives, the Western City finance director. Morgan and Barbara Matlock, assistant to the director of recreation, represented the recreation department. Winger opened the session by informing Komives that since the authority of his office had been cited to validate Morgan's cost calculations, the Barracudas had some questions that they hoped he could clarify regarding USAC budgeting and accounting procedures. Winger was careful to point out that he had already consulted several experts who had reinforced his misgivings. He declared that if Komives endorsed Morgan's accounting system after considering his queries, the Barracudas would press the issue no further. He then proceeded to work through the three-page list of questions he had prepared to illustrate the flaws in the USAC accounting system and budget data. Morgan had little to say until near the end of the meeting, when he offered a brief defense of the program-hour methodology and tried to show that Winger had an incomplete understanding of the concept. He pointed out that Winger had mistakenly assumed that a program-hour of pool costs represented ten lane-hours of usage, whereas in fact a program-hour for the Barracudas was any clock-hour during which the team was swimming in any number of lanes.

Now the full implications of the program-hour concept became clear to Winger. The Barracudas had been upset when they believed that the system was attributing to them the costs of operating ten fifty-meter lanes when in fact they were using only ten twenty-five-yard lanes. Now Winger was being told that the Barracudas' hourly share of USAC operating expenses was the same regardless of whether they used the entire fifty-meter capacity of the pool or only two or three twenty-five-yard lanes while other users occupied the remainder. Winger pounced on this revelation and made certain that its implications were not lost on those in attendance.

Komives was attentive but noncommittal during the meeting; he said that he would need time to review the material Winger had presented and that he would get back to him. Winger hoped that the finance director would see that the administration had a potential problem on its hands and would counsel the city manager to avoid a public fight over such a minor issue.

October 6 was the date set for the Western City Council to adopt the recreation fee schedule for the coming year. Despite a follow-up phone call, Winger was unable to obtain a response from Komives prior to the council meeting. He hoped that Komives's silence indicated that he could not endorse Morgan's accounting system but was reluctant to admit it publicly. If that were the case, Komives would likely alert the city manager to the potentially embarrassing situation that was developing.

Winger's optimism was well-founded. As he sat in the audience at the October 6 council meeting, he heard Mayor Charles Franklin announce that consideration of the recreation fee schedule was being deferred until a subsequent meeting. The city manager had requested additional time to work out mutually acceptable fees with certain unnamed "affiliated groups." Franklin was looking directly at Winger as he spoke.

Winger was curious to learn what had transpired behind the scenes to produce this last-minute reprieve. He made an appointment to have coffee two days later with Blaine Perry, the council member with whom he had established the closest rapport. Perry was circumspect in responding to his inquiries; however, he left Winger with the distinct impression that at least some council members had become persuaded that Morgan's cost-accounting system was flawed and that the council had been more than a passive actor in the decision to defer consideration of the fees. Perry also suggested obliquely that the Barracudas give some thought to a fee schedule that would provide lower-cost pool fees for nonpeak demand hours, thereby signaling that the general principles of a compromise solution already had been discussed.

Moving toward a compromise

On October 15 Roger Young, the assistant city manager, called a meeting in his office. He invited Matlock and Morgan from the recreation department and Winger and Art Neighbors, the Barracuda vice president, to represent the swim team. Young had been directed by the city manager to negotiate a speedy resolution to the pool fee controversy.

Like the city manager, Young was concerned that the question of pool fees had escalated into a public dispute, and he sympathized with the swim team's desire to keep membership fees affordable to families of modest means. At the same time, he felt that the Barracudas were being stubborn in the face of the increasing financial pressures on the city. The council had sent a clear message to the administrative staff that user fees were to be set high enough to cover a substantial share of the city's actual costs of providing recreation and other services.

Young also had mixed feelings about the substance of the dispute. He had personal questions about the program-hour concept that Morgan had used to establish the proposed fees, and he was annoyed that the methodology had been allowed to become the focus of a public controversy because he now had to defend it. Even if the methodology was sound, he understood why it had the appearance of inequity to users of the pool. In short, he felt that the credibility and commitment of the city administration were under serious question by this vocal and assertive group of citizens.

Young set out to determine how much ground the Barracudas might be persuaded to yield in arriving at a compromise. Winger and Neighbors were steadfast in challenging USAC cost calculations and supporting their alternative approach. While they reiterated the belief that their proposed lane charges of $2.50 and $4.75 were fair, they conceded that upward adjustments could be acceptable if they were supported by accurate operating cost data and an appropriate cost recovery formula. Young explained that the cost-accounting system could not be changed but asked the Barracudas if they would be receptive to the principle of reduced fees during low-demand hours of the day. They accepted, with the qualification that the baseline fees be determined on the basis of valid cost calculations. As the negotiating session ended, the participants agreed to continue their discussions one week later.

On October 22 Young convened the second and final meeting. He opened the meeting by restating their earlier agreement in principle to a two-tiered fee structure. He then tried one final time to dissuade the Barracudas from their explicit rejection of Morgan's cost-accounting system. Winger and Neighbors refused to yield. Young knew that the city could not accept an open rejection of the accounting system and therefore would be forced to concede on the issue of pool fees rather than back down on its costing methodology. He was relieved, therefore, when Winger suggested that they agree to disagree over accounting methodology for the time being and get on with the task of addressing the fees directly.

Young then asked Morgan how soon he could work up a new fee schedule based on some slight modifications of his cost calculations and incorporating an appropriate fee reduction for nonpeak hours. Morgan said he could have the figures in about one month. Young was livid. He had just won a major face-saving concession from the Barracudas, and a resolution to the controversy was at hand. He immediately called a five-minute recess and summoned Matlock to confer with him.

The decision problem

Now Young was faced with a problem. Both the city manager and the city council expected a settlement of the controversy by the next council meeting, which was only twelve days away. He had the pieces of a successful solution in hand but had just been undermined by one of the city's own players. Several options occurred to him.

1. He could accept Morgan's one-month delay and hope that he could convince the city manager and the council that the delay was warranted.
2. He could give Morgan one week to produce the requested figures.
3. He could reaffirm the recreation department's fees of $4.00 and $6.50 but provide a modest reduction during nonpeak hours.
4. He could accept the Barracudas' proposed fees of $2.50 and $4.75, thereby tacitly acknowledging the inappropriateness of Morgan's accounting system.
5. He could devise an alternative fee structure that would include the discount for nonpeak hours, would be acceptable to the Barracudas, and would produce more revenue for the city than option 3.

Discussion questions

1. How should Young deal with Morgan when the meeting reconvenes? How should he deal with him after the meeting? Should he have invited Morgan to join him and Matlock in the meeting during the recess?
2. How should the following considerations be ordered in terms of priority: increasing program revenues, protecting the recreation department from embarrassment, and settling the controversy? What steps should Young take to accomplish each one?
3. What other considerations should Young weigh?
4. To what degree should Young protect Morgan and his program-hour accounting system?
5. What would Young gain by postponing the negotiations for one month? What would he lose?
6. Should Young's personal views regarding the flexibility/inflexibility or the reasonableness/unreasonableness of the Barracudas' negotiators have any role in his decision making? If so, what role? If not, why not?

Part four: Intergovernmental relations

Introduction to part four:
Intergovernmental relations

Local governments are the primary providers of the public services enjoyed by citizens on a daily basis, but they do not perform that function alone or in isolation. Local governments work with federal and state agencies to deliver a wide range of services. They also work with one another; perhaps a dozen or more different units of local government provide services to each local resident and each parcel of property.

To make the task of coordinating services among these many units of government still more difficult, most communities also house a number of not-for-profit agencies—publicly owned private corporations supported by government grants, private donations, and fees from those who can afford to pay for their services. These agencies share in the task of providing such human services as education, mental health assistance, family counseling, senior citizens' programs, and youth activities. Thus, any particular community may have several governments and any number of not-for-profit groups providing public services.

Because they are so visible and have the broadest grant of authority at the local level, county and city governments usually have the added responsibility for supplementing the funds available to not-for-profit organizations and for coordinating the activities of these diverse service providers. Since counties and cities almost never have the authority to require compliance from these other organizations, their coordinating role only adds to the size and political complexity of the jobs of their administrators.

It goes without saying, of course, that even organizations operated by people of good intentions, possessed of public service motivations, and acting rationally will sometimes find themselves locked in bitter conflict with one another. Such is the situation in the first case presented in this part. "A Jail in City Center" describes a major land use controversy between a city and a county, each of which has legitimate and reasonable plans for the development of a particular parcel, and each of which has the strong support of its citizens in the dispute. Conflicts between nations rarely reach an impasse as severe as the stalemate confronting the city of Rollins and the county of St. Regis, and even the presence of the state government, which has jurisdiction over both local units, fails to ameliorate the conflict.

The next case, "Housing the Homeless in Willow County," explores a more common intergovernmental conflict—one involving the county, its major city, and a large not-for-profit agency active in the housing field. In this case, the agencies all agree generally on the goal of more and better housing for the indigent and on the methods for achieving the goal. The disagreements involve the specific strategies and especially the financial role of the county in the joint housing effort. As is often the case in government decision making, the ultimate problem for the county is not one of policy intent, but one of budgetary reality.

Problems involving intergovernmental relations at the local level have one thing in common with other local problems: although they require the policy involvement of elected officials, it is the professional administrators of the affected agencies and governments who ultimately must undertake the negotiations, balance the political interests, and produce the solutions that keep services flowing to the public. The need to reconcile the interests of many different service providers, like the need to reconcile the interests of many different political groups, adds to the complexity of decision making and thus to the professional challenge of local government administration.

6 A jail in City Center

Bill R. Adams, Glen W. Sparrow, Ronald L. Ballard

Editor's introduction

Gov. James R. Thompson of Illinois has been known to say that the hard part of government is that decision makers rarely get to choose between good ideas and bad ideas; instead, they have to choose between good ideas. Such is the situation in this case: a county and a city both have proposals for the development of a parcel of land in the center of the city. Both proposals make good sense, and both enjoy widespread public support from the governments' respective constituencies.

The case is described from the vantage point of the city, and the decision problem is posed as one that the city manager must resolve. His task is complicated by the structural differences between the city and county governments, the different constituencies to which each responds, and the presence of a court order forcing action by the elected county sheriff.

From an intergovernmental perspective, the central issue is the resolution of a conflict between two local governments, each legally independent of the other but with overlapping jurisdiction. Each pursues its separate interests, but each is clearly also pursuing the public interest. What is best for the county and its residents is not what is best for the city and its residents. Which side should prevail? Which set of public interests should the professional local government administrator, with his commitment to democratic principles, pursue: the interests of the county, which represents more people, or the interests of the city, which employs him?

Questions of principle and ethics abound in this case. How should the manager act? What kind of authorization does he need from the city council? Should a lack of time to consult the council affect his inclination to act in accordance with the council's clear mandate, even when the proposed action has not been specifically considered by the council? What is the extent of a manager's freedom to take action in the public interest?

The city's objective is to promote its economic development. The county's objective is to improve its public safety services. Does the difference in objective make a difference in the manager's freedom to act?

Also involved in the case are two other units of government: the state, which empowers both the city and the county, and a special district, which supplies water to the property in question. Their presence adds to the complexity of the problem and further challenges the resourcefulness of the public officials involved.

Case 6
A jail in City Center

Background

The residents of St. Regis County were whipped into a frenzy as news of jail overcrowding became public. The sheriff, Horace Farley, began beating the drums for a solution, claiming that the jails were powder kegs about to blow. More jails were needed now, or prisoners would have to be unleashed onto the streets. Overcrowding was especially serious at the county's jail in the city of St. Regis.

The media, taking its cue from Farley, dutifully announced that there was indeed a jail crisis and that, of course, something must be done about it. The citizens concurred: something should be done. And so pressure was placed on the St. Regis County Board of Supervisors, the governing body charged with building jails for the entire county. The hysteria reached such a crescendo that the supervisors, who had neglected the issue for two decades, were compelled to declare the jail situation an emergency, and to calm mounting public frustration, county officials searched frantically for a quick-fix solution.

During the flap, citizens of the city of Rollins went about business as usual, unperturbed by the hubbub over villains and jail overcrowding. And why not? The jail issue was of marginal interest to Rollins residents, who were rarely visited by crime in their outlying city of 50,000. However, interest rose precipitously when the county declared Rollins to be the ideal spot for a new, temporary, six-hundred-bed men's jail. This proposal seemed reasonable to most of the county, which perceived Rollins as an outback, representing cowboys, country, western music, and people who did not mind long commutes. Rollins, as might be expected, became quite agitated at the decision, swearing to pit itself against the county juggernaut. Undaunted, the county reiterated its resolve to build, accusing the city of undermining "law and order" and obstructing a necessary solution to the problem. Both governments prepared for conflict.

And, indeed, they did fight. Events that led to this clash had been festering for about two decades. Eventually, the jail overcrowding became so bad that the American Civil Liberties Union filed a class-action suit on behalf of jail inmates. The U.S. District Court ultimately ruled that crowding in the county's city-of-St.-Regis jail was "cruel and unusual punishment" and ordered the sheriff and the county board of supervisors to find a solution to it. The search for a solution became even more urgent when the court imposed a 750-inmate cap on the facility.

There was no denying that the problem had become a monster because of the inaction of former boards. Lack of money, competing crises, and public dissatisfaction with earlier proposed solutions had allowed the issue to be continually set aside. Finally, the county responded by declaring a jail emergency and launching attempts to erect a temporary men's facility in the middle of Rollins, adjacent to the existing, but unobtrusive, women's jail.

The proposed jail was to be placed on county-owned land within the redevelopment area known as City Center, a project envisioned as the city's future commercial hub. The Rollins master plan called for a multiuse project focusing on a vibrant commercial core, pedestrian paths and walkways, lush landscaping, open space, fountains, and ponds—a dramatic recreational, commercial, and residential mix along the St. Regis River. For the city, this project was a matter of pride as well as of economic vitality. It was central to Rollins's attempt to show its sophistication, to overcome its "west-county cowboy" image, and to establish a solid commercial base that would carry it in relative economic comfort into the next century.

In contrast, the county was seeking a low-cost, low-conflict "fix" and, in the process, proposed a planner's nightmare: an open compound, warehousing six hundred inmates in ten barracks, and featuring dual chain-link fencing capped with coils of razor wire, guard towers, and minimal landscaping. From a marketing perspective, the facility was hardly considered a draw for the 706-acre City Center redevelopment area.

The county's assurance that the facility would be temporary held no currency with the city. Aside from the county supervisors' refusal to give a definite termination date, there was little likelihood that, in the rapidly growing county, there would ever be enough empty beds to transfer six hundred or more inmates to other, yet-to-be-built facilities. Would the county give up an operating jail site, knowing that it was getting progressively harder to find communities willing to tolerate new jails? To Rollins, the answer seemed clear.

The problem confronting the city was, what, if anything, could be done to derail the proposal? State law seemed to back the county's contention that it could erect anything without city approval if the land were used for public purposes. The irony was that a major reason for Rollins's incorporation years earlier had been to escape this type of external control. Legally, the county, owner of 371 acres in the northeastern sector of City Center, could destroy City Center by introducing all manner of unwanted public projects.

Rollins

It could be convincingly argued that Rollins, prior to its incorporation seven years earlier, had been a victim of benign neglect by the county of St. Regis, a neglect that had incited a revolt and sparked a home-rule movement in Rollins. The county's policy of approving strip zoning and high-density residential projects in Rollins had left a scar that became the major focus of city policy during Rollins's early postincorporation existence. Only time could heal much of the damage previously visited upon the community by unpopular county land use decisions, but a well-planned downtown could be built from scratch in a relatively short period.

At the beginning of the century, Rollins was a quiet, rural farming and dairy community, remaining so through World War II. It had taken the city almost seventy-five years to reach its 1950 population of 2,000. However, the winds of change struck as Rollins entered the late 1950s. To the chagrin of some and the glee of others (particularly developers), water and sewer lines were extended to the area, inviting development. Two water districts were formed in the region and eventually merged to become an independent special district, the Indian Valley Dam Municipal Water District. The Indian Valley Dam District provided both water and sewage treatment services for much of the urbanized western county, including Rollins.

In the 1950s, when the urbanization of Rollins began, a nebulous community began to take on a form dictated by topography. Except to the south, where the growing city of Rock Hill was located, large rocky hills isolated the Rollins valley from neighboring communities, including the city of St. Regis to the east, most of the sprawling community of Riverfront to the west, and the rugged northern lands. Soaring land values quickly transformed the farming community into a suburb, albeit a distant one, of downtown St. Regis. Land had simply become too expensive to farm. New homes and small shops began sprouting around the community of Rollins—projects marked by high density and strip zoning. Eventually, runaway growth and questionable planning ignited Rollins's home-rule movement.

As Rollins had evolved from a rural to an urban community, its leaders, disturbed by county actions, began to wonder whether county policy was indeed a form of benign neglect or a device to turn Rollins into a receptacle for projects shunned by other communities.

Although the idea of incorporation continued to grow in popularity, Rollins voters rejected the proposition to incorporate in the elections of 1976. Undaunted, home-rule advocates continued the struggle for city status, redrawing boundaries and correcting other objections aired by voters. In 1980 the question again went before the voters. This time it passed; in December Rollins officially became one of sixteen municipalities in St. Regis County. Like all the other cities, it adopted the council-manager form of government.

The creation of City Center

The center of Rollins was mostly vacant land surrounded by homes and small businesses. To Rollins's new city planners, it was almost too good to be true. Here was a chance to build a planned downtown—City Center—in a redevelopment area without first having to tear down existing structures. Adding to the lure was the St. Regis River, which bisected the property, making the land that much more attractive and valuable.

As one of its first major actions, the city council formed the Rollins Redevelopment Agency and became its policy board. Under state law, a city government, as a redevelopment agency, could issue bonds for revenue and use the proceeds to attract new development (through financial incentives) or otherwise improve a blighted or redevelopment area, hence increasing property values, quality of life, and the local tax base. The declaration of City Center as a redevelopment area would freeze property tax revenues from the area for all governments (including the county). The bonds would be repaid through property tax increments accruing from upgraded property values, with all of the increment for the ensuing twenty years going to the redevelopment agency. In the case of Rollins, the redevelopment agency acquired $6.4 million in debt to ensure the success of City Center. If the project failed, the city would be responsible for the entire amount, plus interest.

With the redevelopment process defined, the Rollins Redevelopment Agency (the city council) went about the task of identifying the boundaries of City Center, which consisted of 706 contiguous acres of redevelopment land. This area included all of the property around two county facilities in the City Center area. One facility, Broadview, was the only county geriatric hospital and senior-citizens' home in St. Regis County. In 1966, across the street from Broadview, the county had opened Safe Haven, a "permanent" reform school for delinquent girls. The promise that it would remain a girls' reform school was breached a decade later when the structure was converted to a lockup for women—the first and only one in the county.

Several years later, the city began to tackle the tough questions concerning City Center land use. It took two hectic years for the city to approve a comprehensive land use package, called the City Center Specific Plan. During that period, the city council walked a thin line among groups of every political stripe: slow-growth advocates, free marketers, environmentalists, landowners, and developers. "Get everyone involved from the start and negotiate a comprehensive, if compromise, master plan," was the city's strategy.

Complications

For the most part, the scheme worked. For two years, the city held open meetings, discussions, workshops, conferences, and public hearings on City Center. At the start of the process, the county and the city, in a written pact, agreed to plan City Center together.

Had it not been for structural differences between the city and the county, the cooperative planning venture for City Center might have worked. Both the city and the county had professional administrative leadership: the city with a city manager, Jerry Swanson, the county with a chief administrative officer, Jim Marshall. In theory, the resolution of differences between the city and the county should have been aided by negotiations between the city manager and the county administrator—professional peers.

The jurisdiction of the county administrator, however, was limited by the county's governmental structure, which provided for several elected administrative officers, including the county sheriff. The governmental responsibilities assigned to the elected officers fell outside the purview of the administrator; while the administrator could and did attempt to work with, and influence, the elected officials, his influence varied. On politically sensitive matters, the administrator frequently had limited influence with his elected colleagues.

The county jail was such a matter. Since the county's jails fell within the jurisdiction of the county sheriff, decisions regarding them were made by either the sheriff alone or the sheriff in consultation with the board of supervisors. Pressured by the courts, the press, local law enforcement agencies, and his own staff on the problem of jail overcrowding, Sheriff Farley was not inclined to work with the county administrator. He needed a new jail, he needed it now, and he was not going to waste time with what he regarded as extraneous concerns as he worked to get it. His ability to win reelection in a countywide race demanded that he resolve the jail crisis—and do it before the next election.

The case

As the planning for City Center trudged along and the plan began to take form, the county—City Center's largest single landholder—objected to two related proposals: the amount of park and open space proposed on county land, and the resulting limits on the number of homes permitted on the remaining property. At first county officials protested quietly, but angered that the city was holding fast, they went public, airing their differences openly and in the press.

Two months later, the county announced its plans to build the men's jail in City Center, contending that the project did not require city approval because it was a public facility and not a commercial venture. The city was offended at the county's failure to notify it of the decision before going public. (As a courtesy, local agencies normally give advance notice when a policy decision will affect another's sphere of influence.) Tensions heightened when the city procured pictures of the type of facility planned (barracks, chain-link fencing, razor wire, guard towers) and made them public. However, by year's end, the city had persuaded the county to build elsewhere. A new study was completed, identifying an isolated area along the county's southern border as the new jail site. From outward appearances, Rollins had won.

A second confrontation, increasing the bad feelings between the county and Rollins, occurred a year later in a dispute over one million dollars the county owed the city in unpaid tax moneys. Being short of cash, the county had proposed a swap of some of its City Center real estate to settle the debt. The city, wanting control over as much City Center land as possible, agreed, and a memorandum of understanding was signed by both parties. Unfortunately, they could not agree on the property's worth, and negotiations subsequently collapsed. Apparently agitated by the impasse, the county made a unilateral decision to retain the land and repay the debt in cash. An equally irritated city took the county to court for breach of contract, but lost.

The jail issue resurfaces

Meanwhile, a storm was brewing in the city of St. Regis that would eventually affect Rollins. Because of jail overcrowding, the sheriff's department implemented a policy of book-and-release for misdemeanors, which included prostitution. Residents of neighborhoods with the greatest activity, however, complained to the city council that their streets were being overrun by prostitutes (and their potential customers) and that something had to be done. That sounded reasonable to the council, but what to do? Since all municipalities booked suspected criminals in the county jails, the city of St. Regis turned to the county. It decided to wave a carrot before the county supervisors: expand the women's detention facility at Safe Haven in Rollins so that more prostitutes could be locked up, and the city of St. Regis would cover half of the construction cost.

The county agreed. The Rollins city council, attempting to smooth ruffled feathers, decided to neither oppose nor support the expansion as long as it remained within the existing compound. The county agreed to Rollins's condition.

Nevertheless, fate dealt Rollins a double-cross when the board of supervisors, frustrated in its efforts to procure jail land in the proposed southern location, not only approved the expansion of the women's detention facility by almost two hundred beds, but also ordered construction of the six-hundred-bed men's facility next door.

Rollins was stunned. Had this issue not been resolved less than a year earlier? The Rollins city council, angered by the county's behavior, gave City Manager Swanson a free hand, financially and otherwise, to defend the city from the threat.

Publicly, the county reasoned that the men's temporary jail could be built quickly next to Safe Haven (and removed after permanent facilities were built elsewhere) because the infrastructure—roads, electricity, water, and sewer capacity—was in place and the land already belonged to the county. Rumors that the jail was an excuse to punish Rollins for bucking the county on the City Center plan were denied.

The city argued the emotional issue of security: a male lockup located adjacent to homes, Broadview Hospital, and schools (Rollins Elementary School was only two blocks away) would present a real danger to the community and especially to the schoolchildren. The county waved off these concerns, saying that people would actually be safer with more sheriff's deputies in the area.

Although the county's response to safety issues was anticipated, city officials were puzzled by the county's inability to grasp the economic issue. Both jurisdictions had much to lose financially if the jail were built. With population on the rise in Rollins, healthy commercial development in City Center was needed to expand the city's tax base, which in turn would be used to maintain city services.

The jail, it was feared, could undo all efforts to attract upscale business to Rollins, thereby sinking City Center and conceivably the city's future. City leaders wondered why the county, which was always short of cash, would squander its extremely valuable City Center property on a project guaranteed to scare off money-making ventures. The county answered that the land was not that valuable anymore since a large segment of it had been zoned for park and open space use. Furthermore, the county maintained, the jail would only be temporary and, after it was removed, land values would return to normal.

Crisis management

To respond to the threat, a jail task force, made up of City Manager Swanson, the city attorney, and staff members, formulated a four-pronged strategy—political, administrative, public relations, and legal—all salted with a hefty dose of publicity. The city hoped to sandbag the project with delays—a tactic of attrition.

Swanson was the focal point of Rollins's defense. It fell to him to provide the day-to-day management and coordination of the city's strategy. The city council took the lead on the political front, cajoling county officials and enlisting the aid of sympathetic politicians. The city staff undertook the task of managing the crisis administratively. This included doing technical work, tracking county actions, bird-dogging staff, attending meetings, studying jail-related documents, and publicizing via the media contrary city findings. A public information campaign involved the city's community services coordinator, city council members, and resident activists. It was decided that legal challenges would be used where and when necessary.

To assist in the preparation of its case, the city hired twelve consultants, experts in a range of fields including penal systems, criminology, ecosystems, flood control, fire regulations, socioeconomics, and public relations. The Rollins school board also lashed out at the county for suggesting the placement of a men's lockup so near an elementary school attended by hundreds of children. The board members expressed concern over released and escaped prisoners, visitors, and increased traffic. The school district also hired a consultant to assist the city task force. Further, a Rollins citizens' anti-jail organization regrouped and turned up the heat on the county with letters, telephone calls, rallies, and picketing.

The first legal volley was fired when the city filed in county court for a restraining order, arguing that the county was preparing plans to build before completing an environmental impact report (EIR), as required by state law. This, the city argued, put the cart before the horse; that is, the county should not take steps to build in Rollins until the EIR was completed and had identified the best location for a jail. The county claimed it was following proper procedure—a contention with which the court eventually concurred.

At the same time, Rollins's mayor contacted local legislators and requested state legislation to put an end to the type of unilateral action undertaken by the county. But while legislators expressed sympathy, they introduced no legislation.

Another government gets involved

At about the same time, the Indian Valley Dam District gave the county a scare with news that the sewer trunk line serving the district might be near capacity. If true, this meant that the jail would have to be put on hold until the line was expanded, which could be years down the road. As it turned out, the line was near the limit but not close enough to halt the jail.

While the county went about the business of writing the EIR, the city opened negotiations with the Indian Valley Dam District for control of sewer lines in City Center. Under existing rules, sewer lines could be reserved from the Indian Valley Dam even if landowners had no intention of developing the land. Moreover, the agency sold sewer hookups on a first-come, first-served basis. Landowners merely had to prove ownership and possible future need for the sewer units requested. No city or county approval was necessary, as the Indian Valley Dam was an independent special district. (Sewer units are based on the average service one household requires: one sewer unit equals one household. The jail would require 112 units.)

Once reserved under the Indian Valley Dam scheme, sewer lines were locked to a particular property in perpetuity. This meant that a developer using less than the allotted quota was forbidden to resell, trade, or give away the remaining units to anyone else, including the dam district.

Because of the rapidly dwindling number of available units, the Indian Valley Dam's regulations could have wreaked havoc on City Center development, leaving certain parcels shy of units while others had a surfeit. Such a system had the potential of turning the City Center development into a game of chance, and Rollins had no intention of gambling with its future. Rollins proposed to the dam district that, because of its overriding interest, the city be granted control of the allocation of sewer capacity in the City Center area.

Two events had prompted the city's concern about City Center sewer lines. The first occurred when a major developer, who had become worried by published reports of diminishing sewer capacity, purchased almost half of the remaining sewer capacity (1,460 units) available to Rollins. That left Indian Valley Dam with only 833 units. The precipitous drop in available capacity alarmed Rollins officials, who saw the whole City Center project in double jeopardy. The second event was the county jail proposal: the city would obviously gain significant leverage over the jail location if the county had to go through the city for sewer service.

The city argued before the Indian Valley Dam directors that, jail or no jail, the city must have authority over sewers in order to ensure the integrity of the City Center project. Following the presentation of Rollins's case, the Indian Valley Dam board chose to postpone a decision for two weeks. City officials, concerned that either private developers or the county would purchase the remaining sewer units, countered by requesting a moratorium on the sale of capacity for all locations until the next hearing. The city explained that it feared a "run" on the remaining hookups. Unconvinced, the board denied the request, leaving intact the first-come, first-served policy. County officials had noted in an earlier newspaper interview that they planned to reserve the 112 hookups necessary for the jail in "a day or two."

The decision problem

As he drove home from the meeting with the dam board, Swanson reviewed his handling of the crisis and concluded that time had run out. For two years the city had moved to keep the county from proceeding with a plan that would have seriously, and perhaps permanently, damaged Rollins's economic future. Plans had been created; support mobilized; research undertaken; legal, publicity, and political actions implemented; pleas made; and proposals put forward. Swanson realized, however, that the next morning he would have to act. Further, since there was no opportunity to meet with his council, any action he took would have to be rapid and unilateral.

The problem was more complicated than just stopping the county from proceeding with its plans to place the jail in City Center. While public opinion within Rollins strongly supported action to block the county, public opinion outside Rollins was running just as strongly in favor of the county's plan for the temporary jail location. Which public interest must be served—that of city residents or that of county residents? Although the manager served the city, the population of the county was many times larger than that of the city.

Still more factors were operating against the city. Rollins had lost on legal grounds in the court test; state legislation had not been forthcoming; other cities in St. Regis County had remained relatively silent lest the jail end up in their backyards; the county had the EIR, ownership of the property, and a federal district court order all going for it; and now the Indian Valley Dam board had chosen to vacillate rather than support the city.

The alternatives were limited; most avenues for relief were closed or rapidly closing. Reliance upon other entities, judicial remedies, and political processes seemed to have been exhausted. If the county reserved the remaining sewer hookups, the city's cause would appear to have been lost. Yet no money had been appropriated by the city to pay the $600,000 required to reserve the hookups.

Was there anything Swanson should do? Was there anything he could do?

Discussion questions

1. How should the manager define the public interest in this case? Which group of residents should take priority? Does the interest of the larger jurisdiction always take priority over that of the smaller jurisdiction? If so, why? If not, under what conditions should the smaller jurisdiction prevail?

2. What different governmental agencies are involved in this case? What are their interrelationships? In such a situation, what are the prerogatives of the city to protect the interests of its residents?

3. What principles should govern the behavior of the manager in this case? Which should take priority—his responsibility to his constituents, his commitment to democratic theory and representative government, or the laws of the city and the state? How should these be sorted out?

4. Does the issue under consideration affect the answer to the preceding questions? That is, when the public safety (retention in jail of those accused of crimes) conflicts with community control (the opportunity for economic and land use enhancement), which should take precedence and why?

5. What interpretation would you put on the council's direction that the manager act with "a free hand, financially and otherwise," to defend the city? Does such an authorization enable the manager to spend money without an appropriation? How far does it go in justifying unilateral action by the manager?

6. Given that he is unable to meet with the city council (and regardless of the answer to question 5), are there other efforts at consultation that Swanson ought to make before he acts? If so, what are they?

7. Do the time constraints faced in this situation produce "emergency" conditions? Do such conditions permit the manager to exceed his usual authority? If so, by how much? If not, how does a manager defend governmental inaction in the face of emergency situations?

8. Are there situations in which the urgent need for action justifies a government, or an administrator, ignoring accepted and "normal" procedures and engaging in "guerrilla warfare"? Does this situation, with its long-term economic implications, justify such behavior?

9. What tactical options are available to Swanson? What option should he choose? How can it be defended?

Housing the homeless in Willow County

Jacqueline Byrd, Terry Schutten, Steven A. Sherlock, Susan Von Mosch, Jon A. Walsh, Mary Theresa Karcz

Editor's introduction

Provision of human services is often a focal point for intergovernmental relations. Not only do human services tend to be highly complex, but the number of players—governments and not-for-profit agencies delivering these services—is much greater.

Typically, each not-for-profit agency has been organized to respond to a particular public service need. Each serves a specific constituency, and each has a core of devoted supporters, who usually include capable and influential residents of the local community. Consequently, while each provides a valuable public service, it does so in response to its supporters' perceptions of service needs. Organizational jealousies are common, and the agencies sometimes fail to coordinate their efforts with one another and with governments serving the same constituencies.

Thus, in most communities, the human services area poses major problems of service integration or coordination, a job that usually falls to the city or county government. From the perspective of the city or county, these agencies help get needed jobs done, but at a cost of complicated bureaucratic interaction in an intergovernmental setting.

In this case, Willow County must coordinate county, city, and private agency efforts to provide housing for the homeless. As is so often the case, the need is evident, but the resources to do the job are limited. The county administrator and his staff must coordinate an intergovernmental effort to increase the availability of housing for the homeless without exceeding the county's budgetary resources. They must achieve this goal in a way that simultaneously satisfies the other agencies and the county board. Complicating the problem is a well-meaning and influential member of the board who goes beyond his authority in making commitments to the other agencies involved. Thus, administrator-board relations as well as administrator-community relations are additional factors challenging the administrative staff in Willow County.

Case 7
Housing the homeless in Willow County

Background

Willow County is a completely urbanized county with a five-member elected board of commissioners and an appointed administrator. The county seat is Saul, a large city with more than half of the county's population.

The membership of the county board has been very stable. At the time this case begins, four of the five members had served for more than ten years. The board has had a strong commitment to preserving its formal structure and acting as a group. Good, professional government combined with fiscal conservatism are the values of the Willow County board.

The board uses a committee structure to conduct its business; information affecting potential decisions and requests for action are presented to the relevant committee or committees for review before going to the board for final action. The committees include finance, policy, and human services. A presentation to a committee is formal, with minutes and permanent records. As a result, discussion tends to be limited.

When more extensive discussion is needed on an issue, the county administrator calls an "administrative update," an open, public meeting led by the county board chair. This meeting is less formal than a presentation to a committee and encourages communication between staff and elected officials. Administrative updates are used infrequently and usually for major policy projects.

To support the county's policy makers, the county maintains the Policy Analysis Division, which analyzes issues for the board's consideration and recommendation. Options for action are presented by the staff. The division consists of a director and four analysts; it reports directly to the county administrator (see Figure 1).

Like many county governments, Willow County has a major responsibility for social services. Consequently, it has been addressing the problem of homelessness for a number of years. Historically, both the county and the private

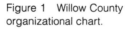

Figure 1   Willow County organizational chart.

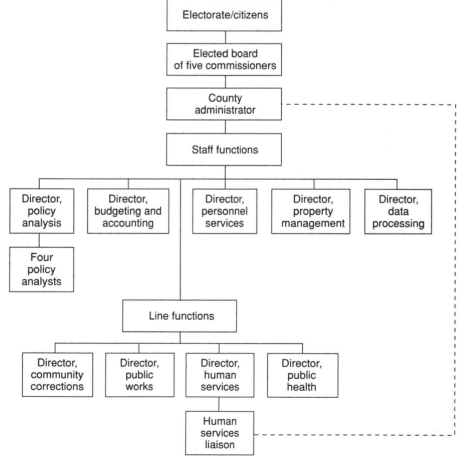

sector have provided food and shelter services for the homeless, and public-private cooperation has been strong. On the public side, for example, in one year Willow County financed $1.04 million in prevention programs that provided support, including emergency assistance, emergency social services, and health service programs, for people in immediate danger of becoming homeless. The county also funded emergency housing, contributing $1.3 million to the WXYZ Association, Adult Shelter Services, several battered-women's shelters, and other such programs that provide immediate shelter to people who have no other housing. The emergency housing is usually short term (one to thirty days), and people are often required to leave the premises during the day. The county does not provide any transitional housing programs that offer shelter for extended periods.

Complementing the county's activity, the private sector finances or provides advocacy and legal services to prevent homelessness, as well as emergency shelter and transitional housing programs that help homeless people get jobs and training.

The case

In the early 1980s, a number of events affected Willow County's services and policies. National economic conditions, severe inflation, high unemployment, and emerging federal policies generally restricted the federal government's role in funding housing and human services.

In response, the Willow County Board of Commissioners appointed the Gold Medal Commission to examine the county's urgent human service needs and to develop recommendations. Represented on the commission were local government; trades and labor; the business, religious, and minority communities; and foundations and private nonprofit organizations. Three county commissioners also served as members, including Commissioner George Goodfellow, chair of the human services committee of the county board.

Commissioner Goodfellow was a powerful, longtime county commissioner with a special interest in addressing human problems, including homelessness. He believed in direct contact with the public and made decisions on that basis. He understood the political process of government and used the system effectively to translate his priorities into action.

The Gold Medal Commission's report made the following recommendations and findings:

• Government has an obligation to address the basic needs of the population.

• The private sector will address the increased need for basic services, such as shelter, only for a maximum of three years, after which government should assume the responsibility.

• Cooperation between the public and private sectors should be increased.

The Willow County Board of Commissioners accepted the Gold Medal Commission's report. Goodfellow, because of his role in developing the commission's recommendations, had particularly strong feelings of ownership toward them.

In response to the report, a local foundation established the Priority Care Fund, whose purpose was to meet the community's critical need for emergency shelter in the short term by funding local shelter providers, such as the Salvation Army. Local governments, including Willow County, and private organizations supported the fund's development and contributed to it.

The next year, the Helping Hand Foundation assumed responsibility for operating the Priority Care Fund but agreed to do so only if use of the fund was restricted to emergency situations.

Two years later, in July, the foundation initiated the Human Development Action Coalition (HuDAC) to study homelessness in the greater Saul metropolitan area and to suggest responsibilities for the ongoing funding of services for the homeless. HuDAC was a committee composed of community, foundation, business, and government representatives. Participants included Goodfellow and one other Willow County commissioner, planning staff from the county's human services department, the vice president of the Helping Hand Foundation, and the chair of the Shelter Board.

HuDAC was composed of diverse groups trying to decide who should do what in the area of emergency services. Intended to function as a proactive, forward-looking catalyst to move social policy toward an emphasis on human development and to address basic needs of society, the coalition's primary objective was to develop strategies for both the public and the private sectors. About a year after its creation, the coalition published the *HuDAC Report,* recommending that

- The Priority Care Fund be phased out

- The county assume responsibility for funding the emergency services that were currently being provided by the Priority Care Fund, such as shelters and food shelves

- The Helping Hand Foundation and the private sector assume responsibility for transitional programs, such as counseling.

The Willow County Board of Commissioners did not formally review, accept, or reject the HuDAC recommendations.

In the months following the *HuDAC Report,* the Helping Hand Foundation announced plans to discontinue the Priority Care Fund at the end of the following year. The rationale for the suggested change was not that the Priority Care Fund dollars were no longer needed but that emergency care needs had ceased to be a temporary crisis. They were an ongoing need and, therefore, a public sector responsibility.

Willow County, particularly the human services department, came under increasing community pressure to expand county financial support for emergency housing and related services. For instance, the WXYZ Association, which operated a housing program for homeless women and children, requested that the county appropriate $400,000 in new funds, as well as about $70,000 in additional funds above the county administrator's proposed budget of $31,200, for emergency shelter services in the forthcoming year, the last year of the Priority Care Fund.

The director of human services, Janet Hamilton, was becoming extremely concerned about the number of requests from private service delivery groups for both increased and new funding of programs and services. In addition, the human services staff was feeling a lack of direction and the need for a comprehensive, countywide policy document for planning and funding emergency services. Hamilton asked the county administrator, Frank Gardner, for a policy recommendation regarding the county's role in providing services to the homeless, particularly in the area of increased funding for emergency services.

During this time, advocates started lobbying county commissioners with phone calls and visits. One of these advocates was the WXYZ Association, which applied pressure when the county's human services department did not immediately agree to fill the gap left by the withdrawal of private sector funds, including the Priority Care Fund. The local press picked up on WXYZ's concerns and published a series of articles discussing the frustrations of social agencies in dealing with the county.

In response to Hamilton's request and to pressure from the community, Gardner appointed a work group to develop policy options for planning and funding emergency housing and related services. The group was composed of staff from the county administrator's office, including the Policy Analysis Division, the Community Development Block Grant program, the human services department, the public health department, the county attorney's office, and the city health department. The group was directed to

• Define the nature and scope of the need for services

• Research additional funding and program options available to the county board and determine potential costs

• Draft a policy report on the provision of emergency housing and related services for the county board's consideration

• Develop funding recommendations, based on policy options, for the next year's budget, and develop recommendations for the possible use of available but undesignated contingency funds in the current budget.

Gardner sent a letter to the commissioners recommending that, pending release of the policy report and the development of a county policy, they not make commitments to community programs for new or additional funding.

Coincidental with the formation of the policy work group, the Helping Hand Foundation sent a letter to the Priority Care Fund agencies informing them that it was phasing out the fund as of December 31 of the following year. The memo went on to state that "the county has agreed, in principle, to assume at that time the role of funder of emergency services currently funded by the Priority Care Fund." The letter was not sent to county commissioners or staff.

The letter frustrated the policy staff. Where did the foundation get the idea that the county had agreed to take over the Priority Care Fund? Craig Beckwith, the director of the Policy Analysis Division, questioned Gardner about the validity of efforts to develop rational policy options if policy decisions were being made before the report was completed.

In response, Gardner sent a letter to Molly Parsons, head of the Helping Hand Foundation, with copies to the commissioners, stating that "Willow County has not committed itself to any action pending the completion of the policy report and recommendations of the board."

Beckwith had first convened the work group in October. The group developed four key questions for analyzing the existing situation as well as the implications of a series of county options for housing-related services. The four questions were as follows:

1. The legal question: What is the legal responsibility of the county and other levels of government (e.g., federal, state, and city) regarding homelessness? Is the county meeting its legal responsibilities?
2. The financial question: How much in resources does the county want to direct toward the problem of homelessness?
3. The philosophical question: What are the nature and extent of the problem of homelessness? What is the appropriate role for the county? For other levels of government? For the private sector? For public-private efforts?
4. The administrative question: How should the county's response to homelessness be structured and administered?

While the work group included staff from a variety of divisions, the policy staff had primary responsibility for coordinating and completing the project. The approach to the study, as well as the report and the options that emerged, were consistent with previous studies from the Policy Analysis Division. However, not all commissioners recognized or endorsed the value of the approach normally taken by policy staff in analyzing an issue.

The controversy builds

In December, a year before the scheduled termination of the Priority Care Fund, Larry Canfield, director of the Shelter Board, convened a meeting of staff from agencies receiving or interested in receiving funds from the McKinney Act, federal legislation that provides funding for services for the homeless. Canfield appeared at the meeting as a general advocate for the homeless rather than for a specific agency or unit of government. His primary concern was that a lack of local, centralized coordination and administration of McKinney funds would result in duplicated or inefficiently delivered services or in the loss of potential funding because no local organization had applied for it.

The meeting was attended by staff from the county's Policy Analysis Division, the city, the state, the Helping Hand Foundation, and private agencies. During the meeting, several participants suggested that the county assume responsibility for calling future meetings of the group and for coordinating McKinney funds and services. County staff could not commit the county to a coordination role, however, in the absence of an approved policy concerning the county's role.

Several days after the meeting, despite the absence of a board directive or policy, Goodfellow, as chair of the county board's human services committee, informed County Administrator Gardner that he wanted the county to take a lead in coordinating the McKinney funds. Gardner maintained that the matter should not be finalized until the board had considered the work group's report on homelessness and defined county policy.

Gardner and Goodfellow had intense exchanges over the establishment of a staff position to coordinate services for the homeless as well as to oversee the McKinney money. When the discussion ended, the issue of the coordinator position was unresolved and remained a point of contention.

Shelter Board director Canfield's concern about coordination and the role of local government in providing services to the homeless resurfaced in January. To advance the discussion, Canfield exerted pressure to have the mayor of Saul, county board chair Nancy Able, and a local U.S. congressman call a press conference to announce the award of McKinney funding and a cooperative city-county effort to address the issue of homelessness.

Able, Gardner, and Beckwith were uncomfortable with the idea of a press conference. Again, the issue was the absence of a formal board statement concerning the county's role. How could the chair publicly discuss the county's role when the board had not defined it? However, the press conference became a moot point when it became clear that the other participants—the mayor and the congressman—were not going to attend.

Meanwhile, during February and early March, the county work group prepared several drafts of the *Homeless Report*. A variety of issues arose during reviews and revisions by the work group and other key county staff.

As the report neared completion, several vendors and agencies providing services to the homeless inquired about it, afraid that the report might adversely affect those services. They thought the report would spell out who would receive funds and who wouldn't. Furthermore, all of the private organizations then providing emergency services and funded by the Priority Care Fund were anxious for the county to acknowledge that it would be assuming responsibility for this fund.

The policy staff met with several noncounty agencies to explain the content of the report. The report presented five options:

- Option 1a: Continuation of Willow County's existing preventive and emergency services.

- Option 1b: Continuation of Willow County's existing preventive and emergency services, with increases in the level of support for emergency services to equal the level of funding provided through the Priority Care Fund.

- Option 2: Continuation of existing preventive and emergency services and addition of intervention services, without continued funding of the agencies currently receiving Priority Care funding. (Intervention services, such as assessment and case management, are provided to individuals who are homeless or at risk of becoming homeless and are not receiving services through the Community Social Services Act.)

- Option 3: Continuation of preventive and emergency services and addition of intervention and transitional services, without continued funding of the agencies currently receiving Priority Care funding.

- Option 4: Continuation of existing preventive and emergency services and addition of intervention, transitional, and long-term housing services, without continued funding of the agencies currently receiving Priority Care funding. (Long-term housing services provide housing on an ongoing basis. Single-room occupancy, or SRO, and public housing are examples of such services. SRO residents often include deinstitutionalized mentally ill persons, chronic alcoholics, and low-income senior citizens.)

The information conveyed in the meetings appeared to dispel some of the concerns of the agencies, especially since none of the options detailed specific amounts of funding for their programs. Policy staff indicated that the report was really designed to deal with policy, not implementation. Before the agency representatives left, however, they pointed out that the *HuDAC Report* recommended that the county assume responsibility for emergency services (e.g., the Priority Care Fund); they said they would continue to worry about this issue.

In early March, shortly before the *Homeless Report* was to be mailed to the county board, Goodfellow requested that policy staff meet with a group, composed of staff from private agencies and the Helping Hand Foundation, that was concerned about homelessness and the current study. At the meeting, Beckwith and staff provided this group with the same information that they had conveyed to staff from other agencies.

A major question from the group was whether a public hearing was to be scheduled. Policy staff responded by explaining that the report would be presented at an administrative update and that a public hearing was not normally part of that process. The private sector participants were not satisfied, however, and expressed their concern to Goodfellow.

The day before the report was to be mailed in preparation for the administrative update, Goodfellow notified Gardner that because the issue was of such importance and urgency, it would come to his committee rather than to an administrative update. Beckwith urged Gardner to try to persuade Goodfellow that the report should be presented at an administrative update. Gardner decided, however, that the issue was not worth fighting about.

Prior to the committee meeting on March 15, Gardner, human services liaison Betsy Markowicz, Beckwith, and policy staff met with Goodfellow to discuss the report. During that meeting, Goodfellow spoke very little about the report but expressed frustration and anger that time was passing and action had not been taken to coordinate the McKinney funds. As staff were working on the report, people were going homeless. "We need to assume responsibility for the Priority Care Fund," he said. "We need action!"

Goodfellow stated that he had made it clear in a previous conversation with Gardner that he wanted a coordinator designated. Gardner acknowledged that they had discussed the issue but that his understanding was that they had agreed to wait for the report and subsequent board action before moving ahead on coordination. The meeting ended without a resolution of the issue, and Goodfellow told Gardner that he was not pleased.

The report

Beckwith presented the report to the county board's human services committee, which was meeting as a committee of the whole with Goodfellow as chair. Goodfellow directed the discussion to coordination of the McKinney funds and the need for a public hearing on the issue.

There was little discussion of and no action on the report. Concern was raised by members of the board about the roles and responsibilities of the other participants—the city and private organizations—in providing services to the homeless. Nancy Able, the county board chair, made it clear that it was important to know what others were going to do before the county decided what it was going to do. The outcome of the meeting was as follows:

- Gardner was to see that staff was designated to coordinate the McKinney funds and programs for the homeless.

- A public hearing on the report and the issue of homelessness was scheduled for May 3.

- Goodfellow was directed to meet with officials from the city, the Helping Hand Foundation, and other organizations, as appropriate, to discuss cooperative roles for addressing the problem of homelessness.

Goodfellow met with the mayor of Saul and other city officials, an executive from Helping Hand, and the author of the *HuDAC Report* in an effort to understand the roles of each. As a result of this meeting, Goodfellow circulated a memo explaining to all the commissioners and representatives who had been at the meeting the agreement that arose from it. He asked for comment but received none.

The public hearing

The next step was the public hearing. Prior to it, Gardner, Beckwith, and human services liaison Markowicz met with Able to discuss the possible results of the public hearing. Able asked whether there was a staff recommendation. Gardner and staff said they were considering option 2 because adding intervention services rather than increasing emergency services was more likely to produce desired changes.

At the public hearing, many of the community's advocates and providers complimented Goodfellow for his support and efforts. Many of the people testifying recommended a combination of options 1b and 2—that the county assume the responsibility for existing preventive services, increased emergency services, and intervention services. Some even recommended that the county provide all services for the homeless.

An important issue was raised during the public hearing. Molly Parsons, executive director of the Helping Hand Foundation, stated that her organization expected the county to assume responsibility for funding not only emergency services, which included shelter and food, but also housing costs associated with transitional services. This surprised Goodfellow, who had assumed that if the county took over emergency services, Helping Hand, together with the city, would take over both the programs and the housing for transitional services. He said that he wanted county staff to meet with city and Helping Hand staff to clarify their roles and responsibilities in the provision of transitional housing services. The board went along with his recommendation.

At the end of the two-and-a-half-hour public hearing, Goodfellow called for staff to cost out an option that he had discussed with the city and the private providers. This option was detailed in a memo indicating what responsibilities the private providers and the city and county might be willing to accept.

After the hearing, Beckwith and Markowicz met with Goodfellow to review his request. It became clear that the option Goodfellow wanted to be costed out was the same as option lb in the *Homeless Report,* with the addition of a half-time coordinator position and a $33,000 rental assistance subsidy.

Within the month, a response to Goodfellow's request was prepared by county staff and sent to the human services committee of the whole for consideration. The committee reviewed the materials and asked staff to (1) meet with city and Helping Hand staff concerning roles in transitional service delivery and summarize the results; and (2) display on one page the costs associated with each option, including the items identified by Goodfellow.

The decision problem

Staff members from the county, the city, and the Helping Hand Foundation met to discuss the continuing matter of providing services to the homeless. During the meeting it became evident that the participants were operating under different assumptions. County staff assumed that the meeting was being held to clarify roles and understandings among the three agencies. City and Helping Hand staff thought all decisions about roles and responsibilities had been made at the meeting between Goodfellow, the mayor, and Helping Hand, and that the current meeting was being held to prepare for program implementation. From Goodfellow's actions, the city and Helping Hand staff members had understood that the county would (1) assume the funding necessary to maintain the Priority Care Fund and (2) fund transitional housing. Helping Hand and city staff indicated that unless the county assumed these responsibilities, they would not take responsibility for the program portion of transitional services or for low-cost housing.

The county staff members were taken aback. Beckwith informed the city and Helping Hand staff that Goodfellow did not have authority to make decisions for the board. He pointed out that the board had directed Goodfellow to discuss respective agency roles but not to make decisions or commitments. All participants left the meeting feeling that they had missed the boat. What had gone wrong? Where should they go from here?

Beckwith and Markowicz met with County Administrator Gardner to explain the outcome of the meeting. Gardner then met with Goodfellow and Able to explain the situation and recommend an administrative update to obtain board direction for further action.

The commissioners agreed to an administrative update, which was held on June 2. Beckwith and Markowicz presented the problem, summarizing the results of the May 27 meeting with staff from the city and the Helping Hand Foundation. Able indicated that she was not happy just to provide "band-aid" services; she wanted county programs that would help people in the long run, programs like option 2 with its intervention services. Some of the other commissioners agreed, arguing that intervention services could save money over time.

Goodfellow urged the board to take over the Priority Care Fund, as recommended by the *HuDAC Report* and the community. This would require the adoption of option lb with Goodfellow's preferred modifications. He reminded the commissioners that at the public hearing, the community had urged the board to assume responsibility for the $200,000–$300,000 gap that would occur when the Priority Care Fund was phased out. He concluded by asking emphatically, "If the county doesn't take over the Priority Care Fund work, who will?"

Another commissioner emphasized that the county could not afford full funding for both options 1b and 2 but must decide which to fund.

Able moved that Gardner be directed to prepare a recommendation consistent with the commissioners' priorities and budgetary constraints, and to work with the human services staff, the Helping Hand Foundation, and the city to develop an effective continuum of services. No mention was made of the role that Goodfellow was to play. The motion was approved.

Gardner was left with the task of finding a solution. He had to choose among the options, knowing full well that the influential Commissioner Goodfellow preferred a modified option 1b but that Able, the board chair, preferred option 2. In addition, he had to consider the preponderance of opinion expressed at the public hearing—that the county should pick up the slack from the termination of the Priority Care Fund. Finally, Goodfellow had clearly demanded that Gardner appoint a coordinator for McKinney fund activity. The expectations of city staff and the thinly veiled ultimatum from the Helping Hand Foundation could not be ignored. Finally, Gardner could not forget the board's admonition that the county could not afford to fund all of the options. He had to act, but how?

Discussion questions

1. What are the values held by the major participants in this case? Where do these values conflict?
2. How should Gardner structure his approach to the county board's directive?
3. Which administrative staff members should be involved in the development of and solution to the commissioners' directive?
4. What key factors would be involved in the development of Gardner's recommendations?
5. How should the objective policy analysis process be balanced against the political dynamics of the situation?
6. What should Gardner recommend to the county board?

Part five:
Planning and economic development

Introduction to part five: Planning and economic development

The late decades of the twentieth century brought increasing pressure on local governments to actively plan for community development and work to achieve economic goals for the community. Counties and cities, in point of fact, became their community's chief agent in the community development process.

Initially, in the 1960s, community development primarily emphasized efforts to plan new development. The goal was to ensure the achievement of community objectives: that development proceed in an orderly manner that protected public health, safety, and well-being while adequate provision was made for essential public facilities, such as water and sewage, roads, parks, and educational facilities. Urban redevelopment was born but was at the time confined largely to the redevelopment of old neighborhoods in the central cities of metropolitan areas.

The last two decades of the century, however, saw a major expansion of local government's role in promoting economic development goals. This change came from many pressures: the economic recession of the 1980s spurred public demands on cities and counties to promote local job creation; the changing nature of the economy left blighted downtown areas and closed factories in its wake, even in rural and suburban areas; changes in public shopping patterns and increasing dependence on sales taxes for local government revenue made local government attention to commercial development a financial necessity; the growing incidence of drugs and crime, particularly in blighted neighborhoods, made the economic and social health of neighborhoods a major concern for localities charged with protecting and promoting the general welfare of their citizenry; and the disappearance of revenue sharing and the increase in citizen demands for tax cuts combined to force local governments to increase both the assessed valuation of property and commercial sales activity in order to generate new revenues with which to meet growing demands for expanded services.

As a result of these trends, planning and economic development moved to the top of most city and county work agendas. Whether the goal was to attract new industrial employment, increase the international trade action of local industries, help finance new hospitals, negotiate with developers for new shopping centers, control new residential subdivisions, or even control and limit growth, local governments were heavily involved at the end of the twentieth century, and that meant more work, more challenges, and more political complications for the professional city or county administrator.

This part of the book describes planning and economic development challenges in two different kinds of communities: a small one outside a metropolitan area and another in the inner core of a major metropolitan center. Both case studies deal with jobs, land use, and economic enhancement; each deals with a common, but different, kind of economic development challenge.

The first case describes the effort to rebuild a blighted and deteriorated area that has lost a theme park that brought both jobs and tourists to the community. It describes the economic considerations involved, the complications posed by the requirements of the developers and landowners, and the politics involved when community residents differ on the kinds of changes they prefer in the area being redeveloped. Finally, it also shows how economic and political philosophies can collide and make problem solving even more difficult.

The second case involves a response to a private sector threat: a major corporation is considering moving its corporate headquarters, together with all the jobs involved, from the central city to a suburban location. Facing the prospect of downtown decimation if the move occurs, the city must decide how to respond. In keeping with common contemporary trends, the issue quickly becomes one of how much of the costs involved in keeping the corporate headquarters downtown the city is willing to pay. Basic principles regarding the use of public funds are involved. And because city administrators ultimately must evaluate and make recommendations regarding the various options, they, too, get caught in the cross fire between principles, economic needs, neighborhood protection, and competition from other governments.

Planning and economic development issues are never easy or clear-cut. Yet they always seem to land on the desks of city administrators.

Redeveloping the waterfront

William R. Bridgeo and Kay W. James

Editor's introduction

Local government administrators work directly for the residents of their communities, taking their direction from the governing board elected by those residents. Thus, they take all their official actions as agents of their councils and the publics these councils represent. Their work is closely controlled by law: they can exercise only the powers given to them by statute or ordinance; they must obey all relevant state/local laws, such as those governing the public's right to know what the government is doing; and they serve as a major intermediary between their governments and other organizations in the public and private sector.

In the economic development field, local government administrators are the primary intermediaries between their government and private sector interests engaged in economic development work within the community. When they begin working with private sector firms, however, they enter a field of activity governed by different expectations and values. Private firms, for instance, operate outside the spotlight of publicity; their business records are not open for public inspection, and, in fact, their business dealings often must be conducted in private to protect the integrity of ongoing negotiations and pending agreements.

When public administrators get involved with economic development, then, they inevitably face the challenges of working in both sectors—public and private—simultaneously. Chief among those challenges is the need to navigate between the sometimes conflicting operating practices of the two sectors, including the need to reconcile the open, public information requirements of the public sector with the closed, confidential requirements of the private sector. Sometimes the line between these two sectors is filled with barriers and obstacles, especially those posed by elected officials representing very different political perspectives and community values.

Such differing political perspectives are often deeply rooted in legitimate, reasonable differences within the community itself. In the following case, for example, the administrators' task is made much more difficult by the reasonable disagreements within the community between those forces seeking redevelopment and economic revitalization and those forces attempting to preserve what they view as important aspects of their community's heritage.

It is appropriate—in fact, perhaps even essential under democratic theory—for reasonable people to reasonably differ, as they do in this case, but the world of public administration becomes infinitely more complicated for administrators who must work with contradictory pressures and operating methods while trying to promote the well-being of the community as a whole. This is the challenge that confronted public administrators Marie Walker and Raymond Williams in the village of Crystal Lake.

Case 8
Redeveloping the waterfront

Background

The village of Crystal Lake (population 12,000) is located at the north end of the scenic lake from which it takes its name, about twenty-five miles from the large metropolitan area of Manchester. Crystal Lake has been the seat of county government and the business and commercial center of the area since its founding, and it continues to be a self-sufficient community, maintaining its small-town character despite the pressures of creeping urbanization.

The lake is the community's most important asset and an essential part of its identity. It serves as a source of drinking water for more than fifty thousand area residents. Moreover, its natural beauty and recreational opportunities have drawn countless vacationers to its shores for two hundred years, making tourism one of the area's most important economic development activities.

The village's lakefront area is about a mile of shoreline, a half mile in depth, and it comprises a mix of residential and commercial uses, parks, and open space. Private property in this district has an assessed value equal to 12 percent of that of the entire village.

Until the 1950s, the main east-west state road passed along the Crystal Lake waterfront, and the area thrived. After a new bypass rerouted travelers, the lakefront commercial area along Lakeside Drive began to decline. Over time, the area badly degenerated. Whereas the natural setting had once readily attracted tourists and their dollars, the deteriorating condition of the lakefront area and the waning revenues from summer visitors made residents desperate to revive the once prosperous resort area.

The low point for the community came when the lakefront amusement park, which had been enjoyed by generations of local residents and regional visitors over its sixty-year history, closed after several seasons of operating deficits. The trauma of this loss to the community was dramatized at an auction that saw the roller-coaster and the beloved carousel go to other communities despite efforts by local residents to raise enough revenue to keep them.

Although the land on which the amusement park was located was, and historically had been, privately owned, the members of the community considered it to be public property because they had access to the waterfront there (even if they had to pay an entrance fee). Residents of neighboring communities as well as seasonal residents also asserted a proprietary interest in the property even though they paid no taxes to support it. Thus, the community, already demoralized by the loss of the amusement park, was stunned by the announcement that the site formerly occupied by the park was to be redeveloped as an exclusive residential area. The plan included the removal of a bridge, which would sever the roadway, closing it to through traffic and allowing the development of a "peninsular community" on the waterfront. This proposal had been developed secretively by a group of local investors, who presented it to the village manager months before any public announcement had been made —indeed, before the amusement park was closed.

The case

The spirited debate over the controversial redevelopment proposal produced in-fighting among village board members and conflict between the prodevelopment village manager and certain board members who feared that this new development would bring unwelcome changes to the community's character.

Information about the project was valued like military intelligence. The local newspaper was filled with articles, editorials, and letters to the editor—some verging on slanderous—regarding the lakefront proposal.

With the support and backing of the local chamber of commerce, the project developers aggressively pushed for village board approval of the rezoning and bridge abandonment, which were needed to make the project possible. After nearly a year of controversy, the project became the focus of the campaigns for village board elections. Candidates from one party were photographed standing on the bridge declaring their commitment to its preservation.

The entire seven-member board was reelected every two years, making the political situation in Crystal Lake somewhat unstable. In this election, three board members, all of whom were without previous government experience and had campaigned together on a platform of opposition to the lakefront development proposal, were swept into office by impressive majorities. Incumbent mayor David Cook, a hard-driving businessman who had generally favored and worked toward the aggressive lakefront development plans, was reelected by the narrowest of margins. Three other incumbent board members who supported lakefront development were also reelected, but again by uncomfortably thin majorities.

But the elections had made it clear that the community did not support the project, as the staunchest supporters of the project not only failed to achieve reelection but were soundly defeated. The would-be developers, seeing the futility of continuing to pursue the project, withdrew their application and abandoned their efforts. The frustrated village manager, who had staked his professional reputation on this project, left the community within a few months to move on to his next career position.

With the withdrawal of the controversial lakefront development proposal, the board focused its efforts on rezoning the lakefront, intent on making it clear to any future developers what kind of waterfront development the community would find acceptable. The rezoning process started while the search for a new manager was under way. Marie Walker, the village's development director and acting village manager during the search, attempted to manage the process in a manner that would take some of the political sting out of the issues but met with limited success.

The government players

There was consensus among the Crystal Lake village board members that Raymond Williams, the city manager of a community in another state, was the best candidate for the village manager post, but board members differed greatly in their reasons for supporting him. Some admired his principled stand on a police labor dispute in his former job and perceived him to be a tough manager who would be able to hold the line on labor costs in village government; others were persuaded to select him because of the community development successes he had achieved in his prior jobs.

Williams himself thoroughly enjoyed the tasks that came with stimulating economic growth in a community. While in the village for his job interview, he had been able to attend one of the public meetings on the proposed lakefront rezoning, and he was impressed by the degree of community interest in the future of its lakefront. Although he was somewhat concerned about the lack of unity on the Crystal Lake village board with regard to development issues, he felt excited about the challenge of realizing the great potential for quality redevelopment on Crystal Lake's waterfront.

Voting for Williams's appointment, but with reservations, was Duke Coleman, the leader of the group of three new board members and a man who wanted to be the next mayor of Crystal Lake. A vocal critic of the lakefront development proposal, he had been elected to an at-large position in the land-slide victory of the development's opponents. It was his first attempt at seeking public office, and he garnered more votes than any other candidate. No one in Crystal Lake was more well liked than "the Duke." The second generation to operate a small grocery store and bakery near the lakefront district, Duke Coleman still delivered groceries to his elderly customers, often waited patiently for payment until social security checks arrived, handed out free candy to his youngest patrons, had a smile for everyone, and thoroughly enjoyed his life in the village.

Coleman was approaching retirement age and had lived in the village all his life. Having grown up in the days when Crystal Lake was governed by a strong mayor, he had never really understood or been comfortable with the idea of an appointed manager serving as the chief executive officer of the village government. Conservative by nature and resistant to change, the Duke had brought two like-minded colleagues onto the board with him at the last election, re-placing prodevelopment board members. All three had gone through Crystal Lake High School together, served in the army in Korea, and remained friends ever since. The "Gang of Three," as Williams's wife Claudia referred to them, all worked locally, had coffee each morning at the same Main Street cafe, and reinforced each other continuously in their political beliefs.

Although Williams had a cordial and open relationship with Duke and his comrades, on the issue of future development within the village there was caution on the part of these board members, to say the least.

Like Mayor Cook, the three incumbents reelected to the board generally favored lakefront development. Mostly apolitical, they tended to vote according to their convictions on specific issues rather than by the party line. All were experienced board members who had barely managed reelection over candidates more skeptical of lakefront changes. While concerned about the welfare of the village, they were, nonetheless, more disposed than the newly elected members to defer to the village manager on day-to-day matters and less apt to question policy recommendations from village staff.

The development problem

The bulk of the land potentially available for development in the lakefront area was owned by Alan Lester. In Crystal Lake, no one was better known, for better or worse, than he. Eighty-three years old, Lester was the epitome of the self-made man. Born in Crystal Lake and raised on a farm just outside the village, he was driven from an early age to succeed in business. Bold, aggressive, and sometimes ruthless, Lester had made money with a start-up farm implement sales business, spun off to an interstate trucking firm, and finally entered into a partnership in a natural gas pipeline construction company. Forty years ago, he had begun purchasing land in Crystal Lake, particularly along the waterfront. He developed the amusement park from the site of a popular dance hall, hot-dog stand, and miniature golf course. Within ten years, Crystal Lake Park had a roller-coaster, water and other mechanical rides, an arcade, and a hand-crafted carousel. It drew summer crowds from throughout the region and provided summer jobs for two generations of Crystal Lake youngsters and adults.

Although admired by many, Alan Lester's tough business demeanor had created substantial ill will with others, including Duke Coleman. Years before, a handshake agreement between the two became a nasty dispute over payment due Duke from Lester. This came at a time when Duke was just taking over the family business and was no match for Lester's sharp business acumen. In the end, Duke lost a substantial sum of money and spent two years making it up. He never forgave Alan Lester for what he saw as a breach of his word. At the public meetings held to discuss the lakefront rezoning proposals, Coleman and Lester frequently exchanged hostile barbs.

The intense public interest in the future of the lakefront was divided between those who wanted the village to acquire the land for a public park; those who wanted private investment but only for recreational uses on the property; and those who were anxious for any community development that would generate business, tax revenue, and jobs.

The influential downtown merchants association, struggling against changing times and competition from surrounding developments such as Walmart, had its own concerns about lakefront redevelopment. While not vehemently opposed to it, the downtown interests wanted to ensure that new lakefront development would complement, rather than compete with, the central business district. Carefully scrutinizing the rezoning proposal, the members of this group, collectively and as individuals, put pressure on the village board to protect its interests.

The media's interest in these issues was equally intense. Owing to the village's history as a summer recreational area enjoyed by people from area communities, local issues were of interest to the regional electronic media, and camera crews and reporters from Manchester's three network affiliate television stations visited Crystal Lake often to chronicle the events affecting the lakefront area. The local and regional daily newspapers competed for stories and quotes, constantly scrambling to be the first to report breaking news. The continuous media inquiries to village board members, which resulted from this competition, provided frequent opportunities to be in the limelight for those who enjoyed such exposure.

In this atmosphere of public concern, the village board, after a fourteen-month process involving eleven different public meetings and the preparation of an environmental impact statement, finally approved a new, comprehensive zoning ordinance for the lakefront. In essence, it limited the type of development that could occur, but it left the door open to reasonable proposals.

A new developer

Into this setting stepped a new developer, the Phoenix Group, headquartered in Manchester. For some time, two of the senior partners of this well-established real estate and commercial development firm had been eyeing Crystal Lake's lakefront as a prime site for a large, multiuse development. Both partners had summer homes on the far shore of the lake and knew the community well. In addition, the company's founder and majority stockholder, Hamlin Ross, had spent his childhood summers on Crystal Lake and enjoyed the idea of establishing in the village a permanent legacy to his national business success.

The Phoenix Group owned shopping plazas and office buildings in eight states. It also owned a large building construction company, an office leasing firm, a broad portfolio of multifamily housing complexes, a half dozen radio and television stations, and a four-star resort hotel in the U.S. Virgin Islands that Hamlin Ross personally inspected with some frequency during the winter months. Phoenix executives relied on long-established relationships with federal and state housing and economic development officials to facilitate most of their larger projects. They were expert in development finance and well regarded by the investment banking community. For his part, Ross cultivated strong personal relationships with members of Congress and the governor of his home state through generous campaign contributions to both parties.

The development proposal

The Phoenix Group's initial multimedia presentation of its new lakefront development proposal was made at a large public meeting attended by hundreds of community residents and with full media coverage. The presentation was well received because the developer was well prepared. The company had closely observed the events of the previous failed development proposal (of which it had no part) and the more recent rezoning effort. It was well-informed about the issues underlying the controversy and about the personalities and apparent motivations of the influential parties. It had also retained the services of a land use planning consultant with a national reputation for designing quality waterfront redevelopment projects. And it had been carefully coached by village manager Raymond Williams and by development director Marie Walker.

The developer had first approached the village manager and development director several months earlier, shortly after Williams had been hired. While the relationship between the administrators and the Phoenix Group was cautious, they got along well from the outset. Acknowledging their responsibility to encourage quality development and understanding the developer's need for confidentiality, but with an eye toward the events of the recent past, Williams and Walker carefully established the ground rules for these initial discussions. They made it clear that their roles as municipal officials were (1) to serve as liaisons between the developer and the decision makers, and (2) to communicate the village's requirements for a new development project. Accordingly, they clarified for the developer the key issues for public acceptance of a new project proposal:

• Continued public access to the waterfront

• Development components designed to promote tourism

• No more than a limited residential component to the project.

Williams and Walker also kept all information the developer presented to them in strict confidence. Wary of being presented with a media freedom-of-information request in the event of a breach of confidentiality, they did not even keep a set of plans for the project in their possession. Concerned that any release of project details without "the full picture" would prejudice public and village board opinion, they told the board members only that they were meeting with a developer concerning a potential lakefront redevelopment project. As a result, when a meeting was finally scheduled for a public presentation of the lakefront development proposal, a great deal of public interest was immediately manifested, in part because of the lack of advance information about the project.

The plan that the Phoenix Group presented to the village board at that public meeting was an $80 million mixed-use proposal for redevelopment of the 100-acre project site, including "heavy" commercial development along the highway bypass (which formed the northern boundary of the site), waterfront and upland townhouses and condominiums, thirty acres of open space, and the "crown jewel"—a "village" of restaurants and retail boutiques, including a first-class, five-story conference hotel, on the lakefront. The commercial lakefront use would ensure the public continued access to the lake at that site, without the need for village purchase of the property and with the additional benefit of revenue generated by sales and property taxes.

However, to create sufficient land on the south side of Lakeside Drive to accommodate the lakefront commercial development, the developer said it would be necessary to move the local road. As a political compromise, the company pledged to preserve the old bridge as a pedestrian walkway and to build the new bridge and new section of relocated roadway at its own expense.

Unlike any other major development project in the administrators' experience, this proposal asked for no government assistance other than the necessary approvals.

At the close of the presentation, there was a momentary stunned silence from the members of the village board and the audience. Then someone started clapping and everyone in the auditorium joined the response. The media reports on that evening's television news and in the newspapers the following day were positive. The whole community was eagerly anticipating the commencement of the project.

Notwithstanding the public enthusiasm for the project, some members of the village board were not pleased with the way in which their staff had handled the release of information about the development proposal. In a executive session following the next board meeting, they expressed to the village manager their great distress at having been left out of the early discussions regarding the project, and they cautioned Williams that full disclosure to the board of all project details in advance of any public release of information was expected in the future.

The public's right to know

Some weeks later, the Phoenix Group advised Williams and Walker that, hoping to attract a Radisson luxury hotel to the site, it had contracted for a market study for the proposed lakefront hotel. They asked the manager and the development director to keep the study and the identity of the potential hotel tenant confidential, as their negotiations with the hotel company were ongoing. Understanding the need for confidentiality under these circumstances, Williams and Walker honored that request and told no one—including the members of the village board—of the market study or the interest of Radisson in the hotel site. However, unknown to them, members of the developer's family were not so discreet.

Mrs. Hamlin Ross Jr. casually mentioned, in a cocktail party conversation with a friend, that her father-in-law's firm was trying to bring a Radisson to the Crystal Lake project. That conversation was overheard by another party guest who happened to live in Crystal Lake, who shared this information with a number of friends, family members, and acquaintances. Soon the rumor had been spread all over the village. A reporter for the local newspaper picked up the rumor, contacted the Radisson Corporation, and was able to confirm the hotel company's interest in the Crystal Lake site. The reporter then contacted Walker and Williams, confronting them with this information and seeking further details, and sought out village board members and the developer for comments on the news. The stunned administrators declined to comment. The village board members were embarrassed to have to admit that they were unaware of the market study and the identity of the hotelier. Hamlin Ross, caught off-guard when he was reached personally by the reporter, who had managed to obtain his home phone number, was furious.

"That's why it's so damn hard to do business in Crystal Lake," he raged. "Nobody can keep their mouth shut." Commenting that he had seen "lots of deals go south" because of bad timing in the release of information, he suggested that this could be the case with the Crystal Lake project. "This deal is only held together with short-term property options," the paper quoted him as saying, "and it might be smarter business to walk away from it than to get mired down in a situation where I can't do business in a normal fashion."

Before that day's afternoon paper had even reached the newsstands, Ray Williams started receiving calls from village board members, and the telephone in his office glowed red for most of the day. The first call came from Mayor Cook, who was clearly annoyed. While he accepted Ray's explanation that he considered the market study to be "no big deal" and therefore not something about which the board members needed to be advised, and that he was honoring the developer's request for confidentiality, Cook cautioned Williams that he doubted that other board members would be as understanding. His words proved to be prophetic.

The next call was from Duke, who was very upset. Being "out of the loop" infuriated him, and he pulled no punches in his phone conversation with Williams, expressing his frustration and anger in uncharacteristically coarse language.

Throughout the day, the calls continued in similar fashion. Williams was exasperated. The elected officials were angry, and the developer blamed him for breaching confidence. Williams had no idea how the story had been leaked, and he didn't believe that his actions had in any way been improper. He stared at the small world globe that he kept on his desk for just such occasions, and tried to put the episode into its proper perspective.

Negotiations continue

Over the ensuing weeks, the furor blew over, and the process of project development and review continued. Lester and Ross arrived at a deal for the purchase of the property and were preparing for a closing on the land sale. Once the deal was closed, the developer would be seriously committed to the project.

At that point, the Phoenix Group approached Williams with a proposal, which it indicated was crucial to closing the deal. Phoenix proposed to convey the thirty acres of the project site planned as "open space" to the village for use as a public park. The acreage was an environmentally sensitive area that could not be developed. Giving the land to the village would relieve the developer of future property taxes and liability for its maintenance. Williams reviewed the proposal with the parks director and Walker, and the staff concluded that, aside from a modest loss of property tax revenues, there would be no significant expense to the village to maintain the forever-wild acreage, and that there were no good reasons not to accept the dedication of the land. Village acceptance of the offer would provide an incentive for the developer to take the final step to close the deal. The improved value of the remaining 70 percent of the property would, even in the most conservative of estimates, provide the village with millions of dollars in new assessed value, several hundred thousand dollars a year in new property and sales tax revenues, and hundreds of new jobs.

Confident that the arrangement being proposed made good sense for the village, Williams scheduled an executive session of the board as part of its next regularly scheduled meeting to explain the proposal and gain authority to sign a binding purchase and sale agreement for the thirty acres of open space. To prepare the board for the discussion, the manager drafted a detailed confidential memorandum and hand delivered it to each board member two weeks before the meeting. With each page stamped "confidential" in bold red print, the first paragraph stressed the importance to the developer and the property owner of keeping the land closing transaction confidential until completed. (The Phoenix Group had bitter competition throughout the state and the year before had lost out on a major shopping mall development—and on hundreds of thousands of dollars in predevelopment costs in the process—from what turned out to be a smear campaign financed behind the scenes by its competitor.)

In the memorandum, Williams and Walker summarized the salient points in the deal and explained that the public assumption of ownership of thirty acres of open space would have minimal financial impact on the village in terms of lost property taxes and increased maintenance costs. As part of the agreement, the developer was willing to grant the village a permanent public easement for walking paths along the lakeshore, a major concession that would limit the future uses of the entire parcel and guarantee, in perpetuity, public access to Crystal Lake. From Hamlin Ross's perspective, keeping thirty acres of open space allowed for greater density in development of the remaining land, reduced his property tax and insurance liability, and drew potential patrons to his commercial properties.

Throughout the process of nurturing this project, Williams had become the key link to the various parties. He had worked hard to establish strong relationships with Hamlin Ross and his associates as well as with Alan Lester. He had positioned himself as the liaison to village department heads and the village board in this matter. More and more, he saw it as his responsibility to facilitate any aspect of the lakefront development, particularly as it related to the Phoenix proposal.

Forty-eight hours after delivery of his confidential memorandum, Williams walked past a downtown newsstand on his way to lunch and lost all appetite when he read the headline in the afternoon *Crystal Lake Daily:* "Village Board Ponders Secret Land Deal." Included in the accompanying story was the complete text of his memorandum. Board members who had been contacted for the story had refused to comment, with the exception of Duke Coleman. "I really don't know much about this. It's the manager's idea. I certainly have a bunch of questions for him, though," he was quoted as saying.

The politics get rough

From this point things just seemed to get worse. Within a couple of hours, a call came to Williams from Hamlin Ross, who was calm but clearly upset. "Look, Ray," he said, "I want to do this project. I really do. But I don't need this type of garbage, and I'm not going to risk a small fortune where I can't even trust that negotiations will be kept out of the papers." He made it clear that any further such occurrences would cause him to cancel the entire project. "And you know as well as I do that you'll be a long time getting anyone else to put up with this foolishness when they read what I went through," he concluded.

The next blow was two-fisted. The following day both the *Crystal Lake Daily* and the *Manchester Journal* ran editorials critical of the upcoming executive session, respectively titled "Who Do Our Village Officials Represent?" and "Secrecy in Government." In essence, they argued that the public's right to know about transactions that affected them outweighed any privacy considerations offered developers. They demanded that the village board conduct its deliberations on this matter publicly.

By the time the executive session was held, what had begun as a project wholeheartedly supported throughout the community had become a source of controversy. Some residents began talking about Hamlin Ross as being "just like any other developer." Alan Lester, in typical curmudgeonly fashion, had commented to a reporter that it was none of the public's business what happened to his land. "The public never paid my taxes on that land. And I never saw the village giving me any tax breaks for the 'public access' that I provided for all those years."

In executive session, the proposed land transaction became secondary to the issue of the leak. Duke Coleman and his two allies favored bringing the entire discussion into public session, but backed away after lengthy discussion about the value of this development project to the future of the village. No one would admit to leaking the memorandum, and tempers flared at statements that sounded like accusations. Ray Williams tried to focus the discussion on the merits of the proposal and, in the end, gained approval from four of the board members to go forward. The Gang of Three argued for deferring the decision "for more study."

Coleman and his two like-minded colleagues on the board began to be more critical of the project after that meeting. During the ensuing weeks, as Williams oversaw the preparations for the land sale, the newspapers ran a series of articles discussing the proposed development. When they had exhausted the material that was based on the limited hard facts available at such an early stage of the revitalization project, both papers ran analysis pieces speculating on what the developer might have in mind for specific elements of the project. Stories also began to surface in the media hinting that the developer had engaged in questionable business practices in other communities. In the midst of all this controversy, the *Manchester Journal* broke a story about the arrest of the mayor of a city in a neighboring state, who had been indicted for soliciting bribes from Hamlin Ross. It was not clear whether Ross was a willing party to the bribery or, as he maintained, was simply cooperating with the state attorney general's office by playing along with the scheme.

A rumor was also circulated in the community that village manager Williams had flown to the Super Bowl on the developer's private jet. When asked by the editor of the *Crystal Lake Daily* to respond to the allegations, Williams was forced to reconstruct his activities on the day in question, eight months earlier. Since he had stayed at home and watched the game on television with his young son, he was hard-pressed to prove that the Super Bowl story wasn't true. While the newspaper refrained from printing the unsubstantiated allegations, the rumor continued to be repeated.

By mid-October, the land sale had still not been closed. Both the buyer and the seller were anxious to close the deal by the end of the calendar year, both for income tax reasons and because of pressure from subleasees, including the Radisson Corporation, to move forward or see them invest elsewhere in the region (most likely with Phoenix's competitors.) This timing was vitally important to the developer, who needed to commit a substantial sum of money by year-end to avoid a significant corporate capital gains tax.

However, by now it was election time again, and the campaigns for village offices were in full swing, with lakefront development again a central issue. Duke Coleman, running for mayor on a platform of "open government," declared that whatever he learned about the development project, the public would also know. "The Duke" campaigned hard. He was in the newspapers almost daily, taking advantage of every photo opportunity that came his way and taking the incumbent mayor to task for failing to devote enough time to his elected office. If elected, Duke promised, he would turn the family business over to his son and retire in order to be a full-time mayor. "There will once again be a mayor's office in the village hall," he declared.

Although Ray Williams's professional ethics demanded that he stay politically neutral, his strong personal feeling was that Crystal Lake would be far better off with Cook remaining in the mayor's seat. And he couldn't help but be concerned over the implications of Coleman's statements about strengthening the mayor's role.

The decision problem

Two weeks before the election, Hamlin Ross requested a meeting with Ray Williams. At that meeting, he told Williams that the hotel market study had been completed and that it indicated that the market would support a maximum of 120 rooms. Because his land options with Lester were contingent upon a market study demonstrating the feasibility of a 200-room hotel, Ross could thus have walked away from the project; however, he preferred to go forward and had devised a plan that would allow him to salvage his investment. To get maximum usage out of the property, he proposed to designate the top two floors of the hotel building for condominiums and to reserve about 25 percent of the proposed public access easement area as private waterfront for the use of the condominium owners. Otherwise, he would not proceed with the project.

Further, he revealed, he had managed to interest Alan Lester, as part of a long-term payment plan for the property, in a leaseback of several of the top-floor units with beautiful views for Lester and his family. Lester was very interested in this proposal, but only if part of the waterfront could be kept as a private beach for the condominium owners.

Knowing that the long-awaited market study, which was due at any time, would finally determine the feasibility of the project, the village board members, as well as the local reporters, regularly asked Williams whether he had received the study results and whether there would be a land closing by year-end. Williams believed that disclosing what he had just learned about the deal and the market study to the village board in the two weeks remaining before the election would guarantee both Coleman's election and the ultimate demise of the lakefront project.

What should he do?

Discussion questions

1. What are the potential consequences of Williams disclosing this information to the village board at this time? What are the potential consequences of deciding to wait until after the election to reveal it?
2. Would it be appropriate for Williams to explain his dilemma to Hamlin Ross and request that he maintain, if asked, that Williams knew nothing of the proposed change in the development plans prior to the election?
3. Should Williams take the mayor into his confidence on this matter? While the mayor would be the logical person with whom to share this information, could doing so be viewed as conspiring with the mayor to influence the outcome of the election?
4. Would failing to disclose this information to the village board in a timely fashion be an attempt on Williams's part to subvert the process of open government?
5. The events leading up to this current dilemma began with Williams's initial private meetings with the developer. Should he have done something different at that point?
6. After Williams got a clear message from the board that he was to share all information about the project with them, was he then exceeding his authority when he agreed to maintain confidentiality regarding the market study?
7. Where is the line between the village manager's obligation to follow the directives of the village board and his sense of obligation to promote the obvious public interest? (In this case, that public interest is in securing the development for the village despite what seem to be obvious "political" attempts by certain village board members to undercut the effort.)

Goodbye, Sampson, Inc.?

Jeffrey A. Raffel and Kevin C. McGonegal

Editor's introduction

Economic development and financial administration are intrinsically related. The pace and kind of economic development affects local government revenues and, in turn, imposes demands for additional government expenditures to pay for new and expanded local services. The relationship is even more serious, however, in communities where the local economy is declining or stagnating. Such communities frequently find it necessary to offer financial incentives— tax breaks or financial support—to attract or, as in this case, retain business firms.

This case examines the linkage between economic development and local government finance, demonstrating the kinds of policy and management decisions that must be made as a result of this linkage. Such decisions cover a broad range of concerns—setting policy precedents, managing intergovernmental and public-private relations, and synthesizing opposing points of view within the management staff itself.

The case also portrays the critical linkage between economic development policies and local neighborhoods. In this case, the proposed development would help revitalize the city's central business district, but at the same time it would have an impact on adjacent residential neighborhoods, with their aging housing stock and diverse racial and socioeconomic makeup. Along with economic development, then, are classic problems of city social and land use planning.

Redevelopment, whether of downtown business districts or of aging residential neighborhoods, has been a vital issue for local governments for more than a half century. The threatened departure of Sampson, Inc., in this case, portends a severe loss of jobs; its retention could be the foundation for downtown redevelopment. But at what cost should the city intervene? Should the costs to affected neighborhoods and displaced residents be considered along with costs to the city treasury?

Economic development rarely proceeds without complex intergovernmental interaction, and this case is no exception. It demonstrates not only the role of different governments, but also the different objectives being pursued by each. Distinct, but also related, is the necessary effort to involve the private business sector in the total development effort.

Most important, however, the case poses the central policy issue of economic development: What is the role of government, and what, if any, incentives should the public sector provide to the private sector in order to promote the overall welfare of the community?

Case 9
Goodbye, Sampson, Inc.?

Background

The city of Metropolis faced a major economic development crisis. Its second-largest employer, Sampson, Inc., was considering a move to the suburbs, and city officials had to decide what actions they could and should take to persuade Sampson to stay.

Metropolis, a city of approximately 80,000 people, is the state's largest city and is Tower County's urban core. Metropolis's 15.77 square miles of land is bounded on the east by a river and on the remaining boundaries by suburban areas. The city's location on the eastern seaboard makes it an important link in the Boston-to-Washington megalopolis; approximately 30 percent of the U.S. population is within a 350-mile radius of the city.

Metropolis is particularly significant to the state's economy, as it is an important center for banking, health and social services, communication, cultural and historical facilities, and education. The city has a thirteen-member elected city council and a mayor elected at-large every four years at the same time as the national presidential election.

At the time this case unfolds, Metropolis had been experiencing problems similar to those of other cities in the Northeast in the 1960s and 1970s—a declining population and tax base; a loss of business and industry; obsolescence of its manufacturing facilities, housing stock, and public facilities; and a concentration of elderly, poor, and disadvantaged populations within the city. The number of manufacturing jobs was declining, while managerial, professional, and clerical jobs held by suburban commuters increased as a proportion of total city jobs. No new nonmanufacturing firms had been established since 1950, and the twelve major nonmanufacturing firms in the city had shown negligible growth in that period. Unemployment in Metropolis was significantly higher than in the surrounding county and in the rest of the state.

Metropolis's central business district, in particular, was aging and economically threatened. It was located between two rivers, the picturesque Lamar River on the north and the Lomax River on the south. Residential neighborhoods bordered the district on its east and west sides. The district sorely needed to keep the level of business activity in the city, not only to retain and increase its own employment levels but also to provide jobs for the residents of surrounding neighborhoods and to encourage redevelopment efforts in the area.

Sampson, Inc., which began life as a divested part of the well-known and huge Clemson Chemical Company, had spent its entire existence in the shadow of the larger company. A successful Fortune 500 firm in its own right, Sampson was a diversified chemical company that developed and manufactured plastics, synthetic fibers, textiles, agricultural chemicals, detergents, and protective coatings. Originally named the Sampson Firepowder Company, it had expanded greatly from its beginnings as a manufacturer of explosives, but it still maintained a significant presence in that field with products for mining, quarrying, and even ballistic missiles.

When Harold Hammer, an experienced and dynamic executive, took the reins at Sampson as president and chief executive officer, he was determined to establish a stronger, separate corporate identity for the company.

Sampson, which was leasing 360,000 square feet of office space in Metropolis, needed 600,000 square feet for a new corporate headquarters. Its 1,350 employees at the downtown location made it the second-largest employer in the city after Clemson. It was considering various relocation options, including a suburban location that was already home to its research center and its country club.

Hammer was particularly upset with the state's personal income tax structure, which taxed top income levels at 20 percent. His feeling, and that of other business leaders, was that this high rate of taxation kept other corporations out of the state, thus hurting the state's image as a business center. He went so far as to threaten to move the corporate headquarters out of state and, in fact, was talking to a city in California about relocating there. Excerpts from a newspaper article written the day after President Hammer's speech to the Metropolis Rotary Club describe his position (see Exhibit 1).

Whether or not he would have followed through on his threats, Hammer certainly got the attention of the governor and the general assembly. Work was begun on a state income tax cut, which subsequently passed, dropping the top rate from 20 percent to 14 percent. The governor also realized that the eco-

---

Exhibit 1 Excerpts from newspaper article Sampson, Inc., an important element in the state's economy since its founding in 1913, could well sever the historic relationship to find a better business climate elsewhere, its chief executive made clear in a carefully worded speech yesterday.

Though avoiding any explicit threat, President and Chief Executive Harold H. Hammer left no doubt that the financially struggling chemical company was giving real thought to uprooting its highly paid 1,350 employees currently headquartered in downtown Metropolis.

The state's business leaders have for some time been grumbling that the state's policies, especially the personal income tax, hurt economic development, but this week could go down as the time they went public.

In a speech to the Rotary Club, Hammer centered his attack on the top rate of 20 percent in the state's personal income tax structure.

Sprinkling the talk with general references to business moves, Hammer rammed home his point by saying Sampson would be watching the state legislature's tax action and noting that the headquarters occupies leased space.

"There is a greater tendency on the part of business today to maintain flexibility. Many companies rent or lease office space instead of building on their own. This, of course, gives greater flexibility. Sampson, for example, leases its space in the Sampson Tower. . . ."

The lease expires a year from December for the offices occupied by 1,350 employees in the Sampson Tower building. "No new lease has been signed," a spokesman said, adding, "It's not even time to sign one."

After the speech, a reporter asked Hammer whether he was threatening to leave. "We have no plan to pull out of the state at this time," he replied. "I will not voice threats. We will do what business prudence tells us to do."

Describing the state as a perfect geographic location that was being shunned by business, Hammer said state government was making little effort to solve basic revenue problems.

Apparently agreeing were the more than two hundred corporate executives, lawyers, surgeons, insurance representatives, and others who jammed the Rotary meeting. Hearty applause continued for twenty-five seconds at the end, and several came to their feet clapping.

Sampson will study the revenue committee's recommendations for tax legislation, Hammer said.

nomic health of the state's major city was crucial to the overall economic health of the state. Metropolis was the "core of the apple," and it was in the state's best interest for Metropolis to retain its second-largest employer and stay as self-sufficient as possible.

Following the tax cut, Hammer announced that Sampson intended to remain in the state. But this decision by no means meant that Sampson would remain in the city.

Another article in the *Metropolis News* reported Hammer's decision to move the company from the Sampson Tower building into a new leased complex, but Hammer said that no decision had been made as to whether it would be in Metropolis.

"I think one of the reasons we're not talking about building ourselves a building, but rather about leasing, is because we're a little skeptical about the long range," said Hammer. In the same press conference, he went on to point out that the corporate office of Sampson, Inc., represented an annual contribution to Metropolis of about $100 million. He also dropped broad hints that Sampson was being courted by industrial development officials from other states but denied that he was seriously considering an out-of-state move.

The press report went on to say that city and state officials, in an effort to retain Sampson, had hired two consultants to help them make proposals for a Sampson headquarters. They talked to Sampson about several "concepts" in the $70 million price range with government-subsidized financing. Photographs of the proposed building at three different sites had one thing in common: a forty-two-story cylinder that towered over the Clemson Chemical Company's complex.

The case

In its search for a new headquarters site, Sampson soon limited its options to two. One was the suburban land already owned by the corporation. The other was a city site made up of two parcels on the northern edge of the downtown area along the Lamar River; one parcel was a vacant lot owned by the Clemson Chemical Company, and the other was occupied by an old vocational/technical school building. The company offered to remain in Metropolis if the costs of the city site were made comparable to those of the suburban location.

Immediately adjacent to the city site, and to the west, was a residential neighborhood called Midtown Lamar, which had been undergoing a transition with fairly extensive housing renovations and rehabilitation. It was now populated with young African-American and white professionals and lower-income African-American renters and home owners (Table 1). Only 3.9 percent of the families in this neighborhood were below poverty level, and the median income equaled the mean for the entire city. A strong neighborhood organization attempted to maintain the racial and economic mix.

To the east of the site was Eastside, a predominantly African-American, lower-income neighborhood composed of a large number of long-term home owners and some elderly renters. According to the U.S. census, the median income of Eastside families was one-third less than that of the whole city, and about 30 percent of the families had an income below the poverty level. The area had experienced a 41 percent decline in population in the decade between the last two census counts; urban renewal was the cause of about half of this figure.

The residents of these two areas expressed a number of concerns to city officials regarding the possibility of a major office structure in their midst. Construction problems for the neighborhoods, such as dirt and construction debris, were short-term issues; of more significance were the longer-term issues such as traffic congestion, design considerations, and displacement. Related

Table 1   Demographic data.

	Census tract		
	City	Eastside	Midtown Lamar
Population (total)	80,386	2,945	787
White, #	44,901	94	266
African American, # (%)	35,072 (43.6)	3,844 (96.6)	511 (64.9)
Ages 16–21 years and over, not high school graduates, not enrolled in school, %	20.7	21.0	11.8
Persons 25 years and over	46,204	1,816	444
Median school years competed, #	10.9	8.8	11.2
High school graduates, %	39.7	20.9	43.2
Male, 16 years and over, #	25,317	1,046	265
In labor force, #	18,462	626	224
Female, 16 years and over, #	32,123	1,176	296
In labor force, #	14,549	688	187
Income below poverty level			
Families, # (% of all families)	3,084 (16.0)	201 (29.7)	6 (3.9)
Persons, # (% of all persons)	16,991 (21.4)	1,111 (37.9)	59 (8.1)
Households, # (% of all households)	5,245 (21.0)	270 (36.5)	43 (15.0)

Source: U.S. Census of Population and Housing.

concerns included the high unemployment rate among Eastside residents and the deterioration of certain parts of the neighborhoods.

The cost differential between the urban and suburban sites was substantial. First, the cost of the city parcel owned by Clemson was $3.9 million. Since Sampson owned the land outside the city, there would be no out-of-pocket expense for purchasing land for a suburban headquarters. Of course, choosing the suburban site would mean a lost opportunity for other development on that site. Second, since the downtown location would be a high-rise structure rather than a low-rise office park structure, the construction costs would be $9.7 million more in the city. Third, a parking garage would be needed in the city, adding $12.7 million to the project cost. Fourth, costs that were proportional to the total project costs, such as contingencies, architects' and engineers' fees, transfer taxes, and financing expenses, all increased roughly in proportion to the overall budget. All in all, the cost of the city location was higher by $32.3 million, or 42 percent, than the cost of the suburban location (Table 2).

Metropolis had several models to draw on. A few economic development projects had been undertaken in the city, although not really as part of an overall development plan. Most notable among these were a pedestrian shopping mall on Main Street and a hotel constructed over a downtown parking garage, a project that had been financed in part by a federal grant. This grant was part of a federal program to encourage urban development projects by making low-interest loans available to businesses locating in economically depressed areas. The process was competitive among cities, and the cities receiving the grants could, in turn, loan the funds to the project businesses. The businesses would repay the loans to the city over a period of time. Other federal grants had been used by the city to aid development in recent years, including grants for community development, public works, urban parks, and job-training programs.

City administrators estimated that approximately $10–$20 million could be available through various federal programs to help close the gap between the costs of a city site and the costs of a suburban site for Sampson. A primary goal of the federal government was to create long-term economic growth opportunities for distressed cities like Metropolis; therefore, the government would evaluate any proposal on the extent to which it involved a partnership

Table 2 Proposed Sampson headquarters building: Cost differential between urban and suburban sites.

Cost component	Urban	Suburban	Differential
Building	$ 45,967,000	$36,256,000	$ 9,711,000
Fixed equipment	1,552,000	1,552,000	—
Site development	1,694,000	2,971,000	1,277,000
Parking landscaping	1,200,000	—	1,200,000
Parking garage	12,700,000	—	12,700,000
Architects' and engineers' fees	3,443,000	2,447,000	996,000
Construction/contractor	3,000,000	3,000,000	—
Owners' administrative expenses	976,000	930,000	46,000
Land	3,878,000	—	3,878,000
Furnishing	10,750,000	10,750,000	—
Interior designer fee	850,000	850,000	—
Contingency	6,352,000	4,700,000	1,652,000
Legal fees	72,500	65,800	6,700
Closing costs	10,000	10,000	—
Title insurance	63,000	47,500	15,500
Transfer tax	2,100,000	1,054,000	1,046,000
Construction financing	14,201,000	12,045,000	2,156,000
Application fee	160,000	—	160,000
Total	$108,968,500	$76,678,300	$32,290,200

with the private sector that would increase investment in the city and lead to new long-term employment opportunities, especially for the city's unemployed minorities. To secure the investment from Sampson and to reduce the city-suburban gap, the city realized that it would need to provide incentives or concessions. These might be in the form of a property tax abatement (a new Sampson headquarters was expected to increase Sampson's property taxes by $360,000 per year), a waiver of the property transfer tax, or other actions that might lower the cost of the city site.

Modest state funds, perhaps as much as $5 million, also could be available for this project. The state's interest, however, had been limited ever since Hammer announced that Sampson was staying in the state.

Thus, outside funds could be available to the city, but city officials would have to determine what they would be willing to "pay" for them and under what conditions. Furthermore, officials would have to decide how to make the development package as attractive as possible to these funding sources.

The loss of the Sampson corporation would be a severe blow to Metropolis. First, the company was the second-largest employer in the city. Its 1,350 employees represented more than $92,000 in "head-tax" payments (levied on employers according to the number of employees over a minimum of five) and $300,000 in wage tax payments (levied on all employees living or working in the city at 1 percent of annual wages). The city depended a great deal on this wage or "municipal user tax," receiving about 30 percent of its $30 million budget from it. Second, a ripple effect on the city economy would be felt by the numerous services employed by the company, such as copying firms, travel agencies, and janitorial services. Third, Sampson employees had a significant impact on retail sales in the central business district. The city planning department estimated that each Sampson employee spent an average of $830 per year downtown, totaling about $1.1 million annually.

The decision problem

David Dunworthy, chief administrative officer of Metropolis and the top aide to Mayor William Williams, was charged with recommending a strategy to meet the Sampson threat. The members of the mayor's administrative cabinet who were involved in this decision had different views and concerns regarding the situation.

The budget director was concerned with the price that the city might have to pay to keep Sampson in town. Trying to reduce the cost of the city site might set a precedent for which the city would pay dearly in later years when other corporations tried to gain similar advantages. He did not feel that the city was in a financial position to make tax concessions to Sampson to compensate for the added cost to Sampson of remaining in the city. Yet, the budget director reasoned, the city must also be concerned about the loss of taxes and revenue that the flight of Sampson would inflict on the city tax base. He thought that Hammer might well be bluffing, and at times he advocated calling his bluff.

The commerce director believed that it was imperative to keep Sampson in the city. If Metropolis's number two employer left town, who knew what firm might be next? And word would get around that Metropolis couldn't hold its own corporations. He therefore advocated doing whatever was necessary to keep Sampson in the city.

The planning director viewed the situation as an opportunity to develop the downtown area more rationally. However, he was concerned about the objections of the neighborhoods adjacent to the site; he did not want an antidevelopment mood to dominate the city's political life for the next five years. He estimated that ten families and businesses would need to be relocated if the headquarters were to be built on the vocational school site.

The mayor was adamantly against "losing Sampson," but he was also concerned about losing the good will of the adjacent neighborhoods. The city of Metropolis, therefore, had a classic dilemma: it could not afford to lose Sampson, nor could it afford to keep Sampson.

City officials determined that if Sampson left for the suburbs, the city would incur the following costs:

- Loss of city wage taxes estimated at $300,000 and head taxes of $92,000

- Loss of retail sales in the central business district totaling about $1.1 million annually

- Loss, not easily measured, of the secondary economic benefits of services employed by the company and the associated wage and head taxes

- Loss of economic development "good-will" and reputation.

Given a total city budget of $30 million and a declining tax and economic base, the loss of more than $400,000 in taxes loomed large.

Yet the city of Metropolis could not afford, by itself, to reduce the city-suburban gap of $32 million to induce Sampson, Inc., to stay. Even if the city's revenue losses were estimated at $1 million per year, the current value of this loss would represent only about $9.1 million at a 10 percent discount rate over twenty-five years. The city could not justify spending much more to keep Sampson. Nor was it clear that Metropolis could raise the money to do this, in any case.

In formulating his recommendation, David Dunworthy had several decisions to make:

1. Should the city take direct action to further influence Sampson to stay in Metropolis?
2. If the city were to take direct action, what strategy should be used and what conditions should be negotiated?
3. What actions could the city take to close the cost differential between the city site and the suburban site? What amount would be enough to convince Sampson to stay? And what cost elements (listed in Table 2) were the most appropriate to alter?

4. What effect would the new Sampson building have on the surrounding neighborhood, and what steps could be taken to mitigate any negative impacts?

Discussion questions

1. Realistically, does Dunworthy have any choice but to recommend that the city work to keep Sampson? If not, why not? If so, how could failure to act be justified to the city's business community? How important are matters of public perception, business attitudes about the city, and precedents when economic development policies are being made?
2. How should Dunworthy handle the department heads in this situation, given the difference in opinion among them?
3. Assuming that a strategy will be developed to attempt to keep Sampson in the city, what principles should guide the city's choice regarding (1) the development costs that the public sector should be asked to assume, and (2) the tax concessions that the city should consider offering to keep Sampson? What alternatives might be considered in each case? What would you recommend?
4. What role could the state be asked to play in an effort to keep Sampson, and what arguments can be advanced to justify the state's cooperation?
5. What role could the private business section in Metropolis be asked to assume in this development effort? How should the business community be approached, and what inducements should be offered?
6. What assistance should be sought from the federal government, and how?
7. How would you organize an effort to keep Sampson? Given the players involved (the city, private organizations such as the chamber of commerce, and other interested parties), where should responsibility for the development of the campaign's policy be located? Who should participate in that policy-making effort? Where should administrative responsibility for the effort be located? What would be the advantages and disadvantages of creating a special economic development organization?
8. What can and should be done to prevent or minimize neighborhood opposition? What should be done to involve the neighborhoods in the process? Are there specific benefits that should be offered to each neighborhood to allay its concerns?

Part six:
Analysis and evaluation

Introduction to part six:
Analysis and evaluation

"Voters are rarely encumbered by concepts
of economic rationality."

This simple statement, uttered privately by the mayor in one of the cases that follow, cogently summarizes the overriding difficulty facing analysis and evaluation in local government. To the extent that management is a science, it is based on an empirical approach to problem solving and decision making. That approach, in turn, relies on such commonly held and widely articulated public values as the desire for efficiency, rationality, economy, and simple "good sense" in government. Yet, as the quotation suggests, the vagaries of a fickle political process result in expressed public preferences that do not always coincide with these values.

It is in these circumstances that the administrative analyst and the administrative decision maker find some of their most difficult challenges. As knowledge of organizational operations has expanded and the technological capacity to process information has increased exponentially, the professional administrator has increasingly tended to rely on empirical analysis of policy and organizational problems as the key to effective decision making.

In so doing, the modern administrator is faithful to a long, widely applauded professional tradition in public management. Woodrow Wilson described the role of the nonpolitical administrator as knowing the best (most efficient) way of implementing policy; Frederick Taylor initiated the search for the "one best way" nearly a century ago; and modern behavioral scientists, such as Nobel Prize–winning economist Herbert A. Simon, have made empirical inquiry the hallmark of competent social science action. The emergence of modern electronic capabilities for managing information and conducting sophisticated analyses of policy options only enhances the administrator's ability and penchant for basing decisions on empirical findings.

Yet, as the cases here demonstrate, the job of organizational and policy management is not based solely on competent analytical work. In a community governed by democratic principles, the will of the voters is the ultimate decision-making criterion, and that will is neither linked to empirical findings nor easy to fathom. Presumably, the will of the voters is translated by elected officials, but, as earlier cases demonstrate, such officials often are reluctant, for understandable political reasons, to make such a translation. The local government administrator will not spend many days in public office before learning that there are many public wills, usually at odds with each other and often at odds with generally acknowledged public values. Elected officials often take positions at odds with their own campaign rhetoric.

Politics not only makes strange bedfellows but also poses strange anomalies for the analyst. Case 10 looks at a situation in which competent analysis was used to solve a difficult service delivery problem. The resulting recommendations were endorsed by the elected officials and then rejected when voter opposition emerged. Case 12 poses similar problems as political considerations apply pressure to alter or ignore analytical findings in the decision-making process. Even in case 11, in which the role of the analysis is dominant, administrative staff cannot ignore the people who will be affected by any decision. All three of these cases afford the student the opportunity to massage data and try to develop their own analytically best solutions.

Throughout, the cases in this section describe the local government administrator at work "running the organization," putting into practice the precepts of organizational theory, and applying decision-making technologies in such diverse activities as designing an emergency medical response system, choosing a residential sanitation technology, and planning the location of human service offices. Even in such purely "administrative" tasks, the reality of politics and political leadership is ever present. Even in these most technical of functions, the administrator must still think politically.

10 Providing a municipal ambulance service

Daniel A. Allen

Editor's introduction

Professional public administration is devoted to the maximization of two principles: responsiveness (to the citizens being served) and efficiency (in the provision of public services). When these two values can be promoted by the same action (e.g., devising a new trash collection system that increases the frequency of collection and permits a simultaneous reduction in collection fees), decisions are easy, citizens are happy, and the administrator enjoys the feeling of accomplishment that goes with a job well done.

Much harder are the decisions that pose a conflict between these principles. That is the situation facing Roger Sims, the administrator in the village of David. Major changes are needed in the village's emergency medical response system, but any changes will cost substantial sums of money and run counter to strong "no new tax" pressures in the community. As is also usual in such circumstances, the available options are limited by political considerations. Administrator Sims, who also doubles as the village's policy analyst, must find a way to improve the community's emergency ambulance services that is politically acceptable to community residents.

The problem in David presents Sims with one of the most common dilemmas that confronts a local government administrator: choosing between doing what is best for the community and doing what the residents want. Such a dilemma has an easy solution: when in doubt, do what the voters want. Unfortunately, as any good policy analyst quickly learns, that solution is almost always a gross oversimplification of the problem. In the case at hand, for example, the typical taxpayer, who has not needed emergency ambulance service in years past and thus has had no personal experience with which to evaluate the importance of speed and quality in medical response, is likely to opt in favor of a lower-cost solution. But the analyst, aware of many case histories and concerned about municipal liability for situations in which emergency medical response is found wanting, is likely to have a different appreciation for the differences that costly upgrades in service quality can make during life-and-death emergencies. Faced with such knowledge, administrators have a difficult time opting for the easy, popular solution.

Other principles get involved in the decision, too. How much of the cost of the service should be paid by user fees and how much by general taxes. Reliance on user fees holds down local taxes but also forces additional medical care cost burdens on low-income persons. Adding to the complications in this case is the past practice of providing ambulance service to persons who reside outside village limits. These persons would benefit from service improvements but could not be required to pay taxes to finance the upgrades.

Clearly, as this case shows so well, the task of policy analysis clearly requires much more than simply "processing the numbers" to find the best-case, most efficient, or even least-cost solution to a problem. As Sims learns in David, it requires skill in reconciling "the numbers" with political realities.

Case 10
Providing a municipal ambulance service

Background

When it hired Roger Sims as the new village manager in David, a rural community of approximately 4,500 persons, one of the village council's primary goals was to have its new chief administrative officer assume a highly visible profile in the community. In addition, the council was anxious to address significant issues of service and infrastructure improvements that had long been given only indifferent attention.

Sims was the third person to occupy the post since it had been created eight years before; the first two village managers had made many internal changes but had not been particularly visible to the public. As a consequence, many citizens in the community were still not sold on the village's need for a professional manager. A small community with more than 125 years of history and experience, David had many residents who were very skeptical about paying the wages and benefits needed to retain a full-time professional manager. The mayor and council were, with an occasional exception, fully in support of the need for a manager. Yet the internal changes and guidance offered by the previous two managers were viewed favorably by the councils that had received them. The current council hoped that the new manager would tackle the village's more "public" needs and would therefore help "sell" the position to the community.

This was the first manager's position for Sims, who had served as an assistant manager for several years in the suburbs of a nearby major metropolitan area. Upon his arrival in the community, Sims made a sincere effort to become well-known and recognized in the community. He also began assessing the various services provided by the village, and identifying and prioritizing the changes he felt needed to be considered to improve the quality and effectiveness of those services.

Because David was a small community, Sims had only a small staff of employees to supervise. A total of twenty-two full- and part-time (nonvolunteer) employees in the police and public works departments and the clerk's office reported to one of four supervisors: the police chief and sergeant, the public works director, and the village clerk.

Of those supervisors, Sims quickly realized that the police chief, Arthur Small, who had been hired away from another community four years earlier to be David's chief of police, was in a very tenuous position. Chief Small was extremely unpopular in the community, both for his personal management style and for his attempt, made a year or so before Sims had been hired as David's manager, to fire a veteran officer of the department after an undercover operation orchestrated by the chief and Sims's predecessor. The "sting" operation resulted in theft charges and a recommendation by Small that the officer be dismissed. After lengthy hearings into the case, the council reduced the discipline imposed to a thirty-day suspension. The officer involved in the case subsequently sued the village, embroiling it in litigation over Small's and the former manager's actions in this matter. The village council had taken a generally supportive view toward the chief, but it had also directed Sims to assess Small's effectiveness and consider whether, in Sims's opinion, Small was able to function effectively in the position.

One of the services for which Chief Small was responsible was that of emergency medical services (EMS) for the community and surrounding area. As a stand-alone community, David was too small to support its own hospital, but it was surrounded by larger communities with hospitals. However, the closest of these hospitals was twenty-two miles away, which meant a long ambulance ride for serious trauma cases. It also meant that whenever a patient had to be transported to one of the surrounding hospitals, David's ambulance attendants were gone from the village for long periods of time.

And David did have an unusually heavy demand for ambulance services. The community was home to a women's prison operated by the state as well as to both a private nursing home for the elderly and a state-operated facility for severely disabled children and young adults. These facilities were the three largest users of David's ambulance service. In addition, David's northern and southern borders included exit and entrance ramps to one of the state's busiest interstate highways, as well as to two other busy state highways, both of which were notorious for their regular high rate of serious traffic accidents.

The case

It did not take long for Sims to realize that the ambulance service was one of the village's services that was most in need of attention. The village had operated its ambulance service since the early 1970s, when the local funeral homes discontinued offering ambulance service and the local fire protection district, operated by volunteers, refused to absorb EMS into its operations. Since David had neither its own hospital nor one close by, the village council concluded that the village's government had an obligation to ensure adequate EMS for the community. Thus, at the council's direction, the village had operated an EMS since that time, using volunteers and police officers to staff the two ambulances on a twenty-four-hour-a-day call basis.

When the new system was established, the council had made the police department responsible for it. The police chief had been given responsibility for managing the ambulance service, and a part-time coordinator had been employed to work for the chief on such matters as scheduling volunteers to be on call and maintaining training records. While dedicated to trying to make the service work, however, Chief Small was not a professional EMS manager and already had his hands full trying to run the daily operations of the police department. Unfortunately, the difficulties Small encountered in trying to manage the ambulance service were compounded by his unpopularity in the community.

Service delivery problems

In the years leading up to Sims's arrival, several problems had developed with the ambulance service, the most notable and serious of these being a shortage of staff to operate it. The number of "volunteers" (who were paid an hourly wage for all time spent actually running calls but were not paid to be on call) had declined to a reliable core group of fewer than twenty persons. Although they were all committed to the ambulance service, many of the volunteers held full-time jobs outside the community and were not in a position to respond to calls except when they were off duty from their regular jobs. Thus, coverage by volunteers during the daytime hours was especially problematic.

In addition, there was a political consideration. While the volunteers were not particularly active as a group politically, many of the current and former members of the volunteer ambulance service were prominent in the community. The organizational structure of the ambulance service, in which the volunteers worked for the chief of police, was a particular bone of contention for many of the volunteers who, correctly or not, perceived the chief as treating the ambulance service and themselves as the "poor relation" of the police department and not giving the service the attention it deserved. These perceptions, along with the chief's style and unpopularity, had almost certainly contributed to the decrease in the number of persons serving on the volunteer service. Most of the remaining, dedicated members of the volunteer corps recognized the need for changes in the operation of the service but hoped that, whatever was done, they would be able to continue serving the community and running ambulance calls.

To ensure the adequate coverage of calls, David's six police officers were required, as a condition of employment, to become certified emergency medical technicians (EMTs). When no volunteers were available, officers were required to come in off duty to run any ambulance calls that came in within the twelve-hour period before their regular shift was set to begin. The officers were not paid for being on backup during these twelve-hour periods but earned overtime for calls run during the preshift periods. On-duty police officers were rarely able to run ambulance calls because, most of the time, there was only one police officer working and that officer could not be pulled off the street. If an ambulance call came when two officers were working together, however, one of the two officers on duty typically wound up having to respond to the call to ensure that there was adequate staff to provide the needed medical services.

Further compounding the personnel problem was the fact that the overtime pay earned by the police officers was more than the hourly wage paid to the volunteers. Thus, as the number of volunteers declined and more of the ambulance service was transferred to off-duty police officers, the amount of overtime being paid out by the village for officers to run calls was becoming a drain on the budget.

Moreover, the situation had become a serious morale problem for the police department as a whole. Many of the officers were not interested in being EMTs, but it was required as a condition of employment. The officers resented constantly being called during their off-duty hours to run ambulance calls. In addition, both the officers and village officials were concerned that running these calls was adversely affecting the officers' ability to function well as police officers when they were on duty.

This was especially true of the officers who worked overnight because they were called more often during the day owing to the lack of available daytime ambulance volunteers. The officers worked twelve-hour shifts overnight, which meant that if an officer was scheduled to work two consecutive days, he or she would be on call for twelve hours for ambulance runs, work for twelve hours as a police officer, be on call again for the twelve-hour period before his or her next shift, and then work for another twelve-hour shift. If multiple ambulance calls came in during these twelve-hour on-call periods, it was conceivable that an officer would be working with little, if any, rest for a period of forty-eight hours. This was clearly not a good situation from a safety standpoint.

Ambulance service parameters

The difficulty in finding people available to run the ambulance calls often extended response times to more than ten minutes, even though the ambulance was in many cases only a minute or two away from the call. Moreover, because of the village's distance to hospitals, ambulance calls averaged one and a half to two hours per call. And the lack of available staff and the length of time for each call was exacerbated by the potential for calls involving severe trauma, given the facilities and highways mentioned above. The longer the response times to these severe trauma calls, the lower the likelihood of a successful outcome on the call.

Finding volunteers willing to receive even a basic EMT-A license had been difficult in David, given the time such training would take. As a result, the ambulance service functioned only at the minimal basic life support (BLS) level. Each year there were a few calls in which patients in need of a higher level of care received only basic care during lengthy ambulance rides to a hospital. With the increasing staffing demands to maintain even the basic EMT-A-level certification by the state, however, it simply was not possible to upgrade the level of care using the current hybrid police officer/volunteer staffing system.

All of these difficulties were compounded by the fact that the number of calls for service had increased dramatically from a previous high of fewer than 300 calls five years earlier to more than 450 per year. This trend was expected to continue because the community was experiencing its most rapid growth since the late 1960s, when its largest employer, biggest utility user, and most prominent corporate citizen had located there.

The number of calls was straining the service to the point where it was very unreliable. At times, it took several minutes to find the people to staff a call. In a number of instances, two calls for ambulance service had come in within a short period, and an ambulance crew from another nearby community had to be summoned to handle the emergency. Response times in these situations occasionally exceeded twenty minutes, which was simply unacceptable to the person who was in need of the service. Because of this situation, the village council was appropriately concerned about the liability risk it was taking when its ambulance service was unable to respond to a call in a timely fashion.

Political considerations

Despite these problems, many persons in the community, most of whom had never needed to use the ambulance service, had no idea of the difficulties the village was having in providing it.

When Sims presented a report to the council on the ambulance service's problems, the council agreed with his conclusion that something had to be done to improve the service for the community. What should be done, however, was not so clear. With the unpopularity of Chief Small, the weight of the complaints and concerns voiced by the current and former members of the volunteer service, and the traditional aversion of David's residents to any increase in taxes, an acceptable solution would clearly be difficult to achieve and, no matter how appropriate, would likely be controversial. Nonetheless, with his council colleagues in agreement, Mayor Charles Franklin told Sims to consider the available options and report back with a recommendation.

Sims first approached the David Fire Protection District, which operated a thriving traditional volunteer fire department, about either working with the village to provide the service or, preferably, assuming total responsibility for its operation. The fire district, though, was not at all interested in doing this, even with village financial aid. In fact, the district's personnel rules did not allow a member of its fire department to participate as a volunteer member of the ambulance service because of what the district perceived as a conflict of interest between fire and EMS duties on calls. The fire department had several certified EMTs among its ranks who gladly would have assisted on the ambulance, but they were forced to choose between the ambulance service and the fire service by the fire district's board. The members of the board, in turn, were beyond the control of the village council since they were appointed to the board by the county board chairman.

Cost considerations

With the refusal of the fire protection district even to discuss expanding its services to include emergency ambulance calls, and with the state's policy of relying strictly on local ambulance companies to service its facilities, Sims knew that the village would have to provide emergency ambulance services to the community.

Since a large proportion of the system's demand came from the women's prison and the home for severely disabled children and young adults, both of which were operated by the state, Sims next approached the state government for a subsidy to help maintain an ambulance service. This request, too, met with summary dismissal. The state acknowledged that it had an obligation to pay for ambulance calls to its facilities, but it refused to consider providing any other kind of support. "If we helped David maintain an ambulance service, we'd end up paying to support similar services in every community in the state that has a state corrections facility," responded an official in the state's Department of Corrections. It was thus obvious to Sims that David not only had to provide ambulance service itself, but would also have to rely on its own resources to cover the cost of the service.

Historically, the village had been billing users of the ambulance service. Such billings, however, had never covered the full costs of the service, and the village council had not increased the billing rate for approximately eight years. The costs of operating the service had increased significantly since that time, as medical supply costs had skyrocketed and wages paid to police officers and volunteers had increased as well. Clearly, some increase in the fee structure was unavoidable, but an increase in fees to cover all of the system's costs would make the fees astronomical. This would pose political and other problems. Since ambulance fees historically have been among the hardest charges to collect, regardless of amount, and high fees would be even harder to collect, Sims expected from the start that any reasonable fee increase would never be sufficient to pay all of the ambulance service's costs.

The year that Sims arrived in David, the village's general fund had to subsidize the ambulance fund with approximately $20,000 so that the fund could balance revenues with expenditures. In a community in which the general fund's total revenue flow amounted to less than a million dollars per year, this subsidy represented a significant amount of money. General fund revenues came primarily from village property tax levies and the village's share of state-levied sales taxes. Under state law, the village could levy a utility tax of up to 5 percent on all bills for electric, natural gas, and intrastate telephone services paid by utility customers located in the village. But, like their peers in almost all of the state's small municipalities, David's council members had never levied the tax.

The village council also had a general aversion to the idea of raising property taxes and had done an admirable job of keeping the rate low for the past several years. In addition, the village was in a fairly healthy financial situation, with adequate excess reserve levels in most funds (but not in the ambulance fund).

The decision problem

With this information in hand, Sims discussed the problem with the village council, with Chief Small, and with ambulance service volunteers. He also consulted with administrators in other communities in his search for other options for improving the ambulance service. Among the possibilities identified were the following:

1. The village could expand the payments to volunteers by going to a paid on-call situation rather than paying volunteers for their time on an hourly basis only when they were actually on an ambulance call. However, there were no guarantees that this approach would accomplish anything more than increase the cost of the service without providing for more manpower and quicker response times.

2. The village could move to a full-time paid service for part of the day. With most of the volunteers unavailable during the weekday to run calls, the village could hire full-time personnel to run calls during the week-days and continue to depend on volunteers during the evening, night, and weekend hours, when there was a greater chance of volunteers being available. However, this could create an inequitable situation in which persons who called for service during certain times of the day would be assured quicker service than those who called at other times. A source of adequate funding for this option was also a concern.

3. The village could move to a full-time paid service twenty-four hours a day, seven days a week. This option would provide for guaranteed cover-age by paid professionals, and it would also ensure faster response times. It might also permit an increase in the level of service to advanced life support (ALS). The nearest potential quarters for personnel working overnight was in the old village hall, located approximately one hundred feet from the building where the ambulances were housed. The old hall was leased by the village to the David Historical Society, which used it to store information on David's history. However, the cost of this option made it problematic: not only would the building require remodeling to house the professionals between calls, but this option would also require a major commitment of new personnel dollars.

4. The village could contract the service to a private provider. Although none was physically located in the community, some private providers in nearby communities had expressed an interest in coming to David to provide the service. One advantage of a private service would be that if manpower from David were not available at any given time, the private contractor could free up additional manpower resources from other com-munities it served, thereby ensuring full coverage of the ambulance. Once again, however, funding for such a contract was a big concern.

5. The village could maintain the volunteer service in its current form while removing it from the management duties of the police chief and giving responsibility over to either a volunteer or a full-time EMS coordinator hired by the village. There were no guarantees, however, that this would solve the manpower problems with the volunteers. In addition, this would set up some potentially problematic situations with police officers reporting to two different supervisors, one for police work and one for EMS work.

6. The village could try to pressure the fire protection district to develop a joint partnership arrangement with it by publicizing the district's indiffer-ence to the ambulance situation. The public pressure on the district's board might then force the district to become involved against its will.

Most of the options under consideration were going to result in significant additional costs to the village, costs that would have to be passed on to its citizens and taxpayers. These costs are summarized in Table 1.

Sims identified several options for funding any changes and upgrades in the village's ambulance service. Among these were the following:

Table 1 Summary of costs for possible service improvement options.	Option cost, $	Additional, $
Current system	80,241	n/a
Paid, on-call volunteers	115,801	35,560
12 hours full time, 12 hours volunteer	248,377	168,136
24 hours full time	310,835	230,594
24 hours contracted	312,539	232,298

1. The billing rate could be increased to generate additional revenue from each call. Although many viewed this as the fairest way to pay for the ambulance service, most users of the service were on state aid or under the control of the state (correctional center residents), so increasing the billing rate was not likely to generate significant additional revenue for a few years until the state's Medicaid system agreed to pay the new rates. Others argued that billings were not a fair way to fund the system, and that a major reason to have an ambulance service available is the simple fact that it is just that—available to *all* in the community regardless of an individual's financial condition. Many protested that the person in need of an ambulance should not be faced with the prospect of having to pay a significant bill for the ambulance service as well as for the other medical bills that are likely to come with the need for the ambulance.

2. The village could increase its corporate levy for property taxes. During a period of rebellion against property taxes, however, and especially in the middle of a statewide effort to enact property tax caps, any such proposed tax increase would be very controversial. Further, David's property tax levy was extremely low, comprising less than 10 percent of the village's overall revenues, so a very large percentage increase would be required to generate significant additional revenue. In addition, the largest users of the ambulance service—the state facilities and the nursing home—were all exempt from paying property taxes, so the residents and businesses would all be asked to carry a larger portion of the load for funding the service while the service's biggest users would not be affected by the increase in taxes.

    Further compounding the tax option, however, was the incidence of the tax increase. Only those persons who resided in the corporate limits of the village would be paying the increased levy. Residents in the outlying areas who received the service would not be included among those paying the additional levy.

3. The village could enact a separate property tax levy specifically to fund the ambulance service, provided that creation of such a levy was approved by a referendum in the village. This would certainly be an uphill battle, as property tax referenda always are. Further, such a levy could, again, be imposed only on village property tax payers; the three largest users and persons residing outside the village boundaries would be exempt from paying it.

4. Because the village did not currently levy one, a tax on utility usage for electricity, natural gas, and telephone service could be enacted without referenda, simply with the passage of an ordinance. A utility tax would be applicable to all utility users in the village, including the three largest users of the ambulance service. However, the largest employer, and also the largest utility user in the village, would be forced to pay a significant portion of these increased revenues even though this employer was not a large user of the ambulance service. Moreover, since few neighboring communities levied utility taxes, such a levy would put David's economic development efforts at a competitive disadvantage.

5. The village could enact a combination of any of the options listed above. However, no other options appeared to be available for financing service enhancements.

Sims knew that from this information, he had to craft a recommendation to present to the village council. As he looked at his options, he ruefully remembered how, as a college student, he had dreamed of being in a position to help make public policies that would improve the quality of people's lives. Now he had that opportunity, but somehow it no longer seemed to be so empowering or desirable. He had to make some hard choices: the best options for protecting health and saving lives seemed to be the same choices that could provoke serious adverse political consequences in the community he served—and thus maybe even for his ability to keep his job.

Sims also knew that he had two kinds of questions to answer. The first were process questions: what information did he need, with whom should he consult, how should he reconcile his own best judgment with the opinions of others, how and when should he release critical information to the public, and how much of a leadership role should he take in selling any recommendation to the public if the members of the council were reluctant to assume such leadership? The second questions were substantive in nature, simple to state and hard to answer: what policy or program changes should ultimately be recommended to correct the problems with the ambulance service?

Discussion questions

1. As an administrative analyst, what additional information would you want before formulating answers to the process questions above?
2. How should Sims proceed? What strategic elements should comprise his "game plan" in moving to resolve the matter?
3. Should the corps of existing ambulance volunteers be included in the decision-making process? If so, how?
4. How, if at all, should the police chief be involved in the decision? To what extent should the chief's unpopularity, some of which was undeserved in Sims's opinion, be a factor in the changes proposed?
5. What role should the largest users of the system have in resolving this situation, if any?
6. How and when should Sims inform the general public of the details of the problem? Should the policy options be opened to public discussion? As an administrator recently arrived in the community, what steps should he take to demonstrate his knowledge of the issue and his sensitivity to "local opinion"?
7. Under what circumstances, if any, should Sims be willing to assume a public leadership role in "selling" a proposed solution to the general public?
8. As an administrative analyst, what additional information would you want before formulating your substantive policy recommendations?
9. Which is more important: finding the right solution from a manpower and response time standpoint or minimizing the increased cost to the citizens and businesses for improvements to the service? Are the two mutually exclusive? If they are, how does an analyst/administrator choose between them? If they are not, how should these two values be reconciled?
10. Sims is not only the village's administrative analyst, he is also the chief administrative officer and thus the one who has to take the heat from the council and perhaps from the public for whatever he recommends. Should this change the way he should proceed to formulate his recommendations? Are the recommendations that he will make as chief administrator likely to be different from those he would make as an administrative analyst reporting to the chief administrator? If so, explain how they might be different and why this might be so. If not, explain why not.
11. If Sims recommends major service improvements that would require a significant increase in local taxes, should he be prepared, in the event that the tax increase proposals generate major public opposition, to take a fallback position in order to salvage his effort to improve services? If so, what might that position be? If not, why not?

12. Should Sims present the policy options to the village council or just a final recommendation?
13. What policy and program changes should Sims recommend to the village council? (If needed, make additional assumptions regarding missing data and then proceed to prepare recommendations.)

11
Contracting for trash
Scott D. Lazenby

Editor's introduction

This case poses an analytical problem that will face most if not all county and city governments in the next decade: how to find the best (i.e., the most cost-efficient and effective) system for collecting residential trash. Solid waste is increasing in volume annually, landfills are nearing their capacity, the public continues to resist higher taxes and garbage collection fees, and recyclable materials must be sorted and collected separately. As a result, virtually every government providing residential sanitation services will be facing decisions nearly identical to the one posed here.

This case also examines a service delivery option that local governments are considering with increasing frequency: contracting with a private firm to provide a public service—in this case, the collection of the city's residential trash.

Unlike many other cases, in which human and political factors are at least as important as analytical findings in the decision process, this case presents a problem in which the decision can rest primarily on the results of analysis. The human and political considerations, while present, are secondary to the need to find a collection method that minimizes both long- and short-term costs. Specifically, when a new collection system is ultimately selected, how can it be implemented so as to minimize adverse effects on employees?

Case 11
Contracting for trash

Background

The city of Newglade is located in a large metropolitan area and has a population of approximately 100,000. At the time the case unfolds, Newglade faced a problem with the collection of solid waste (garbage). Several different methods of collection were used by communities in the metropolitan area, and Newglade found itself forced to evaluate its present collection system and to consider alternatives.

The case has the following cast of characters:

Charles Veracruz, city manager

Chris Smith, assistant city manager

Thomas H. Moses Jr., director of public works

Alfred E. Newhouse, budget director

Pat Chamber, administrative assistant, public works

Kay Hernandez, administrative assistant, finance

The case unfolds through the communication among these officials. The memo that launched the development of this case problem summarizes critical elements of the background.

CITY OF NEWGLADE
MEMORANDUM

DATE: May 2
TO: Charles Veracruz, City Manager
FROM: Pat Chamber, Administrative Assistant II
SUBJECT: Status of Residential Sanitation Operations

Per your request, this report provides information on the status of the residential sanitation operation.

Roughly 80 percent of Newglade's population is served by curbside collection of an unlimited number of cans (the other 20 percent of the population lives in apartments or other forms of housing that are served by the city's commercial sanitation operation). Residential collection is twice a week, as mandated by the state—presumably to keep the fly population down. As you know, parks maintenance staff also collects uncontained waste or "loose trash" twice per month.

The city has taken steps to reduce its garbage collection costs. The three-person rear-loading trucks were replaced with two-person manual side-loading packers. These in turn have been gradually replaced with one-person manual side loaders (the operator gets out of the cab to dump the garbage cans into the packer). In spite of the city's average annual population growth of 10 percent, the sanitation staff has decreased from 43 (including supervisors) two years ago to 25 today (22 driver-loaders and 3 supervisors). No staff members were laid off; positions have been either vacated by normal attrition or transferred to other field operations.

The annual cost of operation is now approaching $1.5 million. Salaries and fringe benefit costs account for $956,000; vehicle maintenance and operation accounts for $241,000; landfill and waste disposal charges are $212,000; and lease-purchase payments on equipment are $44,000. These costs are covered in the general fund through taxes; residents are not billed separately for sanitation service, although separate billing is the practice in some of the other cities in the metro area.

While the reduction in personnel has definitely lowered operating costs, the manual operation is not very efficient. The time taken by the driver to jump out of the cab and load the garbage cans adds to the time taken to complete a route. Of equal concern, the manual operation takes a physical toll on the driver-loaders. Last year there were twenty-two industrial insurance accidents that cost the city $18,000.

Field operations staff has done some preliminary investigation of automating residential collection (i.e., using trucks with equipment that picks up trash cans and dumps them mechanically into the truck), and we have reached the conclusion that this option should be pursued. Perhaps the new public works director will have had some experience in this.

Please feel free to contact me if you desire further information.

The case

WHILE YOU WERE OUT

DATE: 5/3   TIME: 12:50
TO C.V.
Mr. Tractar
Of: City Council called
Message: Said he was contacted by owner of Valley Waste Collection, who was upset that city doesn't contract out residential san. and doesn't allow private companies to provide commercial san. service in city. Call him ASAP.

R.L.

FROM THE DESK OF CHARLES J. VERACRUZ

5/3

Tom, here's a project to help you get your feet wet here! Could you and the public works staff look into contracting out residential garbage collection? There's some interest on the part of council.

C.V.

FROM THE DESK OF CHARLES J. VERACRUZ

5/3

Al, please have your budget staff do some analysis on the pros and cons of billing residents directly for garbage collection. Who pays for it now? What would we have to charge? How would this affect residents?

C.V.

Clipping file, Los Diablos Times, 6/14

NEWGLADE LOOKS AT SOCKING RESIDENTS FOR TRASH

NEWGLADE—In a workshop session, the Newglade City Council on Tuesday considered charging residents as much as $10 per month for collection of garbage.

Citing legal limitations on property taxes and political barriers to raising the sales tax rate, city staff proposed a sanitation "user fee" that would make garbage collection self-supporting and free up $1.5 million in general taxes now dedicated to trash collection.

Budget Director Alfred E. Newhouse stated that reducing general fund support for the residential sanitation operation would allow additional resources to be dedicated to police, fire, streets, and other critical city services. The garbage fee would be phased in over a period of several years, according to a staff report from City Manager Charles Veracruz. Collection service would remain the same under the proposal.

Veracruz also noted that the final rate could be as low as $6.00 per month, depending on cost-saving methods now being investigated by the city. The council took no action but referred the matter to the council budget committee.

CITY OF NEWGLADE
MEMORANDUM

DATE: June 21
TO: Charles Veracruz, City Manager
FROM: Al Newhouse, Budget Director
SUBJECT: Follow-up on Workshop on Garbage Fee

Given the circumstances, the press treated our report on the garbage user fee fairly kindly. One thing we didn't highlight in the report is the shift in tax burden that might result from the user fee. Here's some background:

As you know, the city uses several tax sources to fund sanitation and other city services. The most significant local tax is the 1 percent sales tax. This provides $13 million, or 37 percent of general fund revenues. Staff estimates that less than half of this is paid by local residents through normal retail purchases; the majority is paid by builders through their purchases of home and office building materials and by car buyers, many of whom come from neighboring cities to buy from Newglade dealers.

City property tax revenue for operations (i.e., excluding taxes levied for repayment of principal and interest on bonds) amounts to $2.8 million, only 8 percent of general fund revenues. The tax rate for residential property is $0.60 per $1,000 of value (0.6 mills) for the operating levy (the bond levy rate is 0.5 mills). Commercial and industrial properties are taxed at 2.5 times this rate. State property tax limitations prevent the city from increasing the rate for the operating levy.

About 9 percent of revenue comes from development fees, utility franchise fees, and business licenses, and the remaining 46 percent comes from taxes that are collected by the state and distributed to cities on the basis of population.

While it certainly seems equitable to charge residents for service costs they incur, this does seem to shift the burden of funding from the commercial sector (and nonresidents) to the city residential sector. Further, the user fee can't be deducted for federal tax purposes, unlike some local taxes (notably the property tax).

According to economic theory, people make decisions based on how they would be affected financially. Therefore, the "economically rational" voter would oppose a fee that shifts costs away from businesses and would prefer a tax increase. Should we bring this up with the council?

On a related subject, our commercial sanitation operation more than pays for itself. The fund balance is at 50 percent of annual revenue, and the rates have been set lower than those of many of the surrounding cities in order to avoid building up an excessive balance. As a way of holding down the residential fee, we could combine the two operations into a single fund. Commercial sanitation could subsidize residential sanitation and still be competitive with rates charged by private companies for business garbage pickup.

---

* ELECTRONIC MAIL *

INBOX FOR USERNAME NEWHOUSE
FROM USERNAME: VERACRUZ
POSTED: JUNE 25/8:11:01 AM

Al, thanks for the follow-up report—shared it with the mayor last night. He said that "voters are rarely encumbered by concepts of economic rationality"!
                                                                        C.V.

REPORT ON CONTRACTING FOR SANITATION SERVICES
JULY 6
Thomas H. Moses Jr., Director of Public Works
Pat Chamber, Administrative Assistant

At the direction of the city manager, the Public Works Department has completed an exhaustive and in-depth study of the merits and implications of contracting with the private sector for the provision of residential and commercial sanitation services. The background of this issue and staff recommendations are contained herein.

Commercial sanitation

Cities use several methods for providing commercial sanitation services. In some areas commercial sanitation is unregulated, and each business is free to choose which private company it will use to collect its refuse. Some cities franchise one or more private haulers. Other cities, including Newglade, provide commercial sanitation as a municipal service, following the same philosophy as for the provision of sanitary sewer service.

Notwithstanding the fact that some larger cities divide their service area into several sectors for contracting out commercial sanitation services, it is felt that in an operating area the size of Newglade's, commercial sanitation can be provided most efficiently by a single operator. Moreover, if municipal overhead costs are kept low, the city will be able to compete effectively with the private sector, which must maintain sufficient rates to provide an adequate profit.

To contract for a service, the city must conduct a number of activities. It must draft, review, and advertise specifications. It must devise a selection process that weighs service quality against cost. It must review bids and check references. Following the award of a bid by the city council, the city must develop a service contract that protects the city against inadequate performance of the service; the contract should also include renewal provisions. Finally, the city must administer the contract, including inspecting the quality of the work, resolving service complaints, and providing contract payments.

Contracting out a service previously provided by the municipality has an impact on existing equipment and staff resources. In the case of commercial sanitation, a portion of the staff could be absorbed by other field operations. The successful bidder could also be required to offer jobs to city staff affected by the transition (although salary and benefit levels could not be guaranteed). The equipment would have to be sold; even if the contractor purchased the equipment, it would be at a depreciated value, thus reducing the city's assets.

The city uses service contracts in custodial and parks maintenance services. At one point, the city had to cancel the custodial contract because of poor performance, at a cost to the city of $8,000 for a new contract. The higher administrative costs and potential loss of service quality are felt to be outweighed by the reduced labor cost inherent in the privately provided service.

Residential sanitation

Provision of residential waste collection follows the same patterns as for commercial sanitation, except that municipal provision is more common for residential than for commercial sanitation. Service quality is of potentially greater political concern because of the considerable interaction between the service providers and residents/voters. Prompt and courteous service, including such things as careful handling of waste containers, is a critical component of municipal residential sanitation service.

Recommendations

1. Seek bids for the provision of commercial sanitation service under contract, and compare the bid costs with city costs to determine whether the city should continue to deliver this service.
2. It is felt that current residential operations are competitive with comparable service provided by the private sector, particularly if collection is automated. Service reductions will not be tolerated by residents, especially if a user fee is created, and the Public Works Department does not recommend contracting for this service.

---

* ELECTRONIC MAIL *

INBOX FOR USERNAME NEWHOUSE
FORWARDED BY USERNAME: VERACRUZ
POSTED: JULY 10/2:05:01 PM

FORWARDING COMMENT:
Al, Thought you might be interested in this message. . . .

C.V.

FORWARDED MESSAGE:
TO USERNAME: VERACRUZ
FROM USERNAME: MOSES
POSTED: JULY 10/11:51:20 AM

It has come to my attention that the budget director has proposed combining residential sanitation financing with the commercial sanitation fund. This is totally unacceptable. These must be kept separate to allow separate tracking by the operating managers and to avoid cross subsidies between the services. Charles, you must understand that I will not tolerate this kind of interference in the functioning of the Public Works Department.

—Thomas H. Moses Jr., Director of Public Works

The decision problem

CITY OF NEWGLADE
MEMORANDUM

DATE: July 24
TO: Chris Smith, Assistant City Manager
FROM: Charles Veracruz, City Manager
SUBJECT: The Case Problem

Chris, I need your help in evaluating the city's options in residential sanitation. I will give you my file on the subject; please see other staff as necessary to gather the information you need for your analysis.

Specifically, please analyze and give me your recommendations on the following:

1. Should the residential sanitation operation be automated? What would be the savings to the city in automating? Can you give me an idea of the payback period, net present value, or some other cost-benefit measure? If

we do automate, should it be done at once, or phased in over time? How would we handle the reduced staff needs?

2. As an alternative to automating, should we seek bids for contracting out the provision of residential sanitation services? Again, how would we handle the human resource issues? How would we guard against a decline in service?

3. Under either scenario, how should residential sanitation be financed— i.e., should we continue using general funds or establish a user fee? If the latter, should it be phased in? If user fees are initiated, should the residential and commercial operations be combined in a single fund?

Please summarize your conclusions in a memo that I could share with the mayor.

MEETING NOTES

7/26

Meeting attendees: P. Chamber, K. Hernandez, C. Smith

Garbage Collection Assumptions:

Sixteen manual collection routes for the next two years (1 person per truck), with a route added every other year for population growth. Additional backup labor pool of 6 (to cover absences, training, etc.) for an initial total of 22 driver-collectors. 2.5 FTE supervisors (1 split with commercial san.). Automation would reduce initial routes to 13 and the backup labor pool to 5.

Assume inflation factor of 5 percent per year.

Labor costs (including overtime, uniforms, etc.) are $29,600 per driver and $32,000 per supervisor. Add 30 percent for fringe benefit costs.

Assume workers' comp (industrial accident) insurance at current $18,000, proportional to number of drivers and inflation. Figure workers' comp will be one-quarter of this amount under automated system and also reduced in proportion to the reduction in drivers.

Both manual and automated trucks cost $90,000 each. The acquisition schedule for the current fleet of trucks is to replace two in 1985, one in 1986, two in 1987, and so on at the rate of three trucks every two years. The current fleet could be sold for roughly $576,000 total (assumes trucks have depreciated 50 percent on a straight-line basis and that the city would face a 20 percent price reduction in the used truck market).

New containers for the automated routes would cost $60 each. Would need enough for 80,000 population, assuming 3.5 people per household.

Vehicle operation and maintenance costs are now $241,000 and are assumed to be proportional to the number of routes and inflation.

A new fleet of automated trucks could be financed through a lease-purchase contract. Assume a ten-year term and 10 percent interest rate (annual payment is 0.16 times purchase price).

For net present value calculation, use a discount rate of 10 percent.

Discussion questions

1. What should Assistant Manager Smith recommend to the city manager? (To assist him in his work, Smith prepared a worksheet summarizing the relevant data. That worksheet is presented as Table 1. The last several rows, containing the calculations on which the recommendation should be based, need to be completed.) Complete Table 1 and prepare Smith's recommendation in detail, including the reaction Smith should present to

Table 1   Residential sanitation automation worksheet.

Prepared by C. Smith	Date: August 6				
	Year 1	Year 2	Year 3	Year 4	Year 5
MANUAL SYSTEM					
Labor costs:					
Inflation factor	1.00	1.05	1.10	1.16	1.22
# Routes	16	16	17	17	18
# Drivers	22	22	23	23	24
# Supervisors	2.50	2.50	2.50	2.50	2.50
Labor cost	$950,560	$998,088	$1,090,417	$1,144,937	$1,248,957
Workers' comp.	$18,000	$18,900	$20,747	$21,784	$23,868
Equipment costs:					
# Trucks purchased	2	1	2	1	2
Cost (3 inflator)	$180,000	$94,500	$198,450	$104,186	$218,791
Vehicle O&M	$241,000	$253,050	$282,309	$296,424	$329,554
Total oper. cost	$1,389,560	$1,364,538	$1,591,923	$1,567,332	$1,821,170
AUTOMATED SYSTEM					
Labor costs:					
# Routes	13	13	14	14	14
# Drivers	18	18	19	19	19
# Supervisors	2.50	2.50	2.50	2.50	2.50
Labor cost	$796,640	$836,472	$920,720	$966,756	$1,015,094
Workers' comp.	$3,682	$3,866	$4,285	$4,499	$4,724
Equipment costs:					
Vehicle O&M	$195,813	$205,603	$232,490	$244,114	$256,320
Subtotal, oper. cost	$996,134	$1,045,941	$1,157,494	$1,215,369	$1,276,137
New equipment costs:					
# Trucks purchased	16				
Cost, new trucks	$1,440,000				
Salvage, manual trucks	($576,000)				
New containers	$1,371,429				
Net equipment cost	$2,235,429				
Lease/purchase cost	$363,806	$363,806	$363,806	$363,806	$363,806
Annual savings, automated system, before new equipment investment					
Annual savings	$_____	$_____	$_____	$_____	$_____
Cum. payback period	_____	_____	_____	_____	_____
Simple payback period: _____ years					
Net annual savings, including lease/purchase cost of new equipment					
Net annual savings	$_____	$_____	$_____	$_____	$_____
Discount factor	_____	_____	_____	_____	_____
Discounted savings	$_____	$_____	$_____	$_____	$_____
Net present value over 5 years	$_____	$_____	$_____	$_____	$_____

both automation and privatization, and include a justification for the recommendation in terms of both short- and long-term considerations.

2. City staff in Newglade analyzed the questions of automation and privatization simultaneously. Was this the best way to proceed or should these issues have been addressed separately? Give reasons for your answer.

3. Was the mayor correct in his assessment that voters "are rarely encumbered by concepts of economic rationality" when considering tax and service fee questions? What role should these considerations play in the decision being made here?

4. As the city manager, how would you have responded to the memo of July 10 in which the public works director opposed consideration of a merger of commercial and residential sanitation services? Would you include a combined system in your policy recommendation?

5. Under what circumstances would it be desirable to implement an automated collection system immediately? If such a change should be made, should the entire system be automated at once or gradually over time? Upon what considerations would you make such a decision?

6. Questions of privatization involve both ideological preferences and objective, analytical considerations. List the ideological and analytical considerations. Under what circumstances should ideological considerations weigh more heavily than dispassionate analysis in making such decisions? What factors should weigh most heavily in this decision, and why?

7. How should long-run and short-run cost and savings considerations be weighted in this decision? Are elected officials and professional administrators likely to agree on the answer to this question? If not, how should administrators handle differences in perspective?

12 Moving the multiservice center

Jack Manahan

Editor's introduction

The first case in this section posed a question in which the findings of analysis were subordinated to political and behavioral considerations; the second case dealt with a problem in which analytical findings were the primary basis for decision making. This third case is a synthesis; the question of where the county should relocate one of its multiservice centers pits political considerations against analytical (empirical) ones and, in the process, poses the ultimate ethical dilemma for an analyst.

Simply put, this case explores the appropriate role of the analyst in the decision-making process. The focal point is a conflict between the solution desired by local politicians and the solution found to be most cost-effective by competent analysis. Caught in the middle are the county administrator and an analyst from the county's management and budget office. Furthermore, the analyst does not agree with the strategy favored by her boss.

The result is a decision problem of sustantial complexity. In addition to the relationships between the administrator and the county board and between the administrator and the analyst, the case also focuses on the intergovernmental relationship between the county, which must relocate its multiservice center, and the city in which the center is currently located. Also involved is a concern that the center be located conveniently for the county residents who it will serve, and particularly the poor, who need easy access to the human service offices located there.

Most important, however, the case probes a contemporary question of democratic theory: How should the results of empirical policy analysis, fashioned to maximize public values regarding cost and service effectiveness in the long term, be reconciled with the policy preferences of elected officials who, although their vision may be focused on short-run political considerations, still have ultimate responsibility for policy decisions? Similarly, the case questions the role of the analyst as a participant in the politics of policy making.

Case 12
Moving the multiservice center

Background

Madison County is an urban/rural county of more than 300,000 in a major metropolitan area of the country. About 80 percent of the population lives in two dozen incorporated cities, mostly in the southwest part of the county. The remaining citizens reside in rural areas to the east and the north. At the time of this case, the county had enjoyed excellent growth for several years, and the local economy had been a bright spot in an otherwise depressed state economy. Population growth had been explosive, and the county was rapidly becoming more urbanized. In addition to the courthouse in the county seat and a smaller satellite office building in the urbanized southwest part of the county, the government operated several "multiservice centers" designed to bring county services to citizens in various parts of the county.

At these multiservice centers, citizens could pay taxes, register vehicles, borrow a book from the county's excellent library system, and access various human services programs provided by county offices. Two multiservice centers in the more populated areas of the county provided office space for some staff of the county Department of Human Services and Aging, other state and local agencies, and nonprofit organizations involved in the delivery of human services.

The first multiservice center was opened ten years earlier in the city of Oakridge, one of the oldest cities in the southwest part of the county. The center, which was known as the Southwest center, contained offices for the county's housing authority and housing counseling programs as well as a remote office for the state's welfare department and offices of three local social service agencies. The state welfare department and the social service agencies sublet from the county. The Southwest center was located in a light-industry and warehouse area near the junction of an interstate highway and a major state highway. The rent that the county paid was very low, about $2.50 per square foot annually, owing in part to the fact that the county had paid the cost of initial interior construction and finishing. Newer space in a better location would cost four to five times the current rental expense.

Although the space was more than adequate when the center opened, it had now been badly overcrowded for several years. Moreover, the location was difficult for visitors and clients to find, and flooding and water damage often occurred when the nearby creek overflowed during periods of heavy rain. County staff had hoped for some time not to renew the lease, which was scheduled to expire at the end of the current year. After a tour by the county commission in the spring, the staff was directed to begin looking for a new location for the Southwest center.

A second multiservice center had been opened in the city of Clearview, about four miles west of Oakridge. Many citizens who previously might have visited the Southwest center had begun to use the Clearview center instead, which was in an elementary school building that had been purchased and renovated by the city of Clearview. Despite the nearness of the two centers, the city had persuaded the county commission to cooperate in the Clearview center's management and operation in a spirit of "intergovernmental cooperation."

The case

Sally Adams was the analyst in the county's management and budget office who was assigned to work with the Department of Human Services and Aging on finding a new location for the Southwest multiservice center. Before a request for proposal (RFP) for rental space could be issued, a key decision had to be made regarding the general location of the new center.

The staff did not want to move the Southwest center any closer to the Clearview center because this could result in the underuse of both centers. Because the county's population growth seemed to be occurring to the east and the north, it made some sense to move the Southwest center farther east. However, upon learning that the county might move its center from Oakridge, the city's Republican mayor accused the Oakridge district's Democratic county commissioner of wanting to move the center because the mayor happened to be supporting the commissioner's Republican opponent in the upcoming election. Regardless of whether this was true, the incumbent county commissioner could not afford the perception that he was failing to represent his district and the cities in it by endorsing the removal of county services. The commissioner called Gerald Davis, the county administrator, who then called Adams. Against her better judgment, Adams decided that it would be best to try to relocate the center within the city limits of Oakridge.

While Adams was drafting the RFP for rental space, Davis stopped by her office and related a telephone conversation he had just had with Harry Sheppler, the Oakridge city administrator. Sheppler had called concerning a potential location only two blocks from the Southwest multiservice center's current location. The building he proposed was a three-story native-stone elementary school building. It had been built in the 1920s, and an addition was constructed shortly after World War II. The school district had abandoned the building twenty years earlier. Since then, it had been the home of a trade school, a community college, a preschool, and, most recently, a Christian private school.

Sheppler told Davis that the city council wanted to purchase the building and propose that the county lease the building from the city for use as the new location for the Southwest multiservice center. The council was most anxious to ensure the continued presence of a multiservice center in the city. Davis told Adams that he was aware that the mayor of Oakridge had contacted the chairman of the county commission about the idea.

Davis asked Adams to analyze the proposal to see if the idea was feasible. Her analysis (Table 1) showed that renovation would be costly and that, for Oakridge to purchase and renovate the school building, the city would have to charge the county about $3.00 per square foot more than the going rate for first-class commercial space in the area. In addition, the building was not energy efficient, and operating costs would be high. After reviewing Adams's analysis, Davis asked her to run another set of numbers, this time assuming that the county would pay 50 percent of the cost of renovation and all of the costs of making the building accessible to the handicapped, including installation of an elevator. If the county contributed funds for some of the renovation costs, Oakridge could charge the county less. Davis said that it might be possible to use the county's Community Development Block Grant funds for some of the renovation costs, but he was not certain. Adams challenged the county administrator's assumptions: in her opinion, the county had no business subsidizing a project such as this. Either the project was feasible or it was not—strictly on the basis of the numbers. She told Davis that she believed he was trying to aid the county commission in justifying a course of action that was not in the best interests of the county.

Davis was taken aback by Adams's reaction to his suggestion. He attempted to explain to her that both of them worked for the county commission, that the commissioners were anxious to work with the city in this matter, and that every opportunity to advance the goals of their elected superiors should be explored. He noted that objective analysis of data was certainly an important part of policy making, but he reminded her that all analysis is designed to serve the needs of elected policy makers and that those policy makers were certainly entitled to set the values or assumptions on which the analysis was based.

Davis concluded the discussion by suggesting that Adams rethink her reaction and get back to him.

The decision problem

Adams felt strongly about her position. Like all local governments, the county worked on a tight budget, and spending more money than necessary on an office lease simply to satisfy the city's political leaders seemed to her both unnecessary and unwise. Besides, she reasoned, the county had already made

Table 1 Original cost analysis of alternative sites.

Option 1. City purchases and renovates school building for lease to county. Building is 65 years old, 15,000 sq. ft., three stories. Exterior is native stone; interior is lath/plaster with oak floor. Heating is provided by a natural-gas, gravity-flow furnace. No central air conditioning; some rooms have window units.

Cost of building		$350,000	
Estimated renovation costs:			
Architecture and engineering	$35,000		
Interior walls and ceilings	70,000		
Floor coverings	30,000		
Electrical	10,000		
Plumbing	10,000		
Heating and ventilation	30,000		
Parking, exterior	40,000		
Handicap accessibility	125,000		
Total		350,000	
Total to be financed by city		700,000	
First-year debt payment to be amortized in lease (level principal payments, 10-year bonds at 8.5% interest)		129,500	($8.63/sq. ft.)
Operating costs:			
Utilities @ $4.00/sq. ft.	60,000		
Janitorial service @ $720/mo.	8,640		
Maintenance @ $1.50/sq. ft.	22,500		
Total		91,140	
Total annual costs to county		$220,640	($14.71/sq. ft.)

Option 2. County leases other commercial space. Under a typical commercial lease, the landlord provides building maintenance, but the tenant provides janitorial service. Any renovation required is negotiable, but the landlord will usually provide moderate finish-out to meet tenant needs.

Estimated cost of leasing 15,000 sq. ft. of retail space in the area @ $9.75 per sq. ft.		$146,250	
Operating costs:			
Janitorial service @ $720/mo.	$8,640		
Utilities @ $1.50/sq. ft.	22,500		
Total		31,140	($11.83/sq. ft.)
Total annual costs to county		$177,390	

---

a gesture of goodwill to the city by examining the school site and doing a cost analysis.

Adams also felt that, with population growth in the county occurring in the north and the east, any decision to keep the multiservice center in Oakridge was already a questionable accommodation to local politics. She believed that an optimum site for the center's relocation would be farther north and east of the city, farther from the Clearview center and closer to the new residential areas.

In short, Adams felt that, for reasons of both cost and service accessibility, the proposed school location was not in the best interest of the county or its residents.

On the other hand, Adams also recognized the validity of the point that Davis was trying to make. She understood the political nature of the county government; she recognized that the members of the county commission were elected by the voters and thus felt a responsibility for determining what would be in the best interest of the county. She also recognized that it was reasonable for county officials to desire to cooperate with Oakridge in this project. The proposed building was old, but an adaptive reuse of an old building with unique architecture could benefit the city in many ways.

Adams reminded herself that analysts and administrators function in a representative political environment and that, as a result, they frequently must deal with what is rather than with what, in their opinion, should be. She knew that it is neither unusual nor always bad for governing bodies to pursue goals that the staff does not find important.

Adams also believed that governing bodies tend to emphasize short-range considerations in their decision making and that it is the responsibility of staff to inject a long-term perspective into policy deliberations. In this case, she felt sure, the long-term needs of the county dictated that the multiservice center be located farther north and east than the city of Oakridge.

It was the cost of the project that Adams found most difficult to justify. Why should the county pay a rental cost for the renovated school building that would be as much as 16 percent higher than the cost of regular commercial space— particularly if such space could be found in a location that would better serve the long-term needs of the county? If the city felt that the building, with its architecture, was valuable, the city should subsidize the project and not expect a subsidy from the county. The idea of a county subsidy for the renovation made absolutely no sense to her at all.

Adams thought of Davis's problem. She knew that the county administrator was charged with carrying out the will of the county commission. Should he then feel obligated to justify what the commission wanted to do, even with an analysis that might be based on limited information? Did he have a responsibility to justify the commissioners' preferred course of action, or should his goal be to assist them in determining the best course of action in this situation? Was an ethical question involved if the county administrator was supporting a decision that would benefit the city at the expense of the county?

Adams also had to think about her own situation. What was the proper relationship between an analyst and the county administrator? Was the question of ethics a problem only for the administrator, or was it a problem for her, too? Did her responsibility end when she expressed her views to him, or did she have a responsibility to pursue the issue further? These questions had personal repercussions as well. Her refusal to do what Davis had requested could result in disciplinary action.

For Adams, the situation appeared to be lose-lose. If she did not produce the new analysis, she would be insubordinate. If she produced a new analysis that showed the new option to be still too expensive, Davis might view her as uncooperative at best or, at worse, as a part of the problem itself.

At a minimum, Adams decided, she should do the analysis that Davis requested. It would be easy to do, and it just might produce results that would surprise her and support what the commissioners wanted. Still, there was a risk. If her new cost figures were an improvement over the old ones, Davis and the county commissioners would undoubtedly be even less inclined to listen to her objections to the proposal.

When she finished the analysis of Davis's proposal (Table 2), she knew her worst fears had been realized. The annual cost to the county would be just under the cost of commercial space, but the county would still have to provide $220,000 up front in renovation costs; it would still have to pay a premium to rent space in a sixty-five-year-old building. The county would still be subsi-

Table 2 Revised cost analysis of school building site.

Option 3. Option 1 with county participation in financing renovation. Assumptions:
1. The county would sign a five-year lease for the building with a five-year option.
2. The county would pay 50 percent of the cost of renovation and all of the costs of making the building accessible to the handicapped, including installation of an elevator.

Cost of building		$350,000
Estimated renovation costs:		
Architecture and engineering	$35,000	
Interior walls and ceilings	70,000	
Floor coverings	30,000	
Electrical	10,000	
Plumbing	10,000	
Heating and ventilation	30,000	
Parking, exterior	40,000	
Handicap accessibility	125,000	
Total		350,000
Total project costs		700,000
Less costs paid directly by county:		
Handicap accessibility	125,000	
50% of all other renovation	112,500	
Total		237,500
Total to be financed by city		462,500
First-year debt payment to be amortized in lease (level principal payments, 10-year bonds at 8.5% interest)		84,312 ($5.62/sq. ft.)
Operating costs:		
Utilities @ $4.00/sq. ft.	60,000	
Janitorial @ $720/mo.	8,640	
Maintenance @ $1.50/sq. ft.	22,500	
Total		91,140
Total annual cost to county		$175,452 ($11.70/sq. ft.)

Note: In addition, the county would incur $220,000 of one-time costs for renovation of the building. These costs would have to be taken from the county's contingency funds.

dizing the city under this option but at figures that might be attractive to the commissioners. Adams felt that the $220,000 this option required could be better spent in other ways that would enhance human services or community development in the community.

As a professional dedicated to the public interest, she felt she had a moral obligation to try to sell her position and her first set of numbers (Table 1) to Davis. She asked herself whether her obligation extended beyond that. Sally Adams had to chart a course of action for herself.

Discussion questions

1. If you were Adams, would you have objected to Davis's suggestion that the county contribute to the renovation costs? How would your response have varied, if at all, from hers? Why?
2. During the course of making her decision, Adams asked herself some basic questions about the role of the analyst. Did her responsibility end when she reported her findings to Davis, or did she have a responsibility

to the public to see that her data were used to support sound public policies? Is there an ethical question involved? Explain your view.

3. Would your answer to question 2 have been different if the marginal difference in cost between option 2 (bottom of Table 1) and option 3 (Table 2) had been $5 million rather than $220,000? What dollar figure would justify a different response?

4. How, if at all, should Davis's and Adams's actions be affected by the fact that two different constituencies and two different groups of elected officials—the city and the county—are involved in this decision? Does "promoting the public interest" mean that Davis and Adams should be concerned for the interest of the city or just for the interest of the county? How does the fact that the city's residents are also county residents affect your answer? Explain your reasoning.

5. To what extent does the county government have a responsibility to promote the well-being of the city? How should this responsibility affect the way in which Davis responds to the county commissioners?

6. In her reasoning, Adams gave no consideration to the quality of either the long- or the short-term relationship between the city and the county. To what extent should this consideration be relevant? How should Adams factor this consideration into her decision?

7. If you were Adams, how would you resolve your questions? What course of action would you take on the matter?

Part seven:
Personnel and
labor relations

Introduction to part seven: Personnel and labor relations

Management theorists are fond of proclaiming that administration and management are generic functions, the same in any kind of organization. Nothing could be further from the truth. While technologies might be similar—for example, computer programs for keeping personnel records might work equally well in corporate and government agencies—and human behavior patterns tend to be the same from organization to organization within a given culture, the context in which administration occurs is not the same everywhere. The difference is particularly marked when public sector administration is compared with private sector administration.

A good example is in the field of personnel administration and labor relations. Human nature in public and private sectors might be the same; both sectors need rules and regulations to govern personnel practices, and both must work with employee organizations as well as with individual employees. But public accountability requires that rules be applied much more stringently in the public sector; that many public sector personnel matters, such as salary schedules, must be made public; that public sector labor relations must be conducted in an atmosphere charged with political as well as economic consequences; and that public employees hold a political trump card—the ability to vote their bosses out of office—that has no private sector counterpart.

Part seven demonstrates these unique characteristics of public sector personnel management even as it provides a flavor of the kinds of personnel decisions that confront the local government manager. The first case, for example, presents an ethical dilemma in personnel management that might occur in either the public or private sector. It demonstrates not only that ethics are an integral part of personnel management, but also that they are difficult to apply when a complicated set of individual circumstances obscures questions of right and wrong. But the solution to the problem is more difficult in the public sector, if only because the ultimate decision must be a matter of public record and thus open to public review and commentary. That openness means that the public decision maker faces a greater likelihood of criticism—in the media, from other employees from whom the decision cannot be kept secret, or from both—regardless of whether the decision emphasizes the letter of the moral principle or a humane concern for the employee involved. Such susceptibility might well mean that the public sector decision maker will be more prone to avoid either strict moralism or very humane sensitivity.

The second case describes two common challenges: fulfilling a commitment to affirmative action and designing a better fit between an employee's capabilities and the organization's needs. In trying to accomplish these goals, the local administrator is faced with the need to deal with personality conflicts as well as with stereotypes and prejudices. But the case has political overtones, too, overtones that are much more common in the public sector than in the private one: the employee in question has political (patronage?) connections that limit the supervisor's effective discretion in decision making. Most importantly, this case focuses on difficulties arising from the need to pursue affirmative action goals, a need much more commonly pronounced in public sector management.

Finally, the case offers insight and documentation of the need to pursue affirmative action goals despite obstacles that arise.

But the goldfish bowl of public personnel administration is most clearly demonstrated in the third case, in which the manager must act against the backdrop of an intense, angry, and occasionally violent labor confrontation between local government managers and the city's police officers and firefighters. This case affords an excellent demonstration of the fact that life is not always either fair or reasonable in public management. The employee demands come just after, not just before, the adoption of the new budget and the approval of a new tax levy. The public opposes higher taxes, but the firefighters are able to win significant public sympathy for their demands for higher wages. Caught in the middle between angry taxpayers and angry firefighters, the public managers must try to resolve an untimely dispute, find new moneys in an already tight budget, avoid mistakes that would cost them council support, and hold true to the council's desire not to enter into negotiations with employee groups. Not surprisingly, their first choice of a solution, contracting with the private sector for fire protection services, sparks political opposition. Their second choice raises problems within their own administrative leadership core.

Following these cases, the final case poses an obvious question. If the requisites of public personnel management are too difficult, too burdensome, or too expensive, might not the obvious answer—one that is being suggested at the present time with increasing frequency and political force and that was first considered in the previous case—be the privatization of public services? On the surface, privatization has much appeal, especially when it can result in significant cost savings. But upon deeper reflection, as this case demonstrates, the case for privatization is much more complicated, particularly because of its personnel implications.

Whoever said that the life of a public manager would be easy?

13 Personnel or people?

John Doe

Editor's introduction

The principal task of personnel administration is the management of people. People are, after all, the heart, brains, and backbone of management. Indeed, the classic definition of administration is the organization of people to achieve more collectively than they can achieve individually.

A major objective of the personnel management is to ensure that all of the organization's employees are treated in a fair, humane, and sensitive manner. This is accomplished through the establishment and application of rules and guidelines based upon considerations of ethics and respect for human dignity. These rules and guidelines are intended to guide the way people behave toward their employers, toward the public being served, and toward each other in the course of daily activities. Most personnel issues arise from the way people treat and are treated by other people.

Sometimes this treatment is part of routine transactions, such as promptness in keeping appointments or cordiality in dealings with others. At other times, it arises in the context of special or unusual circumstances: how much time off with pay can a public employee be given to attend to a sick child, for example? Regardless of the circumstances or the answers, the behavior and decisions involved are rooted in the application of personnel rules and ethical principles.

Such is the situation in this case, which calls for a decision about the treatment of a fire chief who is discovered to be appropriating city property for personal use. What appears to be a simple, straightforward application of principle, however, becomes complicated by idiosyncratic circumstances: by alcoholic illness and an opportunity for rehabilitation, by impending retirement, and by special family considerations and needs. Ultimately, the question becomes a classic nightmare for the administrator: should the case be handled "by the book," or should established rules be sacrificed in favor of more sensitive and humane treatment? Posed in this fashion, there is no simple, universally applicable answer. Each case must be decided on its own merits.

It is just such a case that now faces the city manager of Annsburg.

Case 13
Personnel or people?

Background

As a result of the national transition from a manufacturing economy to a service economy, many communities faced a sudden and severe loss of their industrial tax base. Annsburg, a one-industry town, was one of those communities; its one industry had closed its doors.

The production process used by the industry had left the facilities unfit for alternative uses, so they had to be completely dismantled, and the site had to be cleared. This loss not only deprived Annsburg of an opportunity for economic recovery based on a reuse of the facility, but it also devastated the city's property tax base. Five years after the company closed its doors, the city was operating on less than one-half of its prior tax base.

Annsburg's political leadership consists of a city council elected on a nonpartisan basis for four-year, overlapping terms. The council annually selects a chairperson, or mayor, from among its ranks. The traditional practice is to rotate the position of chairperson through the council to equalize influence among the council members. The city attorney also serves as the prosecuting attorney, a nonpartisan elected position.

Among appointed officials in any community, the police chief and the fire chief exert significant political force. This was particularly true in Annsburg at the time of this case because of the general political environment and because each man had worked his way up through the ranks during more than twenty years of service.

The loss of the dominant industry in a one-industry town creates a political as well as an economic vacuum. Instability and divisiveness are natural results of the struggle to reestablish political order. In Annsburg a charter election to abandon the council-manager form of government in favor of the strong-mayor form was defeated at the polls, but the referendum was symptomatic of the political instability associated with the changes taking place. Annsburg was a community in transition when Paul Daniels became city manager.

When the previous city manager had left Annsburg, the vacancy sparked an extended public debate on whether the new manager should be a local candidate with knowledge of the community or a professional with education and experience in the field. Finally the city council retained Daniels, a professional city manager who came to Annsburg from a community in another state.

Because of the severely distressed local economy, Daniels's mandate was clear. The decline in the tax base meant that the government must get smaller. Each department must be reduced, and some services and programs must be eliminated.

As he set out, department by department, to address long-term expenditures, Daniels discovered that a major challenge would be the fire chief.

The case

Daniels became familiar with Fire Chief Roger Eleson when he revived a plan first developed by his predecessor to supplement the full-time fire department with volunteer personnel. Although the unionized firefighters had grudgingly agreed to terms that would permit the supplemental use of volunteer firefighters, the environment in the fire hall was such that each time a volunteer was recruited, he was ostracized and eventually quit. These problems made it obvious that change was needed, and the fire chief had to be made a change agent.

Under the charter, the fire chief was a council appointee. The council had appointed Eleson without the previous city manager's support. Prior to Daniels's appointment, Eleson had faced charges three times as a result of performance problems. He had always managed to retain his job, however, because of his political connections, the council's fear of adverse economic consequences (earlier discharges had cost the city tens of thousands of dollars in civil damages), and his retention of an effective attorney to represent him.

Eleson went through periods of good performance and intermittent periods of poor performance. He and Daniels developed a system to add volunteer firefighters to the department that was acceptable to the full-time firefighters. It would permit the number of full-time firefighters to be reduced by attrition, without reducing service levels. Including fringe benefits, each position eliminated could save $40,000 per year. This success temporarily enhanced the fire chief's standing in the city.

Then the police chief, Harold Bales, told Daniels that he suspected the fire chief of stealing city property, including gasoline from the city pumps. Too many five-gallon cans of gasoline were being filled and placed in the fire chief's car for transport. The small power tools at the fire hall could not be using that much gas. Bales and Daniels decided to say nothing about their suspicions but to have Eleson followed the next time he picked up gas.

Several months passed before Bales noticed Eleson at the gas pumps. True to form, Eleson filled two five-gallon cans and placed them in the trunk of the vehicle. Bales directed a patrolman in the police station to follow Eleson and report back by telephone (Eleson had a police radio in his vehicle). As the patrolman followed, Eleson went home, took the gas cans out of the trunk of the city car, and placed them in front of his private vehicle parked off the alley. Eleson then proceeded to the fire hall. The patrolman telephoned Police Chief Bales with his report.

Bales and Daniels discussed the situation and telephoned the city attorney to see whether they could obtain a search warrant, which would be necessary to gather evidence if Eleson were to be prosecuted. The city attorney expressed reluctance because it would be difficult to prosecute a fire chief for the petty theft of ten gallons of gasoline. Bales directed the patrolman to continue visual surveillance pending a decision.

The theft of ten gallons of gasoline, while only petty theft, did constitute a breach of the public trust by a high-ranking, visible public official. By itself, however, it would not be sufficient to uphold a discharge under state statute. Daniels presumed that the theft was a result of the fire chief's problem with alcohol, which had contributed to the charges brought on the three previous occasions.

The problem of alcohol

Daniels suspected, but could not confirm, that Eleson drank on duty. If this were true, it could create enormous liability for the city in light of the chief's public safety responsibilities. Fire department morale, improving since the smooth implementation of the volunteer system, was at stake. If the city manager suspected that the fire chief was an alcoholic, members of the fire department, who worked more closely with the chief, must certainly be aware of related problems. Daniels also considered the fiscal implications. If the chief resigned or were discharged, his position would be filled from within the department, the net result being the elimination of one position. An opportunity for action existed, but it carried risks.

Daniels drafted two letters. The first was a letter of immediate resignation, which would be offered to Eleson. The second was a letter from the city manager to the fire chief announcing Eleson's immediate suspension with intent to prosecute and discharge him.

Daniels summoned the unsuspecting Eleson to his office, explained the facts, and indicated that the fire chief had a choice: either he could sign the letter of resignation, or Daniels would sign the letter of suspension with intent to prosecute and discharge. Eleson said he would take no action until he had telephoned his attorney. He had faced charges before. Unable to contact his attorney, he continued to delay, searching for alternatives. Daniels telephoned the city attorney in the fire chief's presence and directed that a search warrant be issued to impound the evidence. He signed the letter of suspension with intent to prosecute and discharge and handed it to Eleson. Eleson hesitated, then signed the letter of resignation and left, appearing somewhat shaken.

The next day Daniels heard that Eleson had started drinking after this confrontation and had set out to find and get even with the patrolman who had caused him this difficulty. Unable to locate the patrolman, he had gone home to tell his family of the injustice to which he was being subjected. After years of living with an alcoholic, his family gave him no sympathy. Finally confronted at home and at work with the effects of his alcoholism, Eleson broke down. He admitted his alcoholism and asked for help.

Daniels met with the three shift commanders of the fire department. Uncertain whether he could make the previous day's resignation stand up and unclear about exactly what had occurred the previous evening, Daniels advised the shift commanders to treat the situation as if the fire chief were on vacation. No permanent assignments would be made, but the senior fire captain would be acting chief, as would be the case were the chief on vacation leave. Daniels gave a status report to each council member by telephone and discussed the situation with the fire chief's attorney. Rumors began to circulate throughout the community.

Legal and political complications

Eleson entered the hospital for inpatient treatment. After several days, his attorney asked Daniels to meet with him and the doctor to discuss the chief's condition. The doctor indicated that the chief was in the advanced stages of alcoholism but that a more critical problem was the interaction between alcohol and the chief's diabetic condition. The doctor stated that the chief's physical condition was such that he almost certainly lacked the mental capacity to make rational decisions; furthermore, that condition had certainly existed on the day that he had signed his resignation. The attorney then said that since Eleson lacked mental capacity, his resignation was invalid.

Daniels indicated that the attorney was free to argue diminished mental capacity at Eleson's trial for theft, but he pointed out that such a trial would undoubtedly be a very public one, with personal repercussions for the fire chief and his family. Positions were thus established.

At their next meeting, the city council went into executive session to hear an update on the situation. Rumors had reached the local media. One reporter accepted the confidential nature of the incident, but another insisted on full disclosure. When not permitted to attend the executive session, he outlined the various rumors in his next day's article.

The stands taken by the actors in this scenario were related to their positions in the community. The city council generally took a neutral stand on the fire chief's resignation. Eleson had been charged too many times, and his political support had eroded. He had signed a letter of resignation, but it was not clear that the resignation would stand up in light of his "diminished capacity." The council feared that the city might again have to pay thousands of dollars in settlement of a wrongful-discharge suit.

To Police Chief Bales, the case was black and white: he had caught a thief. The prosecuting attorney hoped for a negotiated settlement to avoid having to prosecute Eleson. The city manager was adamant; if Eleson managed to return to active-duty status, Daniels would lose credibility. Eleson's attorney was obligated to represent his client. The public watched expectantly, fed regularly by articles and rumors.

The decision problem

Negotiations began in earnest between Daniels and the fire chief's attorney when the chief was about halfway through his twenty-eight-day inpatient therapy. All parties agreed that it was in their mutual interest to have the matter resolved before the chief was released from the hospital. Daniels needed a definitive answer to satisfy the council and the public. Eleson needed a definitive answer so that his recovery from alcoholism could proceed. The chief's attorney offered extended sick leave as a solution.

Although a medical disability was available, it would provide Eleson with less income than full retirement, for which he would become eligible in just eight months. He had available to him twelve months of sick leave, which would normally be paid out at 25 cents on the dollar at retirement. The attorney proposed that the resignation be redated with the chief's full retirement date and that he be placed on sick leave until that time. That would address the city manager's major concern that the fire chief would never again have active-duty status. Keeping the chief on sick leave would cost about $10,000 more than paying off his sick leave on the basis of his original resignation date. Daniels agreed to put Eleson on sick leave while he was in the hospital but would not accept a $10,000 price for what he perceived to be the discharge of an alcoholic thief. Negotiations broke down.

The city manager met again with the council in executive session to report on the status of negotiations. The following morning's headlines would proclaim a "secret meeting" to discuss the still-unconfirmed status of the fire chief. The meeting itself was inconclusive. Daniels believed that he had enough rope to either tie up the problem or hang himself.

Following additional discussions with Daniels, the fire chief's attorney agreed that it was not in his client's best interest to return to active-duty status. However, Eleson had a family to support, with children in college and in high school. To recover from the disease of alcoholism, he would need the self-esteem associated with supporting that family. He would need full retirement. The attorney asked Daniels to meet with Eleson's family so that he could understand the situation better. Reluctantly, Daniels agreed to do so and asked that the council chairperson also attend. Meeting with the wife and children of an employee he was trying to force out was bound to be uncomfortable.

Daniels was taken by surprise when the chief's wife started by thanking him for what he had done. For the first time in their married life, her husband had admitted that he was an alcoholic, and she had hope for a recovery. Because of what Daniels had done, the family now had a chance at a new beginning, a chance to have a real father and husband. The children expressed the same hope.

But in order to recover, the children told Daniels, their father would need help in retraining and finding a new job. And this would require money. The difference between full retirement and medical disability was more than $250 per month for the rest of Eleson's life. That meant college, tuition, books, and a future for them and for their father. Daniels had helped by making their father admit his alcoholism. Couldn't he help a little bit more now and let their father get to a full retirement?

What should Daniels do now?

Discussion questions

1. Should Daniels recommend that the chief be permitted to remain on paid sick leave for eight months in order to prevent him from returning to active duty? Why or why not?
2. How should Daniels weigh the threat of a lawsuit and a possibly expensive damage settlement against his personal determination to uphold matters of principle? What consideration should he give to the city's constituents and taxpayers and to the pleas of the fire chief's family? What consideration should he give to the incident of theft?
3. Does an employer have an obligation to an employee who has been per-

mitted to perform poorly over a long period of time before definitive action is taken? If so, what is that obligation? If not, why not?

4. Of how much concern should the public image of the local government, particularly of the city manager, be in such circumstances? Should public image be a factor in the decision? Why or why not?

5. Evaluate the fiscal impacts of the situation: the up-front cost of $10,000 versus the potential costs of litigation (e.g., the legal fees plus the damages that might have to be paid). Is such a cost-benefit analysis appropriate when matters of principle are under consideration? Why or why not? Explain.

6. How should Daniels estimate the possible nonmonetary costs involved in the situation, including publicity, employee morale, public attitudes regarding the city government, and political repercussions for council members? Are these costs different if Daniels accepts a negotiated settlement in order to avoid possible litigation? What role should these considerations play in Daniels's decision?

14 Affirmatively managing Helen

Mary Timney

Editor's introduction

Affirmative action is often equated with the recruitment of women and minorities into professional positions in an organization, but, as this case points out, there is much more to it than that. Equally important to affirmative action and, indeed, to any good personnel system is the use of individual employees to the maximum advantage of both the employee and the organization.

That is the challenge in this case—the challenge to administrative leadership to secure maximum benefit from a nonproductive but competent employee who has the potential to make important contributions to her department. The task is made more difficult both by the employee's lack of finesse in her dealings with other people and by constraints against her dismissal. Since those constraints are political, the case also explores the nature of administrative leadership in a political setting.

The fact that the employee in question is a woman should be incidental to the larger question of personnel management. In a society emphasizing affirmative action principles in its movement toward equality in the workplace, however, that fact cannot be ignored. Thus, the case also involves the problem of fitting a professional woman into an agency that has traditionally employed only men and in which male prejudices and stereotypes still abound.

The management challenge in the case, then, involves more than just managing affirmative action efforts; it involves educating other employees—in this case, men—who must learn to work with the woman and abandon sexist patterns of behavior.

The case thus involves a multiplicity of issues in organizational theory and human resource management.

Case 14
Affirmatively managing Helen

Background

Rusty City is an aging industrial city with a population of about half a million and a strong-mayor form of government. Since the 1930s, it has been dominated politically by the Democratic party. Today, only remnants of the once-powerful machine remain. In recent years, the party bosses have been embarrassed by members of their own party running successful independent campaigns against the party's endorsed candidates. This not only has created stress throughout the party organization but also has diminished government effectiveness. Successful candidates have found themselves constantly battling potential opponents in their own party, thus reducing their ability to perform effectively in their elected offices.

The city has a modern personnel system, but pockets of patronage remain. All department heads and assistant administrators are appointed by and serve at the pleasure of the mayor. Special positions can be created by the mayor with the consent of the city council. Certain departments, particularly those with a large component of laborers, also tend to have a substantial number of ward chairpersons and party workers. Several of the supervisors of these departments were hired as a result of political patronage. The mayor's office and the city council have been controlled exclusively by Democrats for more than fifty years.

The case

Mayor Sam Hartman, a lifelong Democrat, came to office after running an independent campaign against the party's candidate. Once in office, he set out to rebuild bridges with the party faithful. He was approached shortly after the election by a powerful ward chairperson who asked him to create a position for her daughter, Helen Miller, a mechanical engineer with a graduate degree in energy management. Miller herself had never been interested in politics, but she was having a hard time finding a job in the city and didn't want to leave her family. Mayor Hartman saw the opportunity to achieve several objectives at the same time: soothe some ruffled feathers in the party, demonstrate his concern for energy conservation, and employ a qualified woman at a midlevel position. It seemed to be a golden opportunity, and Hartman happily grabbed it.

The city's engineers were scattered throughout various departments in the organization. There were no other female engineers at the time, although there had been some female student interns in earlier years. Miller was initially placed in the public works department. No one knew exactly what an energy engineer should do, but the mayor was sure that the department could identify an appropriate role for her. Still, the men in the office were more than a little uncertain about how to interact with what they perceived to be a diminutive, fashionably dressed, rather attractive young woman.

Given little direction, Miller tried to define her job. She began to develop a library of energy books and energy management journals. There were many good ideas in these publications, and Miller tried to share them with the other engineers. But these were new ideas that didn't fit the practiced ways of doing things in the department. Nobody seemed to care very much about energy management. They just left her to do her little projects.

Month after month, Miller waited for recognition that never came. Her frustration mounted during budget preparation time, when she failed to get approval for pet projects. Even though she had calculations that could prove that the projects would pay for themselves, she could never convince her superiors that the projects should be given priority. On top of this, she was very uncomfortable in the office. There were no private offices in the department, only cubicles. Her cubicle was located near the director's, and he was a cigar smoker. Finally, unable to stand it any longer, Miller sued the director for polluting her airspace.

Miller's next assignment was in the parks department, which managed and maintained about half of the city's buildings. The engineers there were primarily civil engineers, who, along with a few architects, were responsible for designing recreation centers and swimming pools. They didn't really know what an energy engineer should do, but it seemed a good idea to have her expertise available for consultation, at least.

Now that she was in a department with responsibility for specific buildings, Miller assumed that her job was to identify ways that the city could save money on energy use. She set out to devise conservation strategies for the recreation centers. Although she did find some big problems, such as antiquated heating systems, most often she found that the buildings were poorly maintained and needed simple things like caulking and weather-stripping. She also found several cracked windows. But when she tried to get these conditions corrected, she encountered stiff resistance and even hostility from the maintenance staff. These men had been doing their jobs for years. They were doing the best they could with the resources given to them. Who did this lady think she was to come around and tell them what to do!

The superintendent of maintenance was an old hand who worked closely with the top administrators of the department. Although the administrators thought that energy conservation was a fine idea, they were not inclined to take sides against the maintenance crew just because this woman, who had been forced on the department, couldn't get along. After several clashes with the superintendent of maintenance, Miller expressed her frustration to the mayor loud and clear, as did the department administrators.

Miller was rapidly developing a reputation for being hard to get along with, although it was easy for the mayor to see how a bright woman could ruffle the feathers of the maintenance crew. The mayor felt that she just needed more supervision and perhaps a position where she could influence policy decisions. So she was reassigned to the mayor's office, where she was given the responsibility of developing a strategy to carry out the emergency energy conservation guidelines of the Carter administration.

At last, Miller thought, she had a position where she could accomplish something. She was determined to conserve energy even if she had to turn out everyone's lights herself. Before long, she had alienated a significant number of managers throughout the city government, almost coming to blows with one when she attempted to remove a desk lamp. She finally managed to humiliate the mayor's staff by writing a minority report to the U.S. Department of Energy, accusing the mayor's staff of covering up their lack of commitment to energy policy. Everyone waited for the ax to fall.

The mayor maintained his commitment to keep Miller employed. While he was a good-hearted soul, he was also a pragmatic politician. At that time he was involved in his reelection campaign and did not want to risk the potential fallout from either the party leaders or the feminist and affirmative action groups in the city from firing Miller. So Miller was assigned to the building management department, which had responsibility for the other half of the city's buildings.

The department had a new director, Roger Newton, a civil engineer who had been lured from the private sector and had a reputation for being firm but fair. Newton had management skills honed in business and was confident that he could manage this recalcitrant employee. She had expertise, and Newton welcomed the challenge to put it to good use. Initially they got along well, and for the first time in her career with the city, Miller seemed happy. Newton was not exactly sure what an energy engineer could do, but Miller seemed to have a clear idea of the parameters of the position. He encouraged her to develop ideas and projects for all of the city's buildings and implied that he would provide budgetary support for implementing her projects.

Miller set up visits to all police and fire stations. She discovered that there was no comprehensive set of data on energy use, so she decided to develop basic data on electricity and natural gas use for all city-owned buildings. This was a monumental undertaking since the data had to be obtained from individual gas and electric bills for two hundred buildings.

Miller spent most of her time gathering the data, and a good bit of secretarial time was devoted to typing the reports. She felt very proud each month when she delivered reports that showed, along with the dollar costs, electricity usage in kilowatt hours and natural gas usage in cubic feet. She also calculated the usage in BTUs per degree day to show changes in energy use from year to year. Several copies of these massive lists were made and circulated to the mayor's office and to all department heads, including the police and fire chiefs. But despite her extensive work, recipients of the reports found them almost unreadable. They did not want to take the time to examine all the numbers, and some of the jargon was incomprehensible to them. Newton seemed to appreciate her efforts although he did not have time to read the reports, either.

Miller also spent time in the buildings, identifying potential energy conservation projects. She got along well with the firefighters, who always seemed to appreciate a visit from the "lady engineer." They had lots of ideas on how to save energy and were supportive of her efforts to improve their buildings. This good relationship did not exist with the police, however. In addition to finding her visits a nuisance, police officers remembered the troubles that one precinct had had with a modern building that was supposed to be energy efficient. The building had a fixed thermostat, set by "some dizzy engineer" (not Miller), and the heating and cooling system never worked right. The cops in the station froze in the winter and boiled in the summer. They never could get anyone to fix it right until one officer, in a rage, shot the darn thermostat with his service revolver.

Miller also had clashes with the maintenance staff in the building management department. These hostilities were mollified somewhat by Newton, who was able to establish a truce between Miller and the maintenance superintendent that permitted the two to work together even though they did not like each other. During this time, Miller identified several projects that could pay for themselves and save the city several thousand dollars each year, and she submitted them to Newton for inclusion in the department's capital budget request. But Newton was faced with a budget crunch, and while he thought that she had some good ideas, he felt he could not justify approving these projects if it meant that he would not be able to obtain funding for more critical projects.

The honeymoon in the department ended when the energy projects were not included in Newton's recommendations for capital spending in the next budget. Miller's frustration finally boiled over. She raged publicly at Newton at a staff meeting. He was furious. It seemed that Miller's days were numbered at last.

Once again, the mayor's staff found themselves dealing with the problem of Helen Miller. The mayor was not pleased by this turn of events, but he still did not want to offend his political friend. He insisted that his staff find another place for Miller and a director who would supervise her more closely.

Shortly after the most recent incident, several departments were reorganized. The building management department was eliminated, and many of its functions were placed in the new Department of General Administration. The engineering function was centralized in another new department to streamline operations and coordinate all capital and construction projects. The new director was a highly respected engineer who had been the assistant director of public works. He had heard about Miller and, as part of his agreement with the mayor's office on the reorganization, one engineer—Miller—was excluded from the new arrangement.

Miller was assigned instead to the Department of General Administration, which had been given many of the functions of her former department. The new director, Gloria Asbury, had been assistant director of the budget and finance office. She was known to be a tough administrator who wasn't afraid to fire people. The mayor's staff was convinced that Asbury would be able to handle Miller. Perhaps, after all, Miller just couldn't get along very well with men.

The decision problem

As Asbury began the task of establishing administrative norms and procedures for the new department, she faced the problem of Miller. How could she develop a good working relationship with this person who had alienated everyone with whom she had worked up to now? Was there a way to have peace in the department and make Miller a productive employee? How could she, Gloria Asbury, be any more successful with Miller than all of her predecessors had been? How much control did she really have in light of the mayor's continuing refusal to remove this troublesome employee?

Asbury considered also the needs of the department and the skills that Miller could offer her. As a former budget analyst, Asbury knew how much the city spent for energy each year. Her department budget included $2 million for heating and lighting bills as well as $1.75 million for automotive fuels for the city's vehicles. Miller's expertise, if properly harnessed, could be a way to control the growth of these budgets or even to reduce them. Just a 10 percent difference, which energy experts claim can be obtained with no-cost or low-cost efforts, would mean a decrease of $200,000 in the utility budget. If Miller could find ways to save more than that, it would certainly make Asbury's job easier.

Miller had developed several proposals over the years, but they had never gained budgetary approval. Asbury recognized that part of the problem had been the way Miller had presented her ideas at budget time. As an engineer, she tended to believe that the numbers spoke for themselves; she didn't seem to understand the politics of the budget process. Asbury felt that the presentation of the data could be improved in ways that would make them more understandable. Further, the support of a director who was a budget insider would make it possible for Miller to be more successful at budget time.

But the primary question remained: how would it be possible to get Miller's cooperation? She had a reputation for being very hard to get along with. She didn't really have any friends in the city organization. As a female engineer, she didn't have the opportunity to interact very much with other professional women, and she clearly did not get along with the men.

Within the department, the maintenance superintendent considered Miller a domineering woman. His cooperation would be necessary to carry out any energy maintenance projects, but he resented any suggestion from Miller that smacked of trampling on his territory. In the old building management department, they had had some legendary arguments, and the truce between them was uneasy. Yet Asbury knew him also to be a team player, an old hand who would carry out requests from his director even if he didn't like them. The trick, then, was to establish some ground rules for both of them.

In thinking through how to deal with Miller's outbursts, Asbury had to consider how she would be viewed as a manager—both by Miller and by the rest of the department. She was sensitive to the stereotypes of women as being too emotional to be trusted in management positions, but she was also concerned about being labeled as too hard or rigid, another part of the stereotype of women managers. She would have to walk a fine line, but she had to make it clear to Miller and the rest of the department that her tolerance of certain behaviors was limited. Moreover, she had to do it in such a way that she would be taken seriously but would also be seen as a fair-minded manager.

Finally, there was the problem of the mayor's loyalty to Miller. Others in the city might have fired her long ago, but Asbury knew that it was not unusual for an organization to retain a difficult employee. There was always the possibility of a lawsuit by a disgruntled employee, and it seemed to be cheaper to transfer than to fire. Asbury knew in her heart, then, that it was not likely that Miller would ever be fired. It was far more in Asbury's best interest to find a way to manage Miller so that Miller could exercise her expertise and Asbury could benefit from it.

In considering these factors, Asbury realized that she had few options. If she simply laid down the law to Miller about her behavior, it was not likely to bring about a change in Miller's relationships within the department. Moreover, Asbury would have little recourse if the behavior did not improve. Given no power to fire Miller, Asbury might ultimately be seen as an ineffectual manager and might find her authority with the rest of the staff undermined. Clearly, she had to find a managerial solution that would give Miller a sense of professional accomplishment and bring about cooperation between her and her fellow workers. But what kind of strategy could accomplish those ends after so many past failures?

Discussion questions

1. If you were in Asbury's position, what additional information would you need to make a decision?
2. One of Asbury's options might be to seek an interview with the mayor to see if she could change his mind about retaining Miller. What are the possible outcomes of that strategy?
3. Another of Asbury's options might be to arrange training for staff in communications skills and/or team-building techniques. How would this be likely to work in her department?
4. What contribution could an affirmative action program or an affirmative action officer make to the solution of Asbury's problem?
5. Upon what management tools or skills could Asbury draw in searching for a strategy to solve the problem of Miller?
6. Is there any way that Asbury could solve or reduce the problem by making adjustments in the organizational format of her department or in Miller's organizational assignment? What could she do?
7. Are there behavioral interventions (e.g., getting the affected persons to sit down together with Asbury or with a counselor) that might be attempted? What are the possible outcomes of this strategy?

15 Cedar Valley slowdown

David N. Ammons and M. Lyle Lacy III

Editor's introduction

When they engage in collective action against their employer, local government employees usually have a distinct advantage. First, they can exercise economic leverage through job actions or threatened job actions: strikes where they are allowed, work slowdowns where they are not. Second, they can exercise political leverage by organizing themselves, their families and friends, and local community groups to vote for candidates who support their goals and to apply pressure on elected officials on their behalf.

Local government administrators, on the other hand, must restrict their behavior to actions officially approved by labor relations laws. Even when sympathetic to the demands of their employees, administrators may be constrained by budgetary limitations, the need for equity across departments, or public resistance to higher taxes.

This case describes the plight of the city administration in Cedar Valley as it attempts to respond to ill-timed wage demands, first from its police officers and then from its firefighters. The case has all the elements of a typical local government labor relations controversy: substantial employee demands, tight budgets and taxpayer resistance to tax hikes, lack of experience on both sides of the negotiations, and reluctance on the part of the city to negotiate with employee organizations. The case develops like a chess game—move, countermove; reaction, counterreaction—and finally produces frustration, anger, and lack of trust on the part of all concerned.

In the end, both sides resort to extreme tactics. The firefighters undertake a job action; the city considers contracting with a private firm for fire protection services. This move by the city raises a whole new set of questions: the efficacy of private contracts for public services, the feasibility of public-private partnerships, and the inevitable politics of proposing such an alternative in a labor relations context.

The case also provides a useful insight into a very common reaction by the general public. The firefighters mobilize support for their wage demands from the same public that resists tax increases. Nothing in the American political philosophy or tradition requires consistency from citizens, but the public administration tradition does require consistency and rationality in recommendations and proposals from management. This imbalance gives rise to a classic dilemma for the practicing local government administrator.

From such dilemmas is born the demand for administrative leadership, even in political settings. A characteristic of effective leadership is the ability to produce innovative solutions to seemingly intractable problems. Digging into their storehouse of organizational theory and administrative skills, the local government managers in Cedar Valley must search for such a solution.

Case 15
Cedar Valley slowdown

Background

Hot summer temperatures were mild compared with another kind of heat that plagued city officials well into autumn across the nation, particularly in the mid-South. Walkouts and slowdowns by public safety employees were occurring in rapid succession in several parts of Dixie. Each act of defiance seemed to encourage the next. Even those officials in the South who were not confronted with job actions could see them on all sides.

In that atmosphere, city officials in Cedar Valley probably should not have been caught off guard when police officers staged a work slowdown, but they were. Cedar Valley, a southern city of 30,000 residents, is a major center of employment in a sizable metropolitan area. Its municipal government is supported by significant property tax and sales tax bases and an unusually large component of intergovernmental revenues. It happened that the attention of city officials had been diverted to a hearing on the possible reduction or discontinuation of the intergovernmental revenues when twenty-three officers—one-half of Cedar Valley's total force—declared a work slowdown to dramatize their demands for higher pay, enhanced benefits, and improved working conditions. Among the most important demands were the following:

- An immediate 15 percent increase in pay

- "Hazardous duty" status in the city's classification plan

- Extra pay for evening and midnight shifts as well as time-and-a-half for weekend work

- Incentive pay for education, physical fitness, and marksmanship

- Discontinuation of the merit system in favor of automatic step increases and longevity pay

- Establishment of an exercise facility

- Improved insurance coverage and the elimination of employee contributions for insurance and retirement

- Enhanced benefits for the purchase and maintenance of police uniforms.

The demands, which were presented in a petition to the city council and city manager, were signed by twenty-three police officers. The timing could hardly have been worse.

The day on which the police officers made their declaration, September 7, was slightly more than two months into the city's fiscal year—too late to adjust the tax rate and ten long months before any major changes could be made through the normal budget process. Furthermore, city officials were preoccupied at the moment with the possible loss of a major intergovernmental revenue source, a budding crisis that jeopardized even the current budget and made unthinkable the additional financial pressure that would be imposed if the police officers' demands were met.

Compounding the problem of poor timing was the relative inexperience of two key members of the city's management team. Although both had served previously in other capacities in Cedar Valley, Bill Martin had been city manager for only three months, and his new principal assistant, Larry Bristol, had been director of administration for only one week.

If there was anything fortuitous about the timing of the police slowdown notification, it was that a hearing on intergovernmental revenues had drawn virtually the entire city council together in one place, and Martin was thus able to brief the council immediately on the slowdown. Council members assured Martin that they would avoid making any statements that might undermine his efforts to deal with the problem. Martin appreciated those personal assurances; he was especially pleased that council members made them not in private conversations with him but in the presence of one another.

The case

Martin, Bristol, and Police Chief Carl Angelo met to develop a response to the work slowdown notification. The initial result of the meeting was a memorandum to participating officers that informed them of the difficulties involved in attempting to meet their demands at that point in the fiscal year, cautioned them about the harmful effects that a job action could have on public confidence and cooperation, and ordered them to resume full police activities. Furthermore, the memorandum advised the officers that continuation of the job action might lead the city to cancel the police department's participation in an upcoming in-service training session, thereby jeopardizing the officers' ability to meet the criteria for supplemental pay from the state. Police officers were irritated by the potential loss of supplemental pay but were not persuaded to abandon the slowdown.

In an effort to counteract the adverse effects of the work slowdown, Angelo began assigning officers to high-visibility locations that had been the sites of major accidents. Angelo's intent was to address traffic safety concerns and to compensate for the officers' refusal to take any initiative in traffic patrol. Thus, even officers participating in the slowdown could not help but be perceived by the public as part of the police presence in the community.

On September 12, the city council and city management received another blow. Only four days after the police officers had announced their work slowdown, forty-two members of Cedar Valley's fifty-one-member fire department issued a statement that they were joining the police officers in the slowdown. Unlike the police job action, in which the participants were virtually all nonsupervisory officers, the fire department job action included several ranking officers.

Dealing with employee associations

State law did not regulate labor-management relations in Cedar Valley or in other local governments in the state; the law did not even require that municipal employee unions be recognized. In that environment, Cedar Valley officials staunchly resisted the unionlike tactics of the police and fire groups, groups that officials regarded as merely employee "associations," even though one was affiliated with the Fraternal Order of Police and the other with the International Association of Fire Fighters.

Martin offered to meet with groups of three aggrieved employees at a time but resisted any action that might give the appearance of bargaining with the two or three persons who had emerged as "union" spokespersons. Officer Bob Jacksboro, president of the police association, had assumed that mantle on the police side. The ranking officer in the firefighters' association, Captain Bowie Camp, was its nominal spokesman, but Captain Hal Rockwood was more outspoken and appeared to be that group's driving force. Martin adamantly refused to strengthen their roles as leaders by meeting separately with Jacksboro, Camp, or Rockwood.

On September 14, Jacksboro notified Martin and the city council that individual officers were rejecting Martin's offer to meet with them in small groups rather than with their representatives, and that the police officers and firefighters participating in the job action had voted to merge and pursue their interests as one group. Four days later, the combined group staged a three-block march to city hall and pressed its demands at a meeting of the city council.

In response to the demands, Martin summarized city management's position. First, the salaries of city employees would be given top priority during budget considerations for the next fiscal year; public safety employees, however, would be considered in the context of the entire city workforce. Second, none of the grievances would be addressed as long as the work slowdown continued. Third, the city would not proceed on a course that would, in effect, recognize employee labor unions. The city council formally endorsed Martin's position.

By September 26, police and fire employees had begun to picket the mayor's place of employment as an intended prelude to the picketing of all city council members. However, informal talks between city staff and attorneys representing the two employee groups headed off the second-phase picketing. By September 29, city staff had calculated the projected costs of implementing the group's demands. Those calculations were distributed to aggrieved public safety employees along with an invitation to meet with Martin—not in groups of three, as had been previously offered and rejected, but in entire work shifts. Jacksboro, still hoping to represent the police officers in negotiations with Martin, announced that shiftwide meetings were no more acceptable than meetings with three officers at a time.

Crisis

Police and fire employees aggressively pressed their case in the community and in the local media. Statements of support increased for public servants who were willing to risk their lives for the community; commercial marquees began to urge support for local police officers and firefighters; radio and newspaper coverage and commentary on the subject seemed more and more prominent. Meanwhile, city management had begun to explore options for providing public safety services, including contracting out the fire protection function.

By the end of September, Martin and his staff had grown impatient with the stalemate and with the employees' continued defiance of orders to resume full duties. On October 5, exactly four weeks after police officers had begun the slowdown, participating police officers and firefighters were confronted face to face and ordered to resume full duties. This order was stronger than the order Martin had given the police officers several weeks earlier. This time the participants were told that unless they declared their intention to comply, they would be suspended without pay pending termination for insubordination and neglect of duty, as specified by the city's personnel ordinance.

Martin selected October 5 for the confrontation, not only because it marked the end of the fourth week of the stalemate but also because both Officer Jacksboro and Captain Rockwood were on duty that day. Martin and his staff hoped that, caught off guard, Jacksboro and Rockwood would either discontinue their participation in the slowdown or make a mistake that would undermine the job action. Both, however, held firm.

None of the aggrieved police officers and only three of the aggrieved fire department employees on duty that day decided against continuing. The others were suspended.

Word of the afternoon's events spread rapidly, and city management made final preparations to deal with a very volatile situation. Police Chief Angelo immediately instituted twelve-hour shifts for the remaining police force, which consisted primarily of supervisory employees. Fire Chief Joe Caro consolidated forces at one of the city's three fire stations, relying on a handful of veteran fire officers and firefighters supplemented by employees from other departments who could be persuaded to help.

Picket lines composed of police and fire personnel and members of their families formed late that afternoon. As the evening wore on, emotions ran high. The understaffed fire company was inundated by a rash of false alarms. In the early morning hours of October 6, three fires broke out, all of them later attributed to arson; two homes under construction and a former elementary school serving as a day care center were destroyed. The city's contingency plans had proven sufficient for police services and probably would have been adequate for normal fire responses. However, the rash of false alarms and the triple arson overwhelmed the skeleton firefighting force. Although no arrests were ever made in connection with the arsons, public support for the job action seemed to diminish after the evening's events.

When the next morning dawned, Martin and his staff faced the aftermath of a night that had surpassed everyone's worst-case scenario. All were sickened by the thought that this might be only the first night of several like it. Efforts to prepare for a recurrence were only partially successful. A local industry that operated its own firefighting force agreed to place a pumper and crew at the city's main fire station, and the city manager of a neighboring community assured Martin that he would send a pumper to Cedar Valley on a moment's notice. State officials, however, refused to make the National Guard available, stating simply that the guard could not step in unless fire losses were greater than they had been the first night.

Informal discussions between management staff and attorneys for the employee groups continued throughout the day. By late afternoon, a return-to-work agreement had been reached that reinstated all suspended employees, ended the work slowdown, and instituted a forty-day cooling-off period.

During the cooling-off period, city staff attempted to respond positively to some of the less costly components of the employees' demands. For example, police officers were given access to the weight room of the local high school and a discount on uniform cleaning. Most of management's attention, however, focused on ways to solve the much greater problems of disgruntled employees and limited resources to provide vital public services. From the employees' perspective, the forty-day period passed with little visible progress.

Seeking solutions

Almost from the moment the demands had first been received, city management had been exploring service delivery alternatives. Those efforts continued during the cooling-off period. For two reasons, attention was focused mostly on fire service options. First, because the fire service was a labor-intensive function characterized by extensive idle time, major changes in service delivery patterns would be more manageable and more likely to achieve substantial benefits there than in the police function, where officers presumably spent their time between calls patrolling the community. Second, and perhaps more important, both Director of Administration Bristol and Fire Chief Caro were familiar with the reputation of Smokeater Systems, Inc. (SSI), a private company renowned for providing efficient fire services in a widely publicized contract arrangement in a neighboring state. If the firefighters persisted with their work slowdown, perhaps SSI could provide fire protection to Cedar Valley at a cost equal to or less than the current cost of service provision.

SSI was contacted, and by mid-October the city had a rough proposal in hand that promised to save $135,000 during the first year of operation. By early November that proposal had been refined: it contained a variety of service-level options that provided first-year savings ranging from $135,000 to $280,000.

When local officials checked references, SSI got high marks for service quality and cost-effectiveness.

Knowledge of the city's contact with SSI became widespread by mid-November despite city officials' efforts to remain low-key. Local firefighters were soon writing letters to the city council and the local newspaper editor suggesting that contract service would be unreliable, questioning SSI's willingness and ability to provide fire inspection and allied services, and raising the specter of increasing fire insurance premiums should SSI be hired. One writer asked, "Is the proposal to contract for fire services only another tactic to intimidate city employees?"

By November 20, all doubts about the seriousness of city management's interest in contracting with SSI had vanished. A memorandum from Martin invited the mayor and city council members to view a videotape of a nationally aired television segment on SSI's operation. A resolution authorizing a contract with SSI had been prepared by the city staff, although it was not considered at the council meeting that evening.

By mid-December most city council members had informed Martin, either directly or indirectly, that they were impressed by SSI's operation but that they preferred to make changes in the current operation, if possible, rather than scrap it and turn the fire service over to a contractor. Martin therefore instructed Bristol to continue his analysis of alternative methods of fire service delivery but to direct his attention particularly to the possibility of adapting various characteristics of the SSI operation to local use.

Different perceptions

By January the volatile situation of autumn had settled into an atmosphere of general mistrust. Firefighters and police officers viewed departmental administrators and the city's management staff suspiciously, privately and publicly attributing sinister motives to various actions. For example, they regarded management's unwillingness to negotiate with labor spokespersons and its willingness to consider contracting out fire services not as legitimate management strategies but as affronts to dedicated public safety employees, threats to their employment security, gestures of "bad faith" in the efforts to resolve the crisis, and reflections of management's indifference to the perspective of front-line police officers and firefighters.

Management, on the other hand, saw little to be gained by recognizing a bargaining unit when not required to do so by state law. Martin, Bristol, and many key management officials had little regard for the notion that a major purpose of local government is to provide jobs. They believed instead that the purpose of local government is to provide services and that pay and working conditions are productivity issues rather than humanitarian or social concerns. Accordingly, they viewed the consideration of contractual fire services as an entirely legitimate and even prudent management strategy.

These managers also resented the insinuations by police officers and firefighters that Martin and his colleagues cared little for the security of the community. They were angered by efforts to encourage residents and businesspersons to apply pressure on the city council and city management, and by the inflammatory pronouncements and public appearances that delighted the local media. Particularly irritating were letters to the editor of the local newspaper that purported to speak for "the public" but in fact were written by relatives of police officers and firefighters.

Moreover, city management resented deeply what it believed to be desertion of managerial ranks and responsibilities by fire department middle management. It was true that city management had done little to create a strong sense of "management team" camaraderie with fire captains before or after the job action, but management was nevertheless offended, not by supervisors' sympathy for the firefighters' position (which some of the captains who had stayed on the job also probably felt) but by the overt leadership that some captains exercised in the job action.

Although contradictory, the views of both labor and management had some justification.

The decision problem

Against this backdrop, city management attempted to address what it perceived to be four fundamental problems:

1. Although the desired salary increase had been presented as an ultimatum rather than as a request and had come at a point during the fiscal year when the budget and the tax rate had already been established, Martin agreed fundamentally that salaries of public safety employees should be increased. His primary motivation, however, was to maintain a competitive compensation structure for city employees. The problem, therefore, was not a disagreement over the need for salary adjustments but rather the difficulty of developing a credible strategy to placate, or at least neutralize, disgruntled employees until the next budget cycle.
2. Because city resources were tight, the city council and the citizenry appeared to have little patience with suggestions that property taxes be raised to fund higher salaries. Substantial revenues, therefore, would have to be secured through money-saving changes in current operations.
3. Although Martin never sought a vote from the full city council, conversations between management and individual council members revealed little support for privatization of the fire service despite substantial projected savings. As long as viable in-house options existed, council members appeared to prefer that route—a preference that effectively restricted the alternatives available to management.
4. Labor-management relations within the police and fire departments were severely strained. Each side viewed the other's comments and proposals cynically.

At Martin's request, in late January Bristol presented a staff analysis that explored five options.

The first option, continuation of the current operating mode, offered no solution to any of the existing problems. However, if the city could manage the existing situation until the next budget, it might be able to offer some concessions to the aggrieved employees and perhaps begin the process of rebuilding relationships with them. Furthermore, this option would require no long-term changes and therefore could appeal to anyone who thought the current problems might actually be short term in nature.

The second option, simply cutting the number of fire department employees, would produce cost savings that could be used to make salary and other concessions. It would, however, also result inevitably in reductions in service-level and operating effectiveness. Layoffs or even reductions through attrition would be bitterly opposed, so this option did not even promise improved relations with the police and fire employees.

The third option was the establishment of a public safety officer (PSO) program, in which police officers and firefighters would be cross-trained and deployed on patrol when not otherwise engaged in police or fire activities. Cross-trained public safety officers had been used successfully in some other cities despite chronic opposition from firefighters' associations. Locally, such a plan might produce some cost savings, but it had little administrative appeal to the police chief, the fire chief, or the city management team. Those officials had just experienced the difficulty of dealing with coordinated actions by police officers and firefighters and thus had little inclination to unite the two groups structurally.

The fourth option, contracting out fire protection, was the preference of the management team, but the council would almost certainly reject it. At a minimum, the management team would have to exert substantial effort to sell the council on this option, despite the substantial projected cost savings.

The fifth option was departmental reorganization and the adoption of a "fire specialist" program. As outlined by Bristol, this option would reduce fire department employment by 20 percent, from fifty-one to forty-one full-time employees, and establish new deployment patterns. Under this program, station-based firefighters responding to a structural alarm would be supplemented at the scene by other city employees who had been trained as firefighters and equipped on assigned standby days with a fire department pickup, turnout gear, a two-way radio, and a pager. If the alarm occurred during working hours, the fire specialists from other city departments who were on standby that day would leave their jobs and respond immediately. If the alarm occurred after working hours or on the weekend, they would respond from wherever they happened to be within their assigned response zones. The net effect of the plan was an increase in response strength—from seven or eight firefighters per standard structural alarm under the old system to nine under the new system—despite a reduction in the number of station-based firefighters.

Unlike the rotational pattern used by SSI that required standby personnel to be on call several days in succession, the rotational pattern for standby assignments in Cedar Valley would be one day on and the next two days off. Thus, local firefighters would be able to serve as fire specialists on "off" days in their own work cycle of twenty-four hours on and forty-eight hours off. This arrangement would serve at least three strategic purposes. First and most important, it would tap the most highly trained pool for fire specialist expertise. Second, it would offer firefighters a source of supplemental income that would make use of their skills and impose minimal disruption on normal activities. Third, participation in the fire specialist program by full-time firefighters would do much to blunt criticism of the program, increase the program's chances for long-term survival, and reduce the tendency to view employees from other departments as "scabs" who were seizing jobs from fire department employees. If employees had to be recruited from other departments, it would be because off-duty firefighters had declined to serve as front-line fire specialists.

When fully implemented, the restructured fire service was expected to produce annual savings exceeding $135,000. For two reasons, however, initial savings were expected to be considerably lower. First, city management recommended using normal attrition rather than layoffs to effect employment reductions; in addition, management recommended against salary reductions, even in cases where cutbacks resulted in downward reclassifications of workers. Second, city management recommended that a substantial portion of the first three years' savings be devoted to a smoke detector rebate program to improve fire safety in existing dwellings.

In February, Martin recommended the fifth option—departmental reorganization and adoption of the fire specialist program—to the city council. He and his staff perceived the immediate reaction from the community to be either positive or, at worst, noncommittal, except among firefighters and their friends, their relatives, and others who had been their principal supporters during the autumn work slowdown.

Management staff held meetings with firefighters to describe the plan in detail, discuss its ramifications, and receive suggestions for improvement. The atmosphere of the sessions was tense; most questions from firefighters were designed less to elicit information than to express opinions and challenge the management plan. The response of the firefighters was decidedly negative. A press release in late February stated the firefighters' position:

The Cedar Valley Firefighters Association wants the public to know the truth about the city administration's so-called "reorganization plan" and some of the dangers this plan poses to our community.

The number of professional firefighters on duty during an average shift would be reduced by 20 percent and supplemented by an unspecified number of "civilian specialists" who are not professional firefighters. They have not been trained in the skills and sciences necessary for a successful firefighting operation, such as hydraulics, fire chemistry, rescue and first aid, ventilation, physics, building construction, arson investigation, and fire prevention and inspection.

Members of a fire company *must* train together as a team and work together as a team; they must stay abreast of new techniques and equipment to help them save lives and preserve property. Under our present system, the Cedar Valley Fire Department has an enviable record of success, proving that adequate manpower, responding together as a team, prevents loss. *The saving of lives and the preservation of property are difficult to evaluate in dollars and cents.*

The city administration claims that the proposed plan will cost the taxpayers less than our present, successful system. Actually, implementation of the new plan alone, including the purchase and maintenance of four radio-equipped pickup trucks and between twelve and eighteen pagers, along with the payment of civilian salaries, will negate most, if not all, of the savings.

The Cedar Valley Firefighters Association urges all citizens to read our newspaper ads carefully and to call city council and express concern over this hasty action.

The battle lines of the previous fall were still clearly in place as the focus of attention shifted to the deliberations of the city council. "If they're going to fight me every step of the way," thought Martin, "maybe I should have pushed harder for option 4, the contractual arrangement. Maybe I should revert to that option even now."

Discussion questions

1. Early in the crisis, Martin expressed strong disapproval but nevertheless tolerated a work slowdown for four weeks before forcing action to break the impasse. Was he too patient or too impatient? What action could he have taken earlier that might have produced more favorable results?
2. Was Martin wise in refusing to treat the police and fire employee associations as negotiating units? Why or why not?
3. Did Martin proceed properly? Should he have given in a little more and complied with additional demands? Should he have "battened down the hatches" and attempted to ride out the storm? Should he have focused less on substantive issues and more on smoothing out relationships? Or was he correct in risking further antagonism by considering major changes in the status quo that would be likely to face stiff opposition from firefighters or police officers? In essence, should he have retreated a bit, dug in, sought a truce, or mounted a charge? Explain your answer.
4. Sometimes the most effective political leadership is achieved by keeping a low profile and avoiding confrontation while waiting for a solution to make itself obvious. Is it possible that Martin, as a new city manager, felt that he had to prove his leadership ability by taking direct action? What would you have advised him to do? If he had chosen to keep a low profile, what, if anything, should he have done to speed the emergence of a solution?
5. Are there other options that should have been added to Martin's list? If so, what are they? Evaluate them.
6. Martin's original preference was option 4, contractual fire protection. If

no other option appears as promising, and the firefighters are opposed even to option 5, should Martin return to his first choice and attempt to sell it to the council? If so, how should he proceed? If not, why not?

7. Are there modifications that could be made in either option 4 or option 5 that might make it more acceptable to the firefighters? If so, what are they? What costs might they entail?

8. If you were Martin, how would you proceed? Why?

9. Realistically, what is the best outcome that Martin can hope to achieve?

16 The human side of privatization

James K. Hartmann and Kathryn G. Denhardt

Editor's introduction

Contemporary society—marked by large populations, amorphous communities, very narrow workplace specialization, highly advanced technology, incredibly rapid advances in knowledge, and very short term obsolescence, even of professional work, knowledge, and skills—is increasingly coming to view workers as it views parts of a machine: infinitely replaceable as the need arises.

It is from this society that the suggestion has come that public services can be provided by private sector firms much more economically, and perhaps even more effectively, than by government bureaucracies. Thus, government should be downsized, in part by privatizing the delivery of public services. Privatization, it is argued, reduces service delivery costs to the lowest possible level by engaging the market forces of competition in service delivery pricing and management. And, indeed, a substantial volume of evidence supports the theories and assertions underlying the concept of the privatization of public services.

It is not at all surprising in this era, when human capital (i.e., workers) is considered infinitely replaceable as the need arises, and when evidence can be compiled that privatization often *does* lead to lower service delivery costs, that the advocates of privatization have given little or no consideration to the human consequences of privatization. To be sure, privatization is often accompanied by a requirement that the private firm hire the displaced government workers to continue delivering the public service. What is not usually noted, however, is that the private sector cost savings are largely attributable to the reduction of labor costs resulting from private sector failure to provide the affected workers with such fringe benefits as health insurance and retirement benefits.

This case describes the question of privatization, first raised in this book in the preceding labor relations case, by looking at both the economic and the human consequences of privatization and by raising questions about the trade-offs that accompany privatization efforts. In the process, issues of social justice, public policy ethics, and administrative responsibilities are raised in a new and vitally important context.

Case 16
The human side of privatization

Background

Blaze County has been one of the nation's fastest-growing areas over the past decade. That rapid development has been accompanied by stresses, of course, but revenue growth has generally kept pace, and the county government has been spared many of the hard choices that other governing bodies have faced during the same time period. But that era is fast drawing to a close as the county's economic growth is tapering off and county revenue growth has flattened.

During the past ten years, the number of county employees has more than doubled; it now totals more than seven thousand persons. To attract and maintain a highly qualified and motivated workforce, the county has offered generous salary and benefit packages to all employees. County staff has become accustomed to a high level of benefits, to merit increases that sometimes approach 10 percent annually, and to a manageable amount of work.

The expansion in staff and services over the last ten years has necessitated heavy infrastructure development, accompanied by an increase in staff to maintain these facilities. New facilities have included an administration building, a general office facility, a public works administration complex, and a corrections administration building, adding more than 500,000 square feet of facilities space to be maintained by the Facility Services Department.

A large international union represents many of the blue-collar trade workers employed by the county, including those in Facility Services. The local covers not only the county but also some other area governments and authorities, as well as a few manufacturing plants in the region. Blaze County is located in a "right-to-work" state, and unions traditionally have had limited power. Nonetheless, each year the contract is negotiated in whole or in part, and meaningful collective bargaining occurs. Employees in the Facility Services Department are in the collective bargaining unit for county employees but are not very active members. Public sector unions have sympathetic listeners on the board of county commissioners.

Jim Stuckey has been with the county for eight years and in his current position as director of the Support Services Division for three years. His responsibilities include providing direction to five departments, including the Facility Services Department. He is very gregarious, which has led him to associate freely with all his employees. He enjoys interacting with them and often schedules time each week to visit a variety of work sites. Accessible and unintimidating, Stuckey has an open-door policy and encourages employees to voice their concerns. Although this could give rise to the "Rodney Dangerfield effect" and Jim occasionally complains, "I get no respect!" everyone knows that he is not driven by a need for respect. He enjoys tackling new challenges and is open to new and innovative ideas.

Sam Smith, the manager of the Facility Services Department, has been with the county for nearly twenty years. His approach to managing the department is to maintain the status quo consistently. New ideas for service provision or enhancement rarely emanate from his office, and proposals for change are met with suspicion.

Judy Fundall is the manager of the county's Office of Management and Budget (OMB). Lately she has spent much of her time investigating and promoting enhancements to service delivery that would also lower costs. Like Jim Stuckey, she is open to change and innovative ideas. Both Stuckey and Fundall are in the process of completing their master's in public administration (M.P.A.) degrees.

Government in Blaze County has been highly politicized since a major restructuring took place in the county charter. Under the previous charter, a county commission was elected at-large and a professional county administrator was appointed. The new charter provides for a board of county commissioners elected from single-member districts, with a county chairman elected at-large —essentially a "strong-mayor" form of government. As Edgar Sloan, the new county chairman, has exercised the considerably greater power authorized by the charter, political animosities and power plays have become commonplace.

The highly charged political environment has had a direct impact on administrative staff because, under the new charter, all division directors as well as the county administrator are subject to annual reappointment by the chairman with confirmation by the board of county commissioners. As a division director, Stuckey is accountable to Martha Wright, the county administrator; to Chairman Sloan; and to the elected board of county commissioners.

The case

As local economic growth tapered off and revenues started to decline, county employee benefits, merit increases, and workloads began to receive closer scrutiny. Benefits and merit increases were reduced, and employees started finding themselves doing more with less.

During the previous fiscal year, each organizational unit in Blaze County had been required to achieve a 5 percent budget reduction even though the demand for services continued to grow. At the time of the next year's budget cycle, they were again required to identify substantial reductions. This caused departments to look even more closely at the way services were being delivered, and managers had to make some difficult recommendations such as program reductions and layoffs.

Provision of custodial services for county facilities is primarily the responsibility of the Facility Services Department. At the time of this case, Facility Services had a total staff of 166 personnel, of whom 72 (43 percent) were within the Custodial Maintenance Section, which provides janitorial services to eighteen large facilities totaling approximately 1,150,000 square feet. The lean management staff consisted of the department manager, Sam Smith, along with an assistant manager, a custodial maintenance supervisor, two night custodial supervisors, and two foremen who cleaned as well as supervised. Figure 1 shows the Facility Services Department's organizational chart.

Jim Stuckey knew that his division would face some hard choices as he tried to reduce its budget while maintaining the quality of services, but he was confident that creative solutions could be found. In the Support Services Division, custodial services became the focal point for budget scrutiny. The provision of custodial services, while essential to providing a clean and healthy work environment, was a prime candidate for full evaluation since some service reduction could be obtained without an obvious, short-term adverse effect on citizens or county workplaces. During the previous fiscal year, eight authorized janitorial positions had been eliminated through the implementation of a reduced service program. This year, with little apparent staff reserve to cut, the budget-cutting knife had to find less obvious targets.

The loss of the eight janitorial positions, coupled with the addition of new buildings to the responsibilities of the cleaning staff during the past fiscal year, had come at a cost. A decision was made to ensure that service to the areas accessed by the general public was not affected. To that end, it was department policy that all restrooms, hallways, stairwells, elevators, and meeting and conference rooms would continue to be thoroughly cleaned, dusted, and disinfected daily. However, the janitorial services provided in staff areas was curtailed in a number of ways, including the changes in the following services noted in italics below:

Walls: Dust, clean, or vacuum wall surface, pictures, blinds, clocks, bookcases, doors, light switches, windows. *Clean and dust drapes only when time is available.*

Floors (carpet): Vacuum as required. *Spot clean, shampoo, and steam clean only when absolutely necessary.*

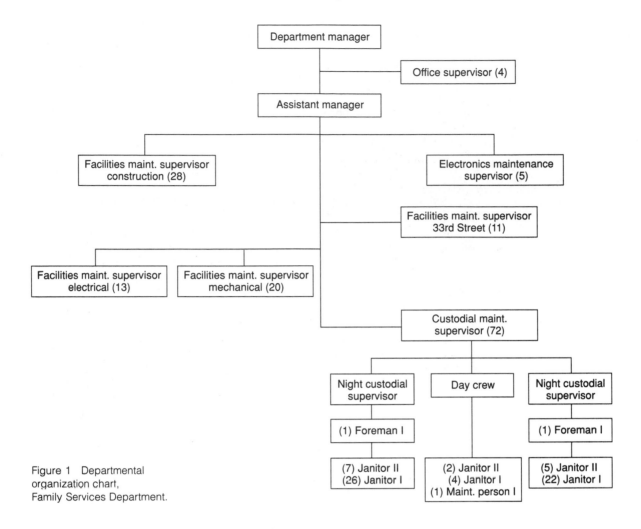

Figure 1 Departmental
organization chart,
Family Services Department.

Floors (hard surface):   Wet mop and dust mop as required; *strip and wax only when absolutely necessary.*

Telephones: *Clean and disinfect only when time is available.*

Personal property and plants: *No service will be performed by janitorial staff.*

Departmental break areas: *Refrigerators, microwaves, vending, and coffee equipment will no longer be cleaned. Employees using these areas are responsible for maintaining them.*

The research project

During this budget preparation period, Stuckey was taking an elective course, Privatization of Public Services, for his M.P.A. degree. Judy Fundall, manager of the county's OMB office, was in the class as well. The course afforded them both the opportunity to work together on a group project exploring the efficiency and effectiveness of privatizing janitorial services. The analysis began with an effort to evaluate the current provision of janitorial services in Blaze County as compared with similar-sized jurisdictions throughout the state. The group sent a questionnaire to governments of comparable size and capacity, as well as to a few private sector agencies operating large facilities.

They received responses to the questionnaire from five comparable counties. The results indicated that Blaze County was paying a much higher rate for janitorial services of comparable quality—$1.66 per square foot versus an average of approximately $.91 per square foot—than any of the other five counties. Table 1 and Figure 2 provide a summary of the results.

The key factor, it turned out, was that all five comparable counties contracted out most if not all of their janitorial services at a substantially lower cost than that incurred by Blaze County. The single private sector agency responding to the questionnaire indicated a cost-per-square-foot of $.76, which fell within the range of those counties that contracted for janitorial services. Most respondents also indicated that the quality of their contracted services was adequate and, in some cases, better than what they had experienced with services provided in-house.

If Blaze County could lower its costs to the average of the other counties, there would be a potential future cost savings of up to $800,000 annually. Upon further analysis, the group of students concluded that Blaze County's costs exceeded those of other counties for two primary reasons. First, personnel costs for Blaze County employees far exceeded those of private sector providers. Second, Blaze County's higher costs could be due to the absence of written standards, performance guidelines, and formal evaluation of efficiency and effectiveness.

The group found that the surveyed local governments' wage rates and generous benefit packages were significantly higher than those paid for comparable positions in the private sector, which limited the governments' ability to be competitive in terms of the cost of providing janitorial services. The starting wage for a Blaze County custodian was $6.35 per hour; that for a similar position in the private sector was $5.25. After benefits and fringes were included for Blaze County employees, the hourly rate increased to $8.91. One reason that benefits raised the labor cost so significantly is mandatory participation in the state retirement system, which added 16.79 percent to the labor cost for employees in the Facility Services Department. When costs of continually rising insurance rates were added, the county could not compete with the prices of private sector providers, who did not have all these mandatory costs. In addition, all county employees also received ten vacation days and eighteen days of paid personal leave to be used for vacation or illness. Combined, this time lost affected both productivity and scheduling.

The group working on the research project concluded that cost savings could be achieved in the Custodial Maintenance Section, and that the private sector could provide the service at a much lower price than its public counterparts. However, effectiveness—especially maintaining cleanliness standards—and meeting service goals and objectives were equally important considerations. Quantifying the effectiveness of janitorial service is difficult at best. To the untrained eye, superficial cleaning can appear the same as deep cleaning. To gauge effectiveness, reliance on the satisfaction level of the occupants and on

Table 1 Blaze County custodial service costs compared with those of other county governments.	County	Total cost	Square feet	Cost per square foot
	Valdu	$ 891,968	1,316,300	$ .68
	Bayside	$ 942,834	1,100,000	$ .86
	South	$2,700,000	3,000,000	$ .90
	Beachview	$1,044,760	1,104,729	$ .95
	Grant	$ 800,000	670,000	$1.19
	Blaze County	$1,909,891	1,150,000	$1.66

Figure 2   Blaze County
custodial service costs:
Graphic comparison of
costs with those of other
county governments.

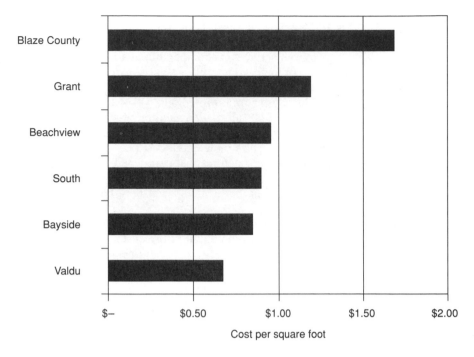

Cost per square foot

general cleanliness as observed by supervisory staff is essential. Both of these
are directly influenced by the type and frequency of services performed.

While the quality of service provided by the Blaze County custodial staff
was considered very good, the county did not have written standards, performance guidelines, or formal evaluation of efficiency and effectiveness for custodial work. The county's facilities, however, were clean and generally considered to be healthful environments.

Still, without documentation regarding the quality and efficiency of custodial
work, no one knew whether the county's janitorial staff might have provided
its services more efficiently if such measures had been in place. What *was*
known was that other counties had established written standards and performance guidelines as a necessary part of contracting with a private vendor, and
had succeeded in lowering costs without sacrificing quality of service.

At the completion of the class project, the group recommended that Blaze
County privatize all or part of its custodial services.

Real people, not abstractions on paper

The findings of the privatization study were striking to Stuckey. He was surprised both at the extent of the cost differences and at the extent to which other
counties were contracting for these services. Fundall enthusiastically supported
moving ahead with contracting for janitorial services in Blaze County. Given
the need to find immediate cost savings, the contracting option became a central
consideration in Stuckey's budget deliberations.

However, to Stuckey, this option was more complicated than a simple management decision based solely on bottom-line dollar savings and maintenance
of quality. There were also people involved, modest-income people, who depended on their county employment for income and other satisfactions connected with employment. The employees who would lose their jobs with the
county were not mere abstractions to him; they were real people with whom
he genuinely enjoyed working. He cared about them, their families, and their
livelihoods. When his report stated that "our in-house services are performed

by talented, loyal, and respected employees," he really meant it. But while he thrived on personal relationships and did not relish the thought of jeopardizing his relationship with members of the custodial staff in order to save money for the county, he was also concerned about the welfare of the county government and the taxpayers. Overall, there did appear to be legitimate concerns about the cost, efficiency, and effectiveness of providing janitorial services in-house.

The decision problem

Contracting for some or all of Blaze County's janitorial services appeared to be a viable option, but not without significant management risks and potential social costs. First, the county lacked both performance standards for janitorial services and experience managing contracts of this type. Both these factors could make contracting difficult and could limit its success. Second, contracting for janitorial services could mean that as many as seventy-two people would lose county jobs at a time when good jobs were very difficult to find. This would be a significant hardship for the individuals affected and could be politically volatile, especially if the union mounted opposition. Stuckey knew from the previous year's experience of laying off just eight employees that morale might decline dramatically throughout the division and even throughout county government. Finally, there was the nagging question of whether the county would be trading off lower, short-term labor costs for higher, long-term social costs as government jobs with moderate wages and good benefits were replaced by private sector jobs with low wages and no benefits. Would the costs saved by the Support Services Division ultimately show up in higher costs for the Health and Human Services Division, for example, as the latter picked up higher costs for indigent health care?

Stuckey knew there were other risks associated with contracting. Sam Smith's probable reaction would be negative, complicating Stuckey's task at best and presenting him with open defiance at worst. Further, if privatization were implemented, service interruption or poor-quality service resulting from either a poor vendor choice or an inadequate contract and monitoring provisions would reflect badly on the county and his division. Clear standards for service were needed, but it was also necessary to allow the vendor sufficient flexibility to pursue cost-effective policies. With no experience in writing or monitoring janitorial performance standards, this could be a difficult balance to achieve initially. But one county responding to the survey had generously provided a copy of the request for proposals (RFP) it had used in contracting out for these services, and that RFP contained a set of performance standards that appeared to meet Blaze County's needs as well.

There were also encouraging considerations. The assistant manager in the Facility Services Department had previously owned and operated a business that provided janitorial services. His experience and expertise could be very valuable in ensuring a successful contracting experience. There were several janitorial service providers in the county, and vendors from surrounding states might also be attracted to such a potentially large contract. Keen competition was expected to help reduce the cost of providing the services and also assist in avoiding the disruption of services. If the ultimate provider could not perform satisfactorily, another provider could be quickly available to assume the task with minimum interruption to the county.

One obvious question was whether the adoption of performance standards for Blaze County's own custodial staff might improve the efficiency and productivity of the in-house provision of services, thereby reducing the need for contracting to achieve cost savings. Stuckey concluded that some cost savings could be achieved in this way, but the primary cost difference was in the labor cost differential between the county and private vendors. The question was not so much whether to recommend contracting for the services but, rather, how to structure a recommendation in the most fair and humane way possible for the affected employees.

If the contracting process were phased in over a period of time, attrition and transfers could minimize the impact on current county employees. During the previous five-year period, attrition of janitor positions had averaged 13.8 employees per year, or approximately 20 percent of the workforce annually. Based on an existing workforce of sixty-seven janitors and assuming a similar attrition rate, most of the phase-in could be completed within a five-year period.[1] Further, employees could be encouraged to cross-train and apply for other county jobs, especially long-term employees concerned about vested retirement benefits. Clear and forthright communication with employees about the change and their options, making very clear the reasons for the decision, could help ease the transition as well. Union reaction might be very negative if the situation was not handled well, and union opposition could be critical.

Even if all these issues were successfully resolved, there remained the larger question of social costs. Most of the private sector firms providing janitorial services offered their nonmanagement employees no health insurance or retirement benefits. Beachview County attempted to address this issue. To minimize the loss of medical benefits by custodial employees discharged because of privatization, Beachview opted to include in its RFP a provision requiring that all employees employed for more than thirty hours per week must be eligible for company-provided health insurance. As it turned out, though, most firms employed nonmanagement janitorial staff on a part-time basis, for fewer than thirty hours per week, which Stuckey found to be the practice among vendors in the Blaze County area as well. When he approached one potential vendor with the idea of an RFP stipulating that health insurance be provided, the vendor said it would refuse to submit a proposal because it could not have one benefit standard for employees working on Blaze County work sites and a lower standard for other employees. To mandate such a requirement would thus compromise the competitiveness of the RFP process by eliminating potential vendors.

Stuckey was concerned about how the board of county commissioners might react to any recommendation he might make. Board members might be tempted by "instant gratification," opting for immediate full-scale privatization in order to maximize cost savings immediately and avert other tough choices in this budget cycle. Yet they could reject the idea of privatization entirely because it would mean a loss of good jobs during hard economic times.

Stuckey was fully aware of the political volatility of the situation. Like every division director, he was subject to the new annual reappointment process, and his job performance and ability to satisfy the county chairman and the board of county commissioners were scrutinized every year. Mishandling this situation by putting the chairman or the commissioners in a difficult political situation could reduce his credibility and even cost him his job. He also realized that the chairman and board would have to discuss this major policy issue in a public forum. There could be intense lobbying for interests on either side of the issue, and the union might seize this issue to strengthen its own position. Regardless, media attention would certainly be focused on his recommendation.

On the other hand, he could be conservative in his handling of the matter,

---

[1] Despite the data, this conclusion is misleading. Job turnover tends to be highest for employees with five or fewer years of service and very low for employees with ten or more years of service. Even with a 5 percent attrition rate, the county could have some janitorial workers who would continue to work for twenty years or more.

avoiding a recommendation but suggesting that the board study the issue. This would avoid immediate jeopardy for himself on this issue, but it would force him to find other budget cuts, a task that would be equally difficult, if less politically volatile.

Although reluctant to face both the political risks involved and the reaction of his janitorial staff to a privatization proposal, Stuckey realized that any substantial, money-saving proposal he offered could cast him as a strong, effective administrator in the eyes of Wright, Sloan, and the commissioners. He also knew that if he failed to seize the initiative, Judy Fundall might recommend privatization of custodial services during the OMB review of his budget requests.

Fundall called to ask Stuckey if he had made a decision about janitorial privatization yet and to remind him that, because of the serious issues involved in meeting this year's lower budget targets, Martha Wright had indicated that she wanted strict enforcement of the deadlines for submission of budget requests and proposals. His budget deadlines were fast approaching, and Stuckey knew he had to decide if and how he wanted to approach this privatization issue. If he did not begin the effort in this year's budget, he would have to sacrifice elsewhere and possibly eliminate other positions or limit valuable services.

If the privatization plan were to move forward and be successful, it had to be comprehensive and sensitive to the political factors guaranteed to surface. But how would those factors play themselves out? Stuckey knew he had to devise both a recommendation and a strategy to build political support for whatever course he chose to follow.

Discussion questions

1. The factors that Stuckey must consider in making his policy decision fall rather neatly into five categories: economic, political, personnel, service delivery, and personal. List the considerations that fall into each of these categories and decide how you would prioritize them in terms of the importance of each to the final decision Stuckey must make.

2. What role, if any, should personnel management concerns play on a policy decision of this magnitude? If such concerns are relevant, how much importance should be attached to them?

3. Are there ethical values of a policy, managerial, or personal nature that should be taken into consideration? Are questions of ethics involved in a trade-off of jobs for cost savings? In a trade-off of jobs for lower taxes?

4. As a manager, should Stuckey be so concerned with the feelings and livelihood of his employees? If so, why? If not, what should he concentrate on?

5. What, if any, ethical obligation does Stuckey have to consider the welfare of the affected janitorial workers? What is his ethical responsibility with regard to the workers' health and retirement benefits? What about the ethical responsibilities of Sam Smith? Judy Fundall? Martha Wright? Edgar Sloan and members of the county board? Does the county government, as a whole, have any ethical responsibility for the janitorial workers?

   If any of the above has such an obligation, what is that obligation? What constraints should ethical considerations place upon each as a decision maker? If none of them has any ethical obligation, why not?

6. Is the delivery of custodial services to public buildings an appropriate government task for privatization? Why or why not? Which of the following are relevant considerations in answering this question: cost savings, tax rates, service delivery standards, welfare of affected workers,

impact of privatization on other county workers, reaction of the workers' union, public relations, political considerations?

7. Should a privatization decision be based solely on short-term considerations? Solely on long-term considerations? On some combination of both? If the latter, how should these be merged? What should be the criteria upon which a privatization decision is made?

8. If all the largest counties in the state have adopted the practice of contracting out for janitorial services, are there larger economic and social implications that should be taken into consideration regarding the nature of jobs being lost and those being created?

9. What factors in the case contributed to the in-house service efficiency problem? What other methods or plans could Stuckey have put into place to increase efficiency and decrease cost without eliminating positions or entering a full privatization effort?

10. Realistically, does Stuckey have a choice other than recommending contracting for janitorial services? If so, what is it? If not, why not?

11. What outside groups (e.g., unions, potential vendors) would be interested in this issue? How strong might their opposition or support be, and why?

12. If privatization is recommended, should Stuckey propose a full implementation or the partial attrition-based plan? Why?

13. If you were in Stuckey's shoes, what would you recommend?

14. What strategy would you follow to promote your recommendation, or at least to minimize and counter opposition to it?

15. How should Stuckey present his recommendation, whatever it is, to the janitors? How can he use this situation to keep employee morale up within his division?

Part eight: Finance and budgeting

Introduction to part eight: Finance and budgeting

Nothing is more vital to the daily process of government than money, and no concern poses a wider range of policy and management issues. Management's job of dealing with those issues requires sophisticated knowledge of accounting, economics, finance, and political science, as well as technical skills in accounting, analysis, and information management. Such knowledge and skills must be applied in the management of revenue, cash, debt, and expenditure policy, and in the implementation of budgeting, policy analysis, and program evaluation functions.

But the critical linkage between finance and local government policy is made in the budgeting process. A government can make any policy it wants, but nothing will change until money is budgeted and spent to implement the policy. A county can establish a zoning ordinance, but no effective zoning will occur until money is budgeted and allocated to hire and empower staff to enforce the ordinance. In a very real sense, the budgetary process is the policy-making process.

Thus, the cases in this part of the book focus on the all-important budgetary process. The first case deals with what might be called macro policy making —the design of the budgeting system itself. It presents the problems facing a new local government administrator, the first chief administrative officer employed by an older rural community, in trying to design a budgeting process that will satisfy both council expectations and administrative needs.

The second case describes the process of budget formulation. It depicts the difficult and critical decisions that are made during the administrative process of preparing a budget proposal that appropriates money to support programs for responding to a community emergency.

The final case focuses on the process of budget implementation. Dealing with issues that are essentially managerial in nature, the case describes the efforts of a budget office staff to ensure that an operating department—a county correctional facility—cooperates in a cost containment program and an effort to develop new administrative policies to reduce the level of public spending.

17 Redesigning the budget process

Samuel E. Tapson

Editor's introduction

The budget is the focal point not only of policy making but also of policy implementation. By appropriating money for specific tasks and programs, the budget authorizes the money needed for each program to proceed, and it also places a critical constraint on program activity: it limits the money that can be spent to accomplish each program's purposes. Further, by dividing inevitably scarce resources among competing programs, the budget also establishes priorities for government activity during the budget period.

Because of its central role, the budget also serves as a major control device: it is a mechanism through which the county board or city council controls administrative operations and, in turn, it is the principal mechanism through which the chief administrative officer directs, influences, and controls departmental operations. The administrator's influence in the government is shaped in major part by two budgetary functions.

The first is the process of budget preparation, described further in the second case. It is during the budget preparation stage that the administrator makes recommendations to guide the budget decisions of the board or council. These recommendations give the administrator a major voice in budget policy making in the council. Further, the way in which the administrator responds to departmental budget requests—that is, the amount of the request the administrator includes in the budget document that is forwarded to the council and the vigor with which he or she serves as an advocate for the department's request—can help shape the administrator's influence over departmental operations.

The second function in which the administrator is influential is the process of budget implementation, described further in case 19. Because budget estimation is, at best, an imprecise science, the administrator plays a central role in making midyear budget adjustments, recommending increases or decreases in budget allocations as needed to stay within budget parameters and to achieve planned program results.

Because of its centrality to their roles as council advisor and program implementor, local government chief administrative officers (CAOs) typically try, formally and informally, to maximize their involvement in the budget process. Thus, in the following case, City Administrator Ted Owens, the first CAO ever employed by the city of Riverview, is pleased to be given the job of designing a new budget process as his first major task for the city. But the challenge of developing a budget process that meets both administrative and legislative expectations produces tensions that underscore the policy importance of the budgetary process.

Case 17
Redesigning the budget process

Background

The city of Riverview is a midwestern community of 9,100 residents located approximately thirty-five miles north of the state's capital city. The state's third oldest city, Riverview is proud of its heritage. The term *tradition* is frequently applied to various facets of its community life and most often applied to its city government.

Benefiting from an expanding regional economy, the city's residential and commercial/industrial base has grown significantly in recent years. Recognizing that local government, like the community itself, has become a more complex environment, the Riverview city council decided that full-time professional leadership was needed.

Joining a growing number of cities statewide, Riverview exercised its home-rule authority to create the position of city administrator. The idea of a city administrator had been subject to debate for nearly six years. Throughout this debate, the current mayor, Cedric Johnson, had steadfastly lobbied against the position. However, as council seats turned over, the mayor's support waned and he finally acceded to the council's wishes. Far from endorsing the concept, though, Mayor Johnson simply agreed not to "stand in the way" of the council

The period of debate finally ended when the council offered the job of city administrator to Ted Owens, an experienced city manager who at the time was serving in a similar capacity as the first administrator in the community where he was currently employed. Owens accepted the council's offer and became Riverview's first city administrator.

The city council

Riverview operates under a traditional mayor-council form of government, with the corporate authority vested in the city council, which is composed of a mayor elected at-large and aldermen elected from districts. The council is recognized to be the policy board (legislative body), and the mayor is the chief executive officer. State statutes also provide for the election of a council president by the seated aldermen. Although the council president is vested with no greater authority than any other alderman, that individual has come to be recognized as the council spokesperson and liaison to the mayor. Arguably this role may be more perceived than real, but the council president in place at the time of Owens's appointment, Roger Scally, clearly viewed his role in this manner. In fact, Scally's leadership and support for the appointment of a city administrator had a significant impact on Mayor Johnson's decision to cease his active opposition to the move.

While its primary function is legislative in nature, the Riverview city council had historically exercised considerable administrative/management authority. Through a system of rigidly departmentalized standing committees, the council was accustomed to a "hands-on" role in managing general municipal operations. The council's penchant for micromanagement was an identifiable weakness in the city's operational mechanism.

In keeping with this concept of administrative committees, the council generally deferred decision making to the respective standing committees. Rarely did the city council, acting as a collective body, pursue a course of action that varied from the committee's recommendations. In fact, committee reports often stood as decision documents without having received formal council concurrence.

The city administrator

Not surprisingly in a community employing its first professional city administrator, the role and powers of that position were issues of some concern among council members. Since the state has no statutory provision for the position of city administrator, many of its cities use their home-rule authority to establish the office by ordinance. Thus, while the degree of administrative authority vested in the office varies from community to community, most local ordinances define relatively limited powers for the position of city administrator. In large part, the popularity of the city administrator form (as opposed to the city manager form) of city government in the state evolved as a reaction to the state's statutory form of council-manager government, which places exceedingly broad powers in the office of the city manager. Like many of the state's cities, Riverview created the position of city administrator rather than city manager in order to limit the administrator's authority.

So wary was the council of the administrator's authority level that, during interviews, Owens was admonished by both Mayor Johnson and Council President Scally to remember the distinction between a "manager" and an "administrator." Although publicly supportive of the administrator position, some council members frankly viewed it as a potential threat to their authority.

The city hall environment

Because of the council's traditional hands-on approach to managing the affairs of city government, the city's management staff voiced considerable frustration to Owens over the level of intervention exhibited by council members. Uncertain as to the council's reaction to staff-initiated decisions, many department heads had learned that "inaction" was a safer, more comfortable posture. As a result, for example, department heads rarely proposed capital projects or purchases, preferring instead to leave all such initiatives to their respective council committees.

If department heads were frustrated, the general staff may have been more so. Accustomed to aldermanic inconsistency and second guessing of decisions, as well as to a high degree of council intervention in daily business, the city hall staff had limited confidence in the council's management of city operations. A fundamentally competent workforce, the staff took few risks and showed limited initiative.

City departments tended to reflect the rigid committee structure of the council, operating as semiautonomous units with minimal interdepartmental cooperation being evident. In part, this situation was attributable to the relationship that existed between committees and operating units. The departmentalized and hands-on nature of the committee system seemed to have contributed to a "turf" atmosphere, with more focus on individual work units than on the city as a whole. Within this atmosphere it was exceedingly difficult for interdepartmental cooperation to flourish.

The case

During the two-year period immediately preceding Owens's appointment, the city's annual budget process had come to be recognized as a source of frustration and conflict among council and staff alike. In fact, the situation had deteriorated to such a degree that the council viewed redesigning the budget process as a priority item on the new administrator's agenda. Focusing on procedural matters more than on financial management issues, the council asked Owens to develop a streamlined budget process and a more useful presentation document.

The budget process

Traditionally, the annual budget was recognized to be the exclusive responsibility of the council's finance committee, which would typically engage each department in a series of line-item review sessions. This approach had become so detailed that the prior year's budget had required meetings on twelve consecutive Monday evenings before it could be presented for council approval.

Reflecting the departmentalized nature of both the council committee system and operating units, budget deliberation tended to focus on each functional unit independent of all other operating units. As a consequence, final budget allocations were often achieved only after negotiated trade-offs among the various departments. Generally this negotiating process tended to favor stronger departments or, more accurately, those departments that enjoyed strong committee representation at the council level. This usually meant gains for police and public works at the expense of parks and recreation, water utility, and administration. These negotiated budget decisions were often made without benefit of input from the affected departments. Quite predictably, this system did not enjoy enthusiastic support among the city's department heads.

Because of the highly competitive and sometimes inexplicable nature of budget decisions, departments exhibited a turf mentality with regard to budgeting. By the time of Owens's appointment, the contentiousness of the annual budget process had become so damaging that it had produced an adversarial relationship among departments.

A somewhat unique feature of the city's annual budget is the funding of numerous local agencies—a general revenue sharing of sorts. During the budget process before Owens's arrival, each of these agencies would be required to appear before the finance committee to present its respective budget requests. Though neither as detailed nor as time-consuming as a departmental review, this local agency budget review added two or three meetings to the overall budget schedule. The community-committee interaction embodied in this process was considered to be an important aspect of the general budget model.

Financial management

The city's general corporate operation derives funding from two primary sources: state-shared revenue and local property taxes. Although all cities in this state are home rule by state charter, the ability to generate revenue from local sources is restricted by statute. Since state-shared revenue allocations are outside the city's influence and alternative local revenue sources are limited, property taxes are the principal source of locally generated revenues. As these cities are located in what is widely regarded as a high property tax state, they are hypersensitive to the issue of property taxes.

Reflecting this sensitivity, the annual budget process had essentially been an exercise in balancing the property tax rate. To achieve a stable property tax rate, the council frequently applied accumulated reserves against current-year operating expenses or simply deferred capital expenditures. However, while either of these budget-balancing techniques may be necessary and occasionally appropriate, their continued use threatens long-term fiscal integrity. This point had been reached in Riverview.

From the council's perspective, fiscal responsibility was measured in terms of the annual property tax rate. The long-term impact of spending down reserves or the deferral of capital requirements was viewed as the natural consequence of exercising fiscal restraint. To Owens, continuing these long-accepted practices clearly posed a major problem; yet altering them appeared to be potentially more problematic.

At the staff level, financial operations were more a bookkeeping function than a matter of management. Owing in part to the limited experience of finance director Tom Rory, the finance department's role in budgeting had recently been limited almost exclusively to one of compiling and reporting data. With Rory exhibiting more than a modicum of uncertainty about his role—he had been in public sector finance for only about eighteen months—the finance committee's role in daily business had probably become more expansive than ever before.

The finance committee

Occupying the preeminent position within the council's standing committee structure, the finance committee assumed an active role in day-to-day financial operations. In fact, the staff had identified the committee or, more specifically, its chairman, Roger Scally, as the council member most prone to micromanagement. To make matters worse, when Owens assumed his duties as city administrator, Scally was also serving as council president, a duality of roles that served to expand even further the committee's range of influence.

If there was one activity over which a committee enjoyed nearly unilateral authority, it was the budgeting process. In keeping with the council's general approach of emphasizing committee-level decision making, the annual budget was clearly the product of the finance committee. The prevailing wisdom among council members was simply to accept the finance committee's judgment in budgetary matters. Unfortunately, this de facto practice of vesting nearly exclusive budgetary responsibility in the finance committee was inconsistent with the budgetary duties and responsibilities now assigned by ordinance to the city administrator. Although a change in practice (policy) was warranted and, in fact, legally authorized, any actual shift in the committee's role and authority, absent the committee's prior endorsement, would undoubtedly result in a strong and immediate backlash. Given historical patterns, the current committee makeup, and the influence of Roger Scally, it was clear to Ted Owens that any substantive change in the city's budget process, in its approach to financial management, and in the role and authority of the finance committee could only begin, and must inevitably end, at the committee level.

The decision problem

The council's apparent support for revised budgeting practices presented Owens with an opportunity and a mechanism for establishing the foundation of council-administrator relations. However, redesigning the city's budget process was a task that also carried with it considerable inherent risk for the new administrator, especially in view of Roger Scally's penchant for micromanagement and his traditional, and obviously enjoyed, pivotal role in the process. Scally was committed in principle to the development of the administrator's position, but Owens had no clear sense that Scally was equally committed to the changes that such a development would normally and optimally entail.

Given the "political" nature of the traditional budget process, change would need to be approached in a manner that preserved a responsible level of aldermanic involvement while transferring primary responsibility to the staff level. In addressing budgeting change, Owens needed to take care so as not to be perceived as "attacking" the council itself.

One of the more interesting, as well as paradoxical, factors confronting

Owens was the role of Roger Scally. As council president, Scally had been an advocate of substantive changes in the budget process as well as a strong proponent of the administrator concept. But as chair of the finance committee, Scally had been a staunch "traditionalist" and inveterate micromanager. Further, Owens sensed that Scally would be protective of the committee's role and authority in financial matters.

Thus, Chairman Scally represented a challenge for Owens, a challenge made even more formidable by the presence of Mayor Johnson, who Owens was convinced would enjoy an opportunity to encourage Scally in a move that would limit the administrator's role and authority. Not having had sufficient time to establish his credibility among council members, nor to assure himself that he enjoyed a consistent level of support among them, Owens could ill-afford to alienate Scally, a recognized ally, at this early juncture. Yet the whole council had explicitly charged Owens with the task of developing a streamlined budget process and a more useful presentation document.

In responding to this charge, Owens also did not want to lose sight of two other concerns high on his personal agenda: (1) encouraging the council to revisit its preferences for postponing needed capital expenditures and for covering operating budget deficits by drawing down reserve funds rather than increasing the property tax rate, and (2) encouraging his department heads to take more initiative in recommending changes they felt would improve the quality of city service delivery.

With the annual budget due in less than six months, Owens needed to decide on an appropriate course of action. How he managed the situation would likely set the tone for council-administrator relations for years to come, and perhaps even determine the fate of the administrator position itself.

Discussion questions

1. Given time constraints and the apparent lack of in-house technical support, would it be advisable for the administrator to adopt a "wait till next year" posture in advancing budgetary change? What risks are there in adopting such an approach?

2. What strategy might be used to achieve a balance between the finance committee's traditional practice of hands-on involvement and the need for a more staff-directed budget process?

3. If you were Owens, how would you deal with Roger Scally on this issue? With the other members of the finance committee? With the council as a whole? With Mayor Johnson? Would you perceive the department heads as critical participants in the change process? How would you involve them?

4. Since procedural elements rather than financial management concerns seem to be the focus of council attention, would you limit the scope of redesigning to simply streamlining procedures, or would you seek to address a full range of budget-related issues? What problems do you perceive to be associated with each approach?

5. In particular, would you use the mandate to begin to address the council's tendencies to delay capital expenditures and draw down operating reserves to cover operating expenses rather than to raise taxes (i.e., increase the property tax rate)?

6. How might changes in the budget process be used as an effective tool for addressing the problems of micromanagement and interdepartmental cooperation?

7. Is there any way in which Owens can use this change process to encourage department heads to take more initiative in formulating policy and operational proposals? If so, how might this be attempted?

18 Welcome to the new town manager?

Mary Jane Kuffner Hirt

Editor's introduction

By focusing on the complexity of budget formulation, this case portrays the linkage between budgeting and policy making. It is in the process of budget formation that the local government policy makers, including the council, the chief administrative officer, and the finance officer, must revisit existing policies regarding service priorities, service levels, tax policy, service charges, capital improvements, and debt management. Linked together in the budget, these policies constitute an operating strategy for the accomplishment of community objectives in a manner consistent with the community's long-term objectives and short-term political preferences.

Each of the policy choices that must be made in this case has an apparently obvious answer, but each answer requires a fundamental change from past policy, and each change would encounter political obstacles. A community grown accustomed to pay-as-you-go capital improvement financing, subsidized water and sewer service, stable tax rates, and established service levels maintained by deficit financing will not easily or willingly accept wholesale changes in such financial policies. Yet, because of a recent natural calamity, all must be reevaluated; business as usual is no longer a viable option for the community.

This case describes every administrator's worst nightmare: an apparently healthy and tranquil community suddenly thrown into crisis conditions with a plethora of hard public policy choices to make and little time in which to make them. The challenge confronting the administrator in this case may sound more fictional than real, but, as in this case, truth is often stranger than fiction. The problems posed by this case are all too familiar to veteran local government administrators. Hard budget choices are more often the rule than the exception in today's local government.

Case 18
Welcome to the new town manager?

Background

Opportunity is a suburban community of 9,200 people located six miles from a declining industrial/corporate center in the mid-Atlantic region. The eight-square-mile municipality, composed of a series of hills and valleys and shaped like a horseshoe, wraps around one of the most affluent communities in the United States. While the municipality is primarily single-family residential in nature, its treasure is a 600-acre regional research and industrial park. The site is home to more than 125 enterprises that employ about 8,000 people and concentrate on light manufacturing; research and development; and wholesale food, beverage, and pharmaceutical distribution. The mostly white-collar community has a low poverty level (1.6 percent), an average elderly population (11.7 percent), and above-average socioeconomic characteristics. Population growth is minimal because of a growing number of empty nesters and smaller-sized families.

The politics

A home-rule community since 1976, Opportunity has a council-manager form of government. Its seven-member council consists of a president and vice president elected at-large and five other members elected by district. The five district representatives, elected last November, include three new members and two incumbents. The president and vice president are in the middle of their terms.

The new council, which has a 4–3 Republican/Democrat split, includes three attorneys, an educator, an engineer/local business operator, a self-employed businessman, and a retiree. The council tends to operate as a group and generally does not split on decisions along political party lines. Most council members adhere to the philosophy that the day-to-day operations belong under the direction of the manager; the council's role is to concentrate on policy and decision responsibilities.

The community has thirty-four full-time and five part-time employees. Services provided by employees include police protection, public works (road, storm, sanitary sewer, and water system services), recreation, zoning, planning and development, and general administration. The town provides financial support to three volunteer fire departments, an ambulance service, a multijurisdictional library, and a community center.

In January, the town manager unexpectedly resigned. The council then spent four months searching for a new manager, ending up with two semifinalist candidates—the current assistant manager and the manager from a nearby community—from a field of ninety. In a vote of 4–2 with one abstention, the council selected the manager from the nearby community.

Town finances

The municipality has strong, stable financial characteristics. The operating and capital budgets for the current year total approximately $3.3 million (Tables 1 and 2). The last tax increase occurred seven years ago, when one mill was added to the property tax. The revenue base primarily is composed of two local taxes: real estate and earned-income taxes (see Table 1). Prior councils created a tax structure that balanced the taxpaying responsibility between residents and the businesses located in the regional industrial park. Consequently, the property tax, at 10.75 mills, is a little over half of the general-purpose maximum rate of 20.00 mills and, with a 97 percent collection rate, generates about 27.0 percent, or $894,640, of total revenues.

In addition, the community has taken advantage of its unlimited authority to set tax rates under home rule and levies a 0.9 percent earned-income tax, which yields $959,000 (see Table 1). (One-tenth percent of earned-income tax produces approximately $106,500.) Water and sewer utility fees provide another 14.5 percent, and grants from the state for highway maintenance, police pensions, and volunteer fire relief funds, plus federal revenue sharing, make up about 5.4 percent of total revenues. Additional tax revenues come from real estate transfer and occupation privilege taxes.

The community is recognized as one with high service levels, and residents have not indicated any dissatisfaction with present taxing levels. Of note on the expenditure side of the current year's budget, as shown in Table 1, are the

Table 1 Current year budget.

	Dollars	Percentage
Revenue		
Real estate tax	894,640	27.0
Earned-income tax	959,000	29.0
Other taxes	105,000	3.0
Licenses, fees, permits	72,490	2.2
Sewer fees	369,000	11.0
Water fees	116,700	3.5
Intergovernmental grants	177,575	5.4
Interest earnings	62,000	2.0
Charges for service	45,750	1.4
Miscellaneous	19,000	0.5
Use of fund balance	491,390	15.0
Total	3,312,545	100.0
Expenditures		
General government	377,181	12.0
Public safety	758,012	23.0
Engineering/code enforcement	154,870	5.0
Sanitation	176,771	5.0
Public works	541,750	16.0
Water service	158,090	6.0
Sewer service	330,800	9.0
Parks/recreation	108,180	3.0
Debt service	168,261	5.0
Capital program	538,630	16.0
Total	3,312,545	100.0

Table 2 Current year capital program.

Road improvements	$253,000	$77,400 (general revenue sharing)
Sanitary sewer	113,000	
Water system	46,280	
Municipal buildings	32,350	
Public works equipment and vehicles	54,000	
Comprehensive plan	10,000	
Fire department subsidy	30,000	
Total	$538,630	

low annual debt-service payment of $168,261 and the planned capital outlay of $538,630, representing 5.0 percent and 16.0 percent of the total budget, respectively. By tradition, the town council tends to follow a practice of "pay-as-you-go" financing for capital improvements.

Ongoing councilmanic debate about annual expenditures has related to the water and sanitary sewer systems' lack of financial self-sufficiency. Revenues provided via sewer and water service fees have covered the town's annual expense for the sewage treatment services provided by a regional sanitary authority, other sewer-related operating costs, and part of the expense of purchasing water from three outside sources for resale to municipal customers. Increases of 37.5 percent in water and 20 percent in sewer rates to raise an additional $90,000 were factored into the revenue estimates for the current year.

Sewer fees for the year have been estimated to generate $369,000 from about 3,000 residential and commercial customers, even though sewer system operating expenses have been estimated at $330,800 and capital expenses at $113,000. Approximately 700 water customers this year are expected to pay about $116,700 to partially offset water operating costs estimated at $158,090 and capital projects of some $46,280. However, as of May 31, the council had taken no action to implement the rate changes.

Other short-term budgetary concerns include

1. Finding money to finance major improvements to the "aging and deteriorating" sewer and water systems and municipal building
2. Coping with the impending loss of $75,000 in intergovernmental funds previously used to finance a portion of the annual road improvement program
3. Identifying new sources of revenue to make up for using accumulated surpluses of approximately $880,000 to balance the annual budget over the preceding four-year period.

Under the home-rule charter, the town manager is charged with responsibility for proposing, implementing, and monitoring the budget adopted by the council. In practice, the operating and capital funds budget has been used as the community's principal tool for establishing short- and long-term service and project priorities. An independent financial audit is performed annually.

The case

The spring in Opportunity was a time of memory-making significance for the community as a whole and for many council and municipal staff members in particular. By mid-May, the council finally had completed its comprehensive and somewhat contentious search for a new town manager and had selected Jennifer Holbrook. With her arrival, municipal operations could resume a regular course of activity. The attention of the council and staff could be refocused on an ambitious agenda of community planning; on the consideration of a newly proposed, mixed-use riverfront zoning district; on the development of a systematic road improvement process; and on the implementation of the annual capital program.

However, within just two weeks—the week before the manager's arrival and her first week on the job—two unanticipated and unrelated disasters occurred that redirected the interests and efforts of the community, council, and staff for the remaining seven months of the year.

The initial disaster was financial. Four months into the fiscal year, the independent audit report for the prior year revealed a closing fund balance of $275,122, approximately $469,000 less than anticipated. During budget preparation, a surplus of $744,456 had been projected, and the council had allocated $491,390 of it to balance the town's current-year budget. The smaller fund balance resulted from a major miscalculation: the month of September's expenditures had not been included in the year-end estimate of total expenses. Consequently, the municipality was looking at a potential year-end deficit of at least $210,000. Holbrook was informed of the situation by the assistant manager in a memo dated May 16. Because the town council had not yet been advised of this financial crisis, it became the manager's responsibility to inform the council at her first workshop meeting on May 27.

The second catastrophe was natural. On May 30, a flash flood fueled by one and one-half inches of rainfall in a little less than an hour devastated an eight-community area. A typically harmless stream became a raging deathtrap for a neighborhood of thirty-eight families, killing eight people and causing millions of dollars of public and private property damage. The initial cost to the town for cleanup operations and repairs to the heavily traveled Brownshill Bridge was about $96,000. Principal among the private problems that later posed significant public responsibilities were the contamination of residential water wells by on-lot septic systems destroyed during the flood, and citizen demands for stream-related flood prevention and protection measures.

A third event, less dramatic but potentially important for the community over the long term, concerned the manner in which planning and evaluation for the annual road improvement program had been conducted. At the council's workshop on May 27, council members had directed Holbrook to develop a comprehensive and systematic process for identifying and funding road improvements. If such a system was not proposed by November 15 and adopted by the council by December 31 of the current year, allocations for subsequent years' road improvements would be reduced by about two-thirds—to $100,000. This ultimatum had resulted from the council's growing frustration over the previous three years, during which three staff engineers had proposed three different road improvement processes for the town.

The decision problem

In the first week of June, Jennifer Holbrook faced an urgent need to develop an effective operating strategy for the next seven months. Given the circumstances, she had to address simultaneously both long- and short-term problems and issues.

The current financial crisis

To minimize the current financial crisis, quick action had to be taken. At mid-year, given the council's failure to authorize the proposed sewer and water fee increases, only significant cuts in operating expenses, capital expenditures, or both would balance the budget. Within the general fund, major reductions could be achieved by deferring the replacement of a police officer and the addition of a new technician in the community development area. Additional general fund savings, though lesser ones, could be accomplished if discretionary expenses within each program area were minimized by department heads for the rest of the year.

Hiring a police officer was more urgent than adding a technician. The police department generally operated with a staff of twelve: nine patrol officers and a sergeant, lieutenant, and superintendent. Forty-seven miles of road stretching across eight square miles required that two officers be on duty during each shift to provide timely response. At this time, the force was down to ten members, with the resignation of one officer and the loss of another for a long time with a back injury. To maintain all shifts with at least two officers required a consistent use of overtime in the first half of the year. With summer vacations further reducing available personnel, overtime costs would certainly exceed budgetary expectations. The civil service commission conducted the screening process for a replacement police officer and posted an eligibility list. The council, civil service commissioners, and local citizens were anxious to see the vacancy filled. To delay in hiring a replacement would be difficult, but potential savings by not paying a full-time salary with benefits could be $30,000.

No action was taken thus far regarding the technician. The position had been requested principally to provide in-house assistance for the town's full-time engineer. The new employee would help prepare plans and perform inspections for water, sewer, and road construction projects. In the past, these services had been procured on an as-needed basis from local engineering firms or independent contractors. With a greater number of capital projects scheduled for the next several years, the staff strongly recommended the addition of a full-time employee. Even though $25,000 had been budgeted for the technician's position, the council had tabled action to initiate the hiring process in March, when it requested a more detailed job description.

Holbrook recognized that discretionary spending across all programs for materials and supplies and minor equipment might be reduced by 5–10 percent, providing $11,000–$22,000 in general operating savings. To achieve this aim, she could direct all department supervisors to review such purchases carefully for the remainder of the year. But given an assessment of prior years' actual spending versus budget allocations, this request likely would not affect service levels.

The major remaining capital projects for the year included the road improvement program ($330,400), sanitary sewer reconstruction in the regional industrial park to replace pumping stations with gravity lines ($113,000), municipal building improvements ($32,350), water system rehabilitation ($46,280), and the purchase of public works trucks and vehicle testing equipment ($54,000). Only one of the projects, sewer reconstruction in the industrial park, was an absolute necessity. County health and state environmental officials had mandated corrective action because twice per day, Monday through Friday, the pumping stations could not keep up with demand, and raw sewage was being discharged directly into a local stream. Construction of gravity lines over a two-year period would eliminate this problem.

Future financial concerns

The current situation was further complicated by the need to address other budget-related concerns in preparation for the next fiscal year. According to the home-rule charter, budget preparation had to start officially in July with the development of a five-year capital plan. The next year's proposed operating and capital budgets had to be presented to the council by November 1.

Three major issues faced Holbrook as she dealt with the current crisis and started planning for the next budget year. The first issue involved financial policy governing utility operations: should general fund revenues continue to subsidize the community's water and sanitary sewer systems? Earlier in the year, the council's reluctance to act decisively to raise sewer and water fees had reflected the complicated nature of the situation. The recommended sewer rate increase of 20 percent would add $60,000, and total revenue generated for sewer services would be $369,000. With the rate increase, revenues would cover annual operating expenses of about $330,000 and leave $39,000 for capital expenses. The $39,000 would partially offset the initial phase of the $226,000 sewer reconstruction project for the industrial park ($113,000 was in the capital budget for the year). A 37.5 percent water rate increase would add $30,000 in water revenues to produce a total of $116,700 for the year. Essentially, this amount would cover two-thirds of the $158,090 annual operating costs although none of the current year's $46,280 capital expense.

Basically, the council was wrestling with whether it could justify rate increases to make the utilities more self-sufficient at the same time that it recognized that previous municipal inaction had created part of the problem. The community had not maintained the water distribution system properly. The leaking system probably had lost 20–25 percent of the water purchased by the town for distribution before it reached customer meters. Rust and sediment in the water provided to about 150 customers routinely ruined laundries and, in many cases, forced residents to buy bottled water for drinking purposes.

The council also hesitated to penalize customers by increasing sewer rates to correct the problems of the poorly designed sanitary sewer system in the twenty-year-old regional industrial park.

To add further difficulty to this dilemma, each year delinquent water and sewer fees had been in the range of 20–25 percent. The auditor's estimate of the accumulated value of uncollected fees at the end of the prior year was about $250,000. Implementation of an effective collection process for delinquent water and sewer fees had been hampered by inconsistencies among computerized payment records and by the absence of an authorized policy to end water services for chronic delinquents.

Dealing with this issue would require balancing fiscal demands with the identification of appropriate community-wide and customer responsibilities. The solution to achieving self-sufficiency or near-sufficiency for either or both services undoubtedly would require rate adjustments, as well as the adoption of a tough stance on delinquencies. It likely would cause a stir within the community.

The second major issue that Holbrook faced dealt with the budget balance: more than $880,000 in surplus funds had been used to balance the municipality's budget in the last four years. The fund balance was now depleted. How should future budgets be balanced? Should services be cut, tax rates increased, new fees for service established, or some combination of options be developed to finance the $200,000–$300,000 annual shortfall caused by the repeated reliance on the fund balance? (A garbage fee of $60 per year, based on 3,000 households to fund the $180,000 garbage collection and disposal contract, had been rejected as a new revenue source for the current fiscal year.)

The third issue concerned financing infrastructure improvements in the community: should the council abandon the previously established policy to fund capital projects on a pay-as-you-go basis? Was it time to look at various debt financing options to address the community's major road, sewer, water, and municipal building projects? The comprehensive road improvement program developed in response to the council's mandate indicated that $5–$6 million should be spent over the next ten years to upgrade the town's forty-seven miles of roads. In addition, reconstruction of major segments of the water distribution system was estimated to cost $750,000, and about $250,000 in municipal building improvements were required, some of which were needed to comply with handicapped-accessibility requirements.

Debt-service expense for the current year was just over $168,000, 5 percent of the total budget. Outstanding principal and interest on existing short- and long-term debt was $525,500 and would be repaid fully within the next five years. For the flood-affected areas, where damaged on-lot septic systems had contaminated about nine out of ten residential water wells, special grants or loans might be available to fund a part of the construction of public water and sanitary sewer systems. Estimated costs for the water and sewer systems were $326,700 and $1.1 million, respectively.

The urgency of the circumstances outlined above precluded Holbrook from assessing with care her new staff's capacity or building a management team. Instead, she essentially had to rely on staff and department heads to provide the necessary assistance and cooperation. Taking time to discuss and establish guidelines to facilitate daily council-manager interaction at workshops and public meetings also was not feasible. As a result, the development of a sound strategy to address the remaining seven months of the year posed a challenge of major proportions for the manager, the existing staff, and the council.

Furthermore, in formulating her plans, Holbrook had to assess the political consequences of various actions. The council had not been willing in the past to make hard decisions on tax and fee increases to keep the budget balanced. Without any chance to test the political climate further, Holbrook had to decide whether to take bold political initiatives, calling for major changes in the town's fiscal policy and using the recent crises to justify recommendations that might cost her needed support on the council. Should she play it safe politically and search for answers that would patch up the town through the immediate crisis while forgoing needed improvements? Or should she find some accommodation between these two courses of action? As a newcomer, she did not know how much support she could expect from the council during her first weeks on the job, how the community would respond to tough new measures, or even how much blame for the current situation could be passed off onto the former manager and former councils. What she *did* know was that the council had not been willing to face up to tough choices on town finances.

In short, Holbrook was not yet settled in the community; she had had no time to build a base of support; and now she had to make immediate decisions that could threaten her future effectiveness as a leader.

Clearly, she had two decisions to make. First, she had to decide how much personal political risk she was willing to take. Then, and most important, she had to devise two sets of financial recommendations: (1) adjustments in the current budget to keep from overspending the community's reserves; and (2) policies that would restore balance to next year's budget. And she had to make these budget recommendations even while responding to the aftermath of the floods. Decisions—lots of them—had to be made fast.

Discussion questions

1. What adjustments should the manager recommend to the council to alleviate Opportunity's projected budget deficit for the current year? (Hint: Revise Tables 1 and 2 in the text.) Should local residents be advised of the financial crisis? If so, what should be communicated, when, how, and by whom?

2. What budget strategy should the manager recommend to the council for the next fiscal year to achieve a balanced budget? Remember that the next year's budget must (1) maintain the community's high level of services; (2) respond to the pressures for infrastructure repairs and improvements created by the flood; and (3) address the need for major water, sewer, and road improvements. What combination of changes, if any, in tax and revenue policies, expenditure policies, capital budget policies, and capital expenditure financing policies would be most likely to produce a balanced budget consistent with the council's and community's expectations?

3. Traditionally, the first few months on the job for a new manager are critical as relationships with the council, staff, volunteer organizations, and community are forged. Given the circumstances of this situation, Holbrook's getting-acquainted opportunity lasted about four days. What operating style should the manager adopt to address the crises faced by Opportunity?

    Are effective managerial styles essentially different for handling crises versus routine operations? If the manager effectively manages these crises, are there any difficulties that might arise to hinder her development of positive, long-term relationships with the council and staff? Explain.

4. Assess the assistant manager's decision to defer any communication of the town's fiscal problem to the council until after the new manager's arrival. What, if any, are the potential implications of this action? How should the manager deal with the assistant manager regarding this matter?

19 County prison overtime

Tom Mills

Editor's introduction

Policy making in the budget process certainly does not end when the budget is adopted. This is particularly true in local governments that operate under mandates—legal, political, and economic—to keep costs within available revenues. As the budget year unfolds, and as changing economic conditions, unanticipated needs, and other circumstances beyond administrative control make their impact felt on both revenues and expenditures, midyear corrections in authorized spending levels are often necessary. Further, every budget requires that line items be stretched over the year, costs contained, budget policies enforced, and economies in spending encouraged.

Thus is the stage set for continuing dialogue, and sometimes confrontation, between the budget office and line departments. This case provides a classic example of the difficulties of budget implementation.

The dispute itself follows a typical pattern. What starts as an exchange of memos between fellow department heads becomes acrimonious. Questions of jurisdiction, expertise, and even motives arise. The dispute soon involves the county administrator, but not before it has come to the attention of the elected chairman of the county board.

As is almost always the case in such management problems, there is no clear right or wrong. And with two valuable and competent subordinates involved, the administrator finds himself searching for a win-win solution, or at least one that will not present an obvious defeat or embarrassment for either party. An overriding consideration is the need for a solution that falls within the constraints posed by budget policy and local politics.

Any solution, furthermore, will have policy implications, both for the budget and for the way in which the county prison system is managed. Policy changes always pose a degree of threat to administrators, especially when they are perceived as being caused by other administrators who lack an understanding of the reasons for the current policy.

This case also provides a glimpse into a little-known and less-understood public service function: the management of a county correctional facility. The dispute centers on overtime pay for correctional officers, and the solution must take into account the undeniable need for, and the working conditions of, such officers. In the case of public safety personnel, any budgetary saving must be accomplished without a serious reduction in service or increased danger to the public.

The solution thus requires good analysis of relevant data, faithfulness to operating budgetary policies, sensitivity to the personalities of those involved, and, as always in local government, an eye on the politicians watching from the sidelines. In short, this case poses a typical challenge to the creativity of the public sector decision maker.

Case 19
County prison overtime

Background

Franklin County is a suburban/rural county located in one of the Mid-Atlantic states. It adjoins a large eastern city and has a land area of 650 square miles, a population of approximately 500,000, and forty-five local governments that consist of boroughs, villages, and townships. The local governments have their own police forces but lack secure holding facilities for defendants arrested and bound over by local magistrates for trial in the county courts.

The county provides all criminal justice system services from the county courthouse located in Franklinville, the county seat. On a tract of county-owned land just outside of Franklinville, the county operates two detention facilities: a small, medium-security facility for juveniles and a large, modern, medium-security facility for both male and female adult detainees. The latter facility, called the county prison, has a capacity of approximately 340 inmates and is maintained and operated by a staff of 181 employees.

Franklin County's chief law-making and administrative authority is the elected county commission, which is vested with both executive and legislative powers. Voters also elect a number of administrative officers—including the sheriff, the controller, and the district attorney—and the judges of the county court, called the supreme court of common pleas.

The county commission consists of three members elected countywide for four-year terms. The county code requires that one of the three commissioners be a member of the opposing, or minority, party. The county is predominantly Republican, and members of that party regularly control the countywide elective offices. The county commission, perhaps owing to its higher visibility, has occasionally been controlled by a Democratic majority.

The county commissioners appoint a county administrator, all nonelected department heads, and the members of most county boards and commissions. The day-to-day operation of the county is the responsibility of the county administrator, who is a professional local government manager recruited and appointed on the basis of technical competence. The county boasts a commitment to professionalism. The county administrator recruits and hires his or her own staff and has been responsible for securing the appointments of the finance director, the personnel director, and the director of purchasing.

The county code constrains the county commissioners' powers of appointment in some instances. The power to appoint the director of the department of corrections, who oversees both the county prison and the juvenile rehabilitation center, is vested in a prison board. The prison board is composed of the president judge of the supreme court of common pleas or that judge's designee, the district attorney, the sheriff, the controller, and the three county commissioners. Five of the seven members of the board were Republicans at the time this case begins.

The case

In the previous election, the Democratic party had won the majority of seats on the county commission by taking what proved to be the more popular position on a critical environmental issue. In hopes of reelection, the Democratic commissioners instituted a cost containment program that, if successful, would enable them to complete their term without raising taxes. The commissioners issued a directive to all department heads instructing them to implement economies wherever possible. The county administrator, George Truly, was given the principal responsibility for implementing the cost containment program. He, in turn, had charged the finance director, Donald Dexter, with much of the program's operating responsibility.

After monitoring the expenditures of the county prison, Dexter was convinced that overtime expenditures were out of control. He had met on several occasions with Charles Goodheart, the director of corrections, and had called him almost weekly in an effort to reduce overtime costs. In Dexter's view, those contacts had been of little value since overtime expenditures continued at what he regarded as an excessive rate. Somewhat reluctantly, he decided to go "on record." He dictated what was to be the first in a series of memorandums.

March 12
TO: Charles R. Goodheart, Director of Corrections
FROM: Donald D. Dexter, Finance Director
SUBJECT: Excessive Prison Overtime

Pursuant to the county commissioners' directive of January 8 establishing the cost containment program, my staff and I have been closely monitoring the overtime expenditures incurred in the operation of the county prison. We have had several meetings and numerous telephone conversations regarding this matter with both you and your key staff members—all to no avail. Overtime expenditures have continued to rise and might well exceed the budget allocation. This I find to be particularly distressing, since we had every hope that this was one area of your operation in which we could effect significant savings.

I would greatly appreciate it if you would provide me, at your first opportunity, with a detailed justification for the current rate of overtime usage and your plans to keep such expenditures to an absolute minimum.

cc: George S. Truly, County Administrator
       Frank Friendly, Personnel Director

Before sending this memorandum, Dexter had given the action considerable thought and had concluded that, even if the memorandum was a bit strong, it was warranted in this case.

In the weeks that followed, Dexter continued to scrutinize the prison payroll records but did not observe any reduction in the use of overtime. He was about to schedule yet another meeting with Goodheart when he received the following memorandum.

April 5
TO: Donald D. Dexter, Finance Director
FROM: Charles R. Goodheart, Director of Corrections
SUBJECT: Response to Your Request for Information Regarding Overtime
                  Expenditures

You indicated in your memorandum of March 12 that you felt we were utilizing an excessive amount of overtime. I welcome the opportunity to explain what might appear to be excessive overtime usage, but which really is no more than prudent prison management.

You will recall that during the budget hearings last year, I shared with you information on overtime usage in the four surrounding counties. Each of these counties has a comparable prison system, and, as I noted then, each uses more overtime than we do.

You must remember that I requested $434,400 as an overtime allocation for the current fiscal year (including holiday overtime). The overtime figure that was allocated to this department was substantially less. When budget allocations were announced, there was no explanation for the reduced overtime figure other than a general statement—which certainly is appropriate for you as finance director to make—that times were difficult, money was tight, and every effort must be made to curtail unnecessary expenditures. Although I accept these comments in the spirit in which they were made, I still am held responsible and accountable to the prison board for operating a safe and secure correctional institution. Prisons are potentially very dangerous, and that danger can be averted only by keeping staffing levels at safe and realistic levels.

As we both know, there are many justifiable causes for overtime usage in a prison setting. In the following paragraphs I'll attempt to identify the major causes.

Turnover   During last year and continuing into this year, we have experienced high levels of turnover among our correctional officers. When staff members leave we are required to fill their posts, which we do through the use of overtime. The problem continues during recruitment for replacements and during the three-week training course to which all recruits are sent. When you add the two- to four-week delay in filling positions to the three-week training period, you can readily see that a considerable amount of overtime might be involved. Turnover is perhaps our most critical problem. Previously I sent you a detailed commentary on our turnover experience. Over the past several years, I have told everyone willing to listen that there is a strong relationship between turnover in a correctional institution and overtime expenditures.

First of all, entry-level correctional officers are poorly paid, and, as I've told the county commissioners at every budget hearing, that is certainly true in our case. Second, this is a very difficult profession, and prison personnel are continually required to work at very high stress levels. Finally, we enjoy very little public esteem, and the working conditions can on occasion be very unpleasant. Small wonder that there is high turnover not only in our prisons but in prisons all across this country. When a staff member leaves, the need to fill the post continues. Unless the prison board tells me that it does not want me to fill vacant posts, I will continue to do so, and I have no choice but to use overtime.

Hospital watches   Whenever an inmate requires inpatient treatment in a local hospital, I must provide the necessary security. Recently, two inmates were hospitalized. For each day of hospitalization, we provided two correctional officers per shift, three shifts per day, for a total of forty-eight hours of coverage. As you can see, the time mounts up rapidly. We have no fat in our shift complements; therefore, when a need like this arises, it must be covered with overtime.

Emergency situations   Whenever there is reason to believe that inmates might be planning an action that could endanger the security of the institution, I adopt an emergency plan that puts all supervisors on twelve-hour shifts. I do not place this institution on an emergency footing for any trivial or illusory cause. Those instances in which I have used emergency overtime have been fully justified, and I stand by my actions.

Sick leave   Our sick leave usage compares favorably with that of other county departments that enjoy less trying working conditions. Still, when a correctional officer calls in sick, his or her position must be filled, and it is usually filled by the use of overtime. We can't call in a replacement on one hour's notice on the person's day off, upset his or her family life, and worsen a bad morale situation simply to cover an eight-hour shift. We feel that the use of overtime in these situations is the most sensible solution.

Workers' compensation   I have frequently remarked on this problem in the past. Today we are filling two posts that are vacant as a result of workers' compensation claims against the county. When an employee is injured on the job and a doctor certifies that he or she may not work, I have no choice but to utilize overtime to fill the post. I simply don't have any slack resources that would permit me to do otherwise.

Reserve duty   Under the laws of this state, all staff members who are members of bona fide military reserve units are authorized to take fifteen days of paid military leave annually. When they depart for their military training, their posts remain, and we are responsible for filling them. The problem is exacerbated by the tendency of both military leave and vacations to cluster in the summer months. Another aspect of military reserve duty also generates overtime. Our correctional officers are scheduled around the clock and frequently are scheduled to work on a weekend when they are expected to attend reserve drills. Under the policy adopted by the county commissioners, the reservists may take "no-pay" time and fulfill their reserve obligations. While the county saves their straight-time pay, I am forced to use overtime to fill their posts.

Vacations   We do make a concerted effort to schedule vacations so as not to result in overtime expenditures. Unfortunately, as a direct result of our lean staffing, on occasion we must resort to overtime to permit our correctional officers to enjoy the vacations they have earned.

Training programs   Compared to the standard advocated by national authorities, our training efforts are extremely modest. We provide equal employment opportunity training, particularly with respect to our female correctional officers, and some supervisory training. In addition, we provide training in interpersonal communication skills—training I regard as essential in an institution such as ours. Since our shift schedules contain no fat, personnel must be brought in for training on their days off, which, of course, results in overtime.

The major causes of our overtime expenditures are as noted above. I have brought these problems and their causes to the attention of the county commissioners at every budget hearing over the past nine years. Our staff utilization records and overtime documentation are available to anyone who wishes to review them. We have nothing to hide.

I don't mean to be flippant or discourteous, but frankly I'm no wizard. I cannot operate this institution without a reasonable overtime allocation any more than the Jews of antiquity could make bricks without straw. For you to insist that I do so strikes me as being every bit as unreasonable as was the order of the Pharaoh's overseer.

If you can provide specific suggestions regarding policies or methodologies that you feel will assist in overtime reduction without compromising safe and efficient operation of this institution, please be assured that we will be happy to work with you in implementing them. We are open to any thoughtful and constructive recommendations that you or your staff may have. In the meantime, you might consider funding a comprehensive study of our staffing needs, including the need for overtime, by a nationally recognized group specializing in the field of corrections.

cc: Members of the County Prison Board
      George S. Truly, County Administrator
      Frank Friendly, Personnel Director

Dexter read the memorandum twice, his feelings alternating between anger and frustration. He regarded Goodheart highly, knowing him to be a caring individual and a respected corrections professional. "But clearly," thought Dexter, "he's no administrator. I asked him for a detailed justification of his use of overtime and his plans to keep those expenditures to a minimum, and what did he do? He offered me a lesson in biblical history and tried to put the monkey on my back with that bit about 'any thoughtful and constructive recommendations' I might have—baloney!" Dexter noted that Goodheart had twice mentioned his accountability to the county prison board and had been ungracious enough to copy the prison board members on the memorandum. "That," thought Dexter sourly, "is just a brazen example of saber rattling. Maybe he thinks that if he can broaden the controversy by bringing in the prison board, he can get me off his case. Not likely!" Still angry, he spun in his chair, picked up the mike of his recording machine, and dictated his reply.

Meanwhile, Jim Kirby, chair of the county commission, was enjoying his new role. He was no stranger to county government; he had been the minority commissioner for eight years under Republican administrations, but that, he felt, was essentially a "nay-sayer" role. Now, as chairman in a Democratic administration, he was in a position to take the lead on policy decisions, and he was enjoying it. He had founded a very successful business in the county and had called the shots there for more than thirty years. Although Kirby had often mused that government and business were much more different than alike—at least on paper—he relished his leadership role in the county.

Kirby prided himself on his capacity for work and made every effort to keep on top of things. He regretted that he had not read Goodheart's memorandum of April 5 before attending the monthly prison board meeting. He hated to be blindsided! The president judge of common pleas court, Harvey Strickland, who was also president of the prison board, had shown Kirby his copy of the memorandum as well as a copy of Dexter's memorandum of March 12, which had prompted Goodheart's reply. Strickland had been his usual amiable self, but Kirby knew from long experience that with him that you worried not about what he said but about what he left unsaid. The fact that Strickland had brought the memorandums with him to the meeting and his oblique references to "those in this life who are penny-wise and pound-foolish" convinced Kirby that trouble was brewing.

As soon as Kirby got back to his office, he called George Truly, the county administrator, and asked him to stop by. Truly was the perfect balance to Kirby. Kirby was "born to lead"—an activist by nature, full of ideas and restless energy and impatient with detail. Truly, on the other hand, was a "doer." A professional administrator with substantial background in local government, he disliked the publicity and pressure of policy leadership, preferring instead the satisfaction that came from making policies work and seeing that services were delivered. The two men understood each other and had developed an effective working relationship. Neither one worried about the line between policy and administration; each one understood the overlap between the two activities and freely advised the other about county problems.

As Truly walked through the doorway, Kirby asked him, "Are you familiar with Don Dexter's memo of March 12 and Charlie Goodheart's reply?"

Truly said that he was and that he had already spoken to Dexter about them, but that he had been too late.

"What do you mean, too late?" Kirby asked. "This thing looks to me like it can still be salvaged."

"Then," Truly replied, "I guess you haven't seen Don's memorandum of April 7."

April 7
TO: Charles R. Goodheart, Director of Corrections
FROM: Donald D. Dexter, Finance Director
SUBJECT: Your Evasive Memorandum of April 5

In a sincere effort to implement the county commissioners' directive establishing a countywide cost containment program, I wrote to you on March 12. In my memorandum I asked you to provide me with a detailed justification for the current rate of overtime usage and your plans to keep such expenditures to an absolute minimum.

In reply, you gave me three pages of generalities and gratuitous comments. You're the prison expert, not me. If I had any good ideas on how you could run your operation more efficiently or economically, you can be sure I'd offer them. But as I see it, that's your job, not mine. My job is to see to the financial well-being of this county, and I can't do my job if I don't get cooperation. That's all I'm asking for—your cooperation in achieving the goals set for all of us by the county commissioners. Your knowledge of the Old Testament is better than mine, but I do know that the Pharaoh didn't pay overtime. As far as I am concerned, you can have all the straw you want, but cut down on the overtime.

cc: George S. Truly, County Administrator
       Frank Friendly, Personnel Director

The decision problem

After Kirby had finished reading Dexter's memo of April 7, he sighed wearily, laid it aside, looked up at Truly, and said, "I see what you mean. Any suggestions?"

Truly was a career administrator who had spent twenty-two years in a series of increasingly demanding city management jobs before being recruited by Kirby to serve as Franklin County administrator. He had been given carte blanche in the recruitment of his administrative staff, and he had picked, among others, Don Dexter. Dexter was extremely bright; he had been the controller for a large manufacturing firm in the county—quite an accomplishment for a man who was not yet thirty. "But," Truly reflected, "he's never swum in political waters before, and there's no question that he's in over his head."

As the two men reviewed the situation, they tried to define the problem specifically, to identify possible courses of action, and to anticipate the probable outcomes of those alternatives.

It was evident that whatever they did, they had to do it quickly. Strickland could not yet have seen Dexter's memorandum of April 7. If he had, he would have had it with him at the meeting, and he would not have been so affable.

The cost containment program was important to Kirby and the other Democrat on the county commission. It was probably their best hope of reelection. If they exempted the county prison from the program for fear of what the prison board might do, the program could be weakened throughout the county. After all, why should the other departments conform if the prison wasn't expected to do its part?

Under the county code, the prison board, not the county commission, was responsible for approving all prison-related expenditures. The board, with its Republican majority, could give Goodheart a blank check if they wanted to, and the commissioners would be able to do nothing about it. "Well not exactly 'nothing,'" groused Kirby. "We could direct the county solicitor to sue the prison board, but since the president of the board is also the president judge, that's more of a theoretical than a practical remedy.''

In fact, it was much more likely that the prison board would wind up suing the county commissioners. If the board alleged that an imminent threat to public safety was created by the refusal of the commissioners and their agents to fund the county prison adequately, it could bring an action *in mandamus*. In that event, the prison board would not be likely to limit the action to the question of prison overtime but would, in all likelihood, open a Pandora's box of problems. Goodheart had documented many of these problems in his memorandum of April 5, and that memo would probably be Exhibit A at a trial. Issues most likely to be litigated included the needs for adequate prison staffing levels, proactive strategies to combat the high rate of turnover, and higher salaries for correctional officers.

Kirby knew that if political warfare broke out, the Republicans would move quickly to seize the high ground. They would allege that the Democrats were jeopardizing the safety and tranquillity of the community for the sake of a few paltry dollars. Kirby was too old a hand to suppose that arguments of efficiency and economy would carry any weight with the public in such a debate— especially if people were convinced that they were going to be murdered in their beds.

Since all the elected officials in the county were Republicans with the exception of Kirby and the other Democratic commissioner, they could really make things untenable. So far, the elected officials had been cooperating in the cost containment program. If, however, they chose to support the prison board in a confrontation with the commission, the cost containment program would be thoroughly scuttled.

"Don Dexter really put us in a box,'' remarked Kirby.

"Yes, but he's young and bright; he won't make the same mistake again,'' replied Truly.

"If the president judge gets him in his sights, he won't have the opportunity,'' observed Kirby solemnly.

"Funny thing,'' Kirby continued, "Don was right; that memorandum from Charlie was evasive, but Don should have known better than to say so. More than that, he shouldn't have written at all. In a situation like that, you go to see the guy. Writing is a very incomplete, very limited way to communicate. It's a lot easier to talk tough to your dictating machine than to an adversary. My rules have always been, never write a letter if you can avoid it, and never throw one away.''

After almost an hour of discussion, the two men had identified five alternative approaches to the problem. Unfortunately, none of them was without risk.

1. Exempt the prison from the cost containment program. Under this alternative, Kirby would contact Strickland informally and intimate that the commission would not be unduly concerned if the prison did not achieve its cost containment objectives. The justification offered would be that, as a public safety and law enforcement agency, the prison ought not be held to the same standard of cost reduction as other agencies, lest public safety suffer. The main problem with this approach was that party loyalty was paramount in this county, and Strickland was certain to share this information with the other elected officials, especially the district attorney and the sheriff, who headed justice system agencies. Once the commissioners had yielded on the prison, it would be difficult for them to hold the line on other justice system agencies, and the cost containment program would be seriously jeopardized. The result could be that the majority commissioners would be branded as weak men of little resolve, and that could have serious spillover effects in other areas.

2.   Fund an in-depth study of the prison by a nationally recognized group specializing in corrections. Since this was a solution proposed by the director of corrections, it would most likely gain the acceptance of the prison board. Apart from the cost of such a study, which could be considerable, its recommendations were not likely to be favorable to the county administration. Through long experience, Kirby and Truly had come to believe that special interest groups of whatever ilk rarely supported anything antithetical to their special interest. Worse yet, a comprehensive study might only document and verify the types of complaints that the director of corrections had been making for years. It was one thing to ignore his complaints; it would be something quite different were the county administration to ignore the studied recommendations of nationally recognized experts.

3.   Conduct an in-house study of the need for prison overtime. This alternative appeared to have a good deal to recommend it. The county had a small management analysis team that reported directly to the county administrator. The supervisor of the team was a thoroughly honest and objective career professional who had been a founding member of the Association of Management Analysts in State and Local Government and was well respected both within the county and beyond its borders. The problem, of course, was one of credibility. Despite his excellent reputation, his objectivity might be questioned in the partisan political climate that prevailed in Franklin County. Moreover, the prison board might refuse to approve such a study. A study could be undertaken without the prison board's concurrence, as a prerogative of the majority commissioners, but in that event, the prison board might view the study as flawed.

4.   Attempt to find an "honest broker" to conduct a study of prison overtime. "Honest" in this context meant someone who would be considered honest in the eyes of the prison board—someone they would perceive as having no ax to grind. Ideally, this person should already work for the county and be known by, and enjoy the confidence of, the prison board. But who? The downside of this alternative, assuming that such a person could be found, was that the honest broker might not be all that honest. Should such a person be selected with the prison board's concurrence, that person might very well take the prison board's side, to the considerable embarrassment of the county administration.

5.   Invite Strickland to undertake the overtime study with members of his staff. The court's administrative staff included several career professionals in court administration who were graduates of the Institute for Court Management. They were undoubtedly capable of conducting the study, and Strickland and the prison board, which he clearly dominated, would certainly find them acceptable. The question, again, was one of objectivity. Truly favored this alternative, arguing that if, as he believed, they were really professionals, they would be objective. Kirby's response was insightful: "I don't recall book and verse, but somewhere in the scripture it is written, 'Whose bread I eat, his song I sing,' and those fellows eat court bread."

What really was needed was a dispassionate review of prison overtime usage, the development of sound recommendations that would reduce overtime expenses without endangering the public, and an appraisal of the adequacy of the current budgetary allocation for prison overtime. This last point was particularly important. Goodheart continually reminded the prison board that his overtime request had been cut arbitrarily by the finance department without consultation or even explanation. True, there were other important questions that the study could appropriately consider, such as the adequacy of entry-level salaries for correctional officers and the appropriateness of current staffing levels. But solutions to both of these problems would be likely to cost the county more money. Given a choice, Kirby would prefer to postpone consideration of all problems that might result in increased cost to the county until after the next election.

Fortunately, the collective bargaining agreement with the local union that represented the correctional officers was due to expire in September. The study would certainly be completed well before then, and any recommendations requiring work-rule changes could be negotiated as part of the contract settlement.

Kirby turned to Truly and said, "George, give this some thought—and quickly! See what you can come up with."

Truly knew he had to work fast to answer two questions: (1) Which of the alternatives should be recommended? and (2) If a study were to be undertaken, what kind of person should be given the assignment?

Discussion questions

1. Judging from the statements and actions of the principal actors in the case, in what ways did their value premises differ?
2. What purposes, if any, are served by "going on record," as Dexter did in his first memorandum?
3. Instead of dictating his reply to Goodheart's memorandum of April 5 while he was still angry, what should Dexter have done?
4. Was Kirby correct in his observation that "writing is a very incomplete, very limited way to communicate"?
5. Are Kirby's and Truly's reservations about the objectivity of a nationally recognized group of corrections experts well-founded? Would the recommendations of such a group be more likely to support or oppose the director of corrections? Why?
6. Which of the five alternatives, or what combination of the alternatives, should Truly recommend?
7. If the county administrator's recommendation involves a study, what kind of person should be selected to head it? Should it be a member of the county staff or an outsider? Should partisan affiliation be a consideration? Should the prison board be consulted on the choice? How important is reputation in such an assignment?
8. If a study is to be commissioned, what instructions or "charge" should be given to the analysts?

Part nine:
Ethics

Introduction to part nine: Ethics

Despite its placement at the end of this book, ethics is neither an afterthought nor a secondary consideration in the professional activities of the local government manager. Quite to the contrary, ethics is a central, all-encompassing, ever-present characteristic of professional local government management. At some level, ethical considerations are a part of every managerial decision or action.

Because of the centrality of ethics in professional management, ethical questions have emerged in many earlier cases in this book. While one can find them at the foundation of any administrative problem, or "case," at least fourteen cases in this book directly involve questions of ethics; of these, seven explicitly pose ethical questions for the reader's consideration. These are cases 1, 6, 12, 13, and 16, as well as cases 20 and 21, which are included in this part of the book.

Taken together, the six cases in which ethical questions are directly posed give a sense of the range of local government matters that have an ethical dimension. For example, case 1 describes a conflict between principle and political expediency; case 6 presents a circumstance in which a manager is tempted to act beyond his legal authority to resolve a crisis; case 12 portrays the ethical dilemma of an analyst who perceives herself under pressure to develop numbers supportive of a policy option that she feels is not in the public interest; case 13 demonstrates the difficulty of applying ethical principles when a complicated set of individual circumstances obscures questions of right and wrong; and case 16 discusses the ethical conflict that arises when a policy is proposed that will save taxpayers dollars but result in the dismissal of a significant number of employees, some of whom have records of long and faithful service.

But the reader is encouraged to find ethical dimensions in other cases as well. For instance, case 3 poses a problem of policy ethics: to what extent is the administrator obligated to follow public opinion and how much of an effort is required to ascertain what that opinion is? Case 8 wrestles with the conflict between the manager's obligations to inform the public and to preserve confidentiality in pending economic development negotiations. Case 9 deals with the use of public funds to aid a private business. Case 19 involves a situation complicated by the way administrators treat each other. And in case 5, a number of ethical principles are involved in the efforts to establish a pricing policy for the delivery of public services to a private group.

The two cases in this section pose particularly severe ethical challenges. Both deal with situations in which the manager is under pressure to act in ways that would violate the code of ethics established for local government managers by the International City/County Management Association (ICMA). (A copy of the code is included as an appendix in this book.) They both pose the ultimate ethical dilemma: what to do when the *right* (read "most legally or morally appropriate") solution to a problem can be achieved only by action that violates ethical principles, or when ethical principles themselves are in conflict.

In the first of these cases, the ethical dilemma arises from the relationship between elected officials and the administrator, a relationship complicated by demands for administrative action in the middle of an election campaign that would, inevitably, draw the administrator into the campaign itself. The second poses a similar dilemma: how should an administrator respond when the council itself is demanding that the administrator act in an unethical manner?

The special virtue of the cases that follow is the message they convey about ethics in government. They underscore the difficulty that even highly ethical people can have in trying to determine right and wrong and in trying to decide how best to respond to particular situations. They clearly communicate that ethical behavior requires, first and foremost, conscious awareness of the ethical dimensions of the problem at hand and thoughtful deliberation in selecting a policy option or an appropriate course of action. Perhaps most of all, these cases suggest that ethical judgments should not be made hastily, either when determining one's own course of action or when judging the decisions, actions, or behavior of others.

20 Principles under pressure

Harry G. Gerken

Editor's introduction

The central characteristic of council-manager government and of professional administration in local government is its nonpolitical nature. True to the description first set forth by Woodrow Wilson, professional local government administrators eschew involvement in local politics. Indeed, the code of ethics set forth by the ICMA specifically rejects such involvement.

What, then, should the local administrator do when external circumstances seem to make it impossible to avoid politics? How does the code apply when normal patterns of relationships between elected officials and the appointed administrator break down? That is the issue posed by this case.

While the instant reaction of most professional administrators would be to condemn political involvement regardless of the circumstances, real-life situations rarely lack mitigating circumstances, and this case is no different. The manager's failure to get involved could undermine the integrity of the council-manager form of government as practiced in the community and probably cost the manager his job as well.

Adding to the complexity of the manager's decision is the potential for codes of ethics—in this case, the ICMA code—to send apparently conflicting signals to the embattled manager. The case thus affords an opportunity not only to apply ethical principles in practice, but also to reconcile different sections of the code with the help of their accompanying guidelines. The ICMA Code of Ethics, together with the guidelines, appears in the appendix to this book.

Case 20
Principles under pressure

Background

In the mid-1970s the ripples of Watergate reached down to many local governments. Perhaps prompted by the almost daily revelations of wrongdoing at the federal level, some citizens of Centerville formed a group known as Taxpayers Against Corruption (TAC).

Centerville, a sprawling community of 35,000, contained large tracts of undeveloped land. Intensive development pressure created immediate growth-related problems, such as insufficient sewer capacity, roads, and schools. With growth came residents demanding services, which inevitably caused property taxes to increase each year.

With a government chartered under the council-manager form, Centerville's citizens alternately elected four at-large and five ward council members in nonpartisan elections every other May. The mayor, chosen by and from members of the council, was elected to serve a one-year term at the annual reorganization meeting held each July 1.

Taxes, development, and the legacy of Watergate provided fuel for a bitter and highly politicized at-large election in May 1975. TAC raised questions about virtually all activity in the municipal building. It also suggested that legitimate bills for consulting engineering services and legal advice were the reasons that property taxes were skyrocketing. TAC-supported candidates made allegations of conflict of interest involving both elected and appointed officials of the community. Republicans, holding a slim 5–4 majority on the council, jumped on the TAC bandwagon by endorsing both the actions and the candidates of TAC.

When the votes were counted, TAC candidates swept the four at-large seats, giving the Republicans an 8–1 majority on the annual reorganization day. After the new council members were sworn in, the city manager asked to be recognized. The next day's headlines read "City Manager Resigns: TAC Takes Control."

Despite Centerville's reputation as a politically explosive community, more than eighty applicants sought the city manager's position. In a move questioned by the press, the public, and city employees, the council hired a local resident with no prior governmental experience.

John Newman, the council's choice for city manager, had impressive credentials in private sector management. His weakness, as voiced by an unidentified city employee in the next day's paper, was his appointment by the TAC-dominated council. Terms such as "hatchet man" and "political hack" appeared in early press reports, always attributed to sources who wished to remain anonymous. In fact, Newman was a two-year resident of Centerville who had no political affiliation. His only contact with local officials was as a volunteer with Centerville's conservation commission.

Newman spent much of his time during his first few months meeting and talking with city employees, community leaders, and appointed officials of Centerville. The bitter election campaign had polarized the community and caused tremendous tension among staff members. Some employees actively supported the TAC candidates while others worked against them. One of Newman's tactics included meeting with small groups of employees to assure them that no one's job was in jeopardy for past political involvement. The caveat was that any future activity would result in appropriate disciplinary action.

During his first eighteen months in office, Newman succeeded in returning some sense of stability to the local government. TAC lost much of its punch once the "reformers" became the policy makers. Concerns over property taxes, corruption, and other perceived evils of government abated as the election approached for the five ward seats on the council.

The case

A few weeks before the candidate filing date for the next ward election, Sue Farwell, a longtime employee in Centerville's accounting department, requested an unpaid leave of absence to campaign for the ward seat on the council in the area in which she lived. Farwell had been an active supporter of the TAC candidates in the previous election, but she had abided by Newman's directive to avoid continued involvement in political activity. After consulting with the city attorney, Newman granted Farwell's request, which expired at her request on the day after the election.

On the second Tuesday in May, voters returned most of the Republicans to office; one ward council seat went Democratic, creating a 7–2 split. Included among the winners was Sue Farwell.

The morning after the election, Newman received a letter from Farwell.

Instead of offering the expected resignation, Farwell informed her soon-to-be subordinate that she was under a doctor's care for physical and mental exhaustion. The letter requested that she be placed on paid sick leave and was accompanied by a letter from her doctor attesting to her condition. The doctor suggested that she could be expected to return in four to six weeks. Farwell's role as a council member was to begin on July 1.

Newman again asked the city attorney for a written opinion on whether the city was required to grant this sick leave. The attorney advised that under the circumstances, Farwell's request could not be denied.

Five weeks later, two days before Farwell was sworn into office, Newman received a letter of resignation from Farwell as an employee so that she could assume her duties as a council member. Along with the letter was a doctor's certification that she was in good health.

With a check for six weeks of sick pay and a letter of best wishes from her former boss, Farwell began a four-year term as an elected member of the Centerville city council. During the first few months of her term, relations between the city manager and his former employee were cordial. In the winter, however, Newman began to detect possible violations of state law governing council-manager relations. A number of residents of Farwell's ward called city offices indicating that they had been promised services that Centerville could not legally provide. In the spring Newman found himself rejecting employment applicants who had been promised positions by Farwell. The manager also learned that Farwell had promised certain employees promotions or raises.

To stop these activities and to avoid public embarrassment of a council member, Newman asked the mayor and other members of the majority party to discuss the city manager's concerns privately with Farwell. But when Farwell's husband approached Newman and other members of Centerville's staff for campaign contributions, Newman realized that his efforts to solve the problem through informal means had been unsuccessful. With the next ward election still eighteen months away, Newman believed he had to take some action.

Newman wrote a personal and confidential letter to Farwell detailing his concerns over the incidents of the previous thirty months. He advised her that any future violation of the state laws governing council members' relations with local government employees and interference in personnel matters would be reported immediately to appropriate state officials.

The final year of Farwell's four-year term was marked by cool and sometimes hostile relations between Farwell and the city manager. Newman's Republican supporters tried to distance themselves from Farwell. As relations deteriorated among members of the governing body, Newman became the frequent target of Farwell's comments to the press. To counter her attacks, the Republican majority strongly backed the manager's performance.

When the Republicans met in January to pick candidates for the ward election in May, Farwell did not receive her party's endorsement. Undaunted by the rejection, she decided to run an independent campaign for her ward seat against a weak Republican and an unknown Democrat.

The election campaign was anything but nonpartisan although nonpartisan elections were required by law. The Democrats, who had gained another seat in the at-large election two years earlier, recognized the lack of unity in their Republican opponents. A Democratic victory in four of the five seats would mean control of the council for the first time in decades. The Republicans needed just two seats to continue control. Clearly, both sides desperately needed to win the ward seat occupied by Farwell.

In the May election, Farwell, running as an Independent, received 48 percent of the vote, the Democratic candidate received 28 percent, and the Republican candidate received 24 percent. State election law dictated that the successful candidate must have 50 percent plus one vote; therefore, a runoff election between Farwell and the Democratic challenger was scheduled for the second Tuesday in June.

In typical Centerville fashion, the May election created chaos for the political parties. Excluding Farwell's seat, each side had won four seats. The Democrats, out of power for years, needed only to pull an upset in the runoff election to become the majority party. The Republicans suddenly found themselves with four seats and no candidate for the runoff election. To retain majority control, the Republicans' only alternative was to support Farwell's candidacy in the June election, just four weeks away.

Given the 4–4 split between the parties, Farwell was in a strong negotiating position. Her terms for continued Republican control of the council were very simple. First, she was to be named mayor. Second, Newman, now in his sixth year as city manager, must be replaced. Should the Republicans not agree to her terms, Farwell would approach the four Democratic members with the same offer. The incumbent Republicans reluctantly agreed to Farwell's terms. The Democratic party put all of its support behind its own candidate.

As the four-week campaign for the remaining seat began, Newman was besieged by the press and the public for comment on the situation. Members of both parties were aware that Newman and Farwell had clashed on a number of issues, and in the first week of the campaign, leaders of the Democratic party demanded that Newman disclose all written memoranda, legal opinions, and personnel records that related to his problems with Farwell.

Newman realized that he was in a bind. To release any information or to comment publicly could easily be construed as partisan political activity because it would be damaging to Farwell. It would also be construed as self-interested, of course, since Newman's only hope of continued employment as city manager rested with a Democratic victory, given the deal struck by the Republicans and Farwell. Failure to release the information or to comment, however, could also be regarded as partisan activity— specifically, as an endorsement of Farwell's past actions, if not of her candidacy.

Looking for guidance and hoping to avoid professional suicide, Newman turned to the ICMA Code of Ethics, which hung prominently on his office wall, and at the guidelines for interpreting the code (see Appendix). Tenet 7 of the code clearly states, "Refrain from all political activities which undermine public confidence in professional administrators. Refrain from participation in the election of the members of the employing legislative body."

Yet tenet 3 required that Newman "be dedicated to the highest ideals of honor and integrity in all public and personal relationships in order that the member may merit the respect and confidence of the elected officials, of other officials and employees, and of the public." Respect, honor, and integrity seemed hollow words in such circumstances.

Tenet 4 affirmed that ICMA members must "recognize that the chief function of local government at all times is to serve the best interests of all the people."

Tenet 10 added another twist, particularly its guideline requiring the manager to "openly share information with the governing body." But what worried Newman the most was tenet 12, with its guideline on confidential information. It stated clearly that "members should not disclose to others, or use to further their personal interest, confidential information acquired by them in the course of their official duties."

The decision problem

Newman faced both a personal and a professional ethical crisis. Releasing the information on Farwell's past activities clearly would give the Democratic party a potent and perhaps valid campaign issue for the runoff election. The Republican members had agreed that should Farwell win, they would make her mayor and discharge Newman from his position.

In considering the code of ethics, Newman decided that from his perspective, the best interests of all of Centerville's residents—as well as his own interests—would probably best be served if Farwell were defeated. He believed that Farwell's conduct throughout her tenure as an elected official was consistently unethical, if not illegal.

The tenet on "honor and integrity" also seemed to support Newman's initial inclination. Did not honor and integrity demand that the city manager release facts about Farwell's unethical conduct? Would silence on the subject be construed as condoning unethical activity on the part of an elected official?

Still, Newman could not reconcile this position with the prohibition against participation in partisan politics. To release the information would be construed by the Republicans as partisan activity. However, not to release the information would also be construed by the Democrats as partisan activity since they would be deprived of a major campaign issue.

To complicate his dilemma further, Newman had an uneasy feeling that the material in question might fall into the category of "confidential information" that he had acquired in the course of his duties, and that to divulge it would certainly further his personal interests.

Weighing all of these considerations, what should Newman do?

Discussion questions

1. In most states, the city manager is required by law to enforce all municipal and state laws in the community. Did Newman violate his oath of office by not contacting law enforcement officers at the first hint of Farwell's unethical and perhaps illegal conduct?

2. Was Newman's response to the request for campaign contributions the most appropriate one? What else might he have done?

3. Newman's initial approach to solve the problem involved a private meeting with the mayor and Farwell's Republican colleagues. Should the two members of the minority party have been included? Why?

4. Were there other steps that Newman could have taken to deal with the Farwell situation prior to the election campaign?

5. Do you agree with Newman that failure to release the information would be construed by the Democrats as partisan?

6. Could Newman have solved his dilemma by seeing that the information was "leaked" to the press anonymously? Is this strategy practical? Is it ethical?

7. What is the best course of action for the manager in this case? Are there other ethically acceptable courses of action? If so, what are they?

21

Fire or be fired

John L. Pape

Editor's introduction

Public administrators typically must confront more complicated ethical dilemmas than their private sector counterparts because they must deal with all the ethical concerns confronting the private sector and, in addition, with the ethical expectations associated with what Woodrow Wilson called their "sacred trust," their obligation under democratic principles to be responsive to the interests, well-being, and preferences of the public at large.

This case demonstrates the level of complexity that can confront public administrators—in this case, a local government administrator. It describes an actual case in which several of the most severe kinds of ethical dilemmas occur simultaneously. At its root, it presents a challenge found in both private and public sectors and at all levels of organizational responsibility: what to do when your boss, in this case the city council, wants you to violate your personal ethical principles. That challenge is particularly severe when, as in this case, the action sought would not only violate the administrator's personal ethics, but his (the ICMA) professional code of ethics as well.

This case also demonstrates the clash between expediency and principle. In this case, the path of least resistance, and certainly the path to the outcome that is almost inevitable, is strewn with serious ethical problems. The manager's bosses—the city council—are demanding that the police chief be terminated despite the fact that there is no legitimate evidence that the chief has done anything to justify his dismissal. The expedient course of action would sacrifice the chief. The manager is left to ponder the extent to which he is ethically obligated to protect his innocent subordinate, keeping in mind the effect of his decision upon the life and well-being of that subordinate.

Either of these issues might afflict a decision maker in the private sector as well. But this case also demonstrates the added ethical complications involved in transacting the public's business. Josh Peters, the administrator in this case, must also deal with the ethical obligations imposed by the nation's system of constitutional democracy. He must measure the impact of his actions on his obligation to serve the best interests of the city's residents. He must consider both the consequences of his actions on his efforts to improve the quality of police services and the need to choose between responsiveness to a very vocal group of voters, on the one hand, and responsiveness to the general public interest, on the other hand.

Peters, the local government administrator, must decide, in short, how to apply the obligations imposed upon him by the tenets of democratic theory and Wilson's "sacred trust."

Case 21
Fire or be fired

Background

Adams, a southwestern city of approximately 17,000 people, has been afflicted with multiple, sometimes contradictory, forces of change. Economically, it has been feeling the effects of several years of economic downturn resulting from the decline of its once-prosperous oil industry. More recently, a local Native American tribe, in an effort to help improve the quality of life for its members, launched a number of new business ventures in the fields of health, transportation, and foreign trade. In an unrelated development, the city also recently became the home of a major new regional health center. The city has thus felt the effects of the serious decline of its major industry as well as the impact of a changing local economy.

As might be expected, these economic changes have been accompanied by changes in the city's politics. The five-member city council, once a relatively cohesive body, found itself increasingly divided as the "old guard" political structure struggled to retain its dominance over emerging political interests linked more closely to the city's new economic interests. Of particular significance, and certainly not unnoticed by the old guard, was the support for the new political forces coming from the city's Native American community.

As if these changes were not enough for the city's government, Adams's recent years of economic difficulty had left a backlog of escalating service needs, deteriorating infrastructure, and declining city services. Such problems are difficult to confront in the best of circumstances. Now, the difficulty of resolving them was exacerbated by political changes within the council. New and unfamiliar divisions among the city's elected leaders left the council unable to develop a clear direction or vision of how to address the community's rapidly increasing service needs. After less than three years on the job, Adams's most recent city manager had resigned out of frustration over the situation.

Moving quickly to recruit a new city manager, the city council named Josh Peters, a city manager from a neighboring state, to fill the post. Although the council vote to hire Peters was unanimous, it was readily apparent from the outset that Peters would have difficulty getting the council's unanimous support for any effort he might propose to address the city's problems.

On his first day on the job, Peters met individually with the department heads. In the meeting with Chief of Police William Maloney, Peters learned that Maloney was planning to retire within a few months. He was also informed that the local police union fully expected that the new chief would be appointed from among the ranks of the department, all of whom were union members. Former police chiefs in Adams had always been promoted from within the department. Hiring an outside chief had simply never been done, at least not in anyone's memory.

Although only 10 percent of the state's workforce was unionized, organized labor had traditionally exerted a great deal of influence on state and local elected officials. As in most of the state's cities, the police and fire departments in Adams were unionized while all other municipal employees were not. The police and fire unions had developed a strong relationship with the old guard council members, which was reflected in the fact that police officers and firefighters had been the only city employees granted a pay raise in recent years.

The new city manager had a strong background in law enforcement and had even served as a chief of police before moving into city management, yet the local police union hierarchy viewed his presence with concern. Peters had made it clear that he would align himself with neither political faction on the city council and would make independent decisions based on community needs. From the outset, he made it clear that Chief Maloney's successor would be recruited through a national search, with the best candidate being hired. Candidates from within the department would be evaluated by the same standard as all others. This move was immediately branded as an attempt at "union busting" by the union's leaders.

Four of the five council members privately commended Peters for his approach, but only the two who were members of the newly emerging faction on the council would publicly support him. The one council member who remained silent on the police chief issue was Mayor Bill Brown, a veteran council member. (Under the city charter, the mayor's position was not elected by the people but was filled each year for a one-year term by a vote of the council. By tradition, the largely ceremonial mayoral post was "rotated" among the council members.) Brown had been chief of the Adams fire department at the time of his retirement from the city. While an Adams firefighter, Brown had been an active member of the local firefighters' union, and he had continued to be a strong proponent of union-supported issues during his council tenure.

The case

With the retirement of Chief Maloney, the recruitment of a new chief began in earnest. Assistant Chief Fred McKenna, a veteran of more than twenty-five years with the Adams police department, was named as interim chief of police. McKenna had disavowed any interest in being appointed chief, but he had been willing to delay his own retirement to serve as interim chief.

Under the city charter, the city manager had exclusive authority over all personnel decisions and city council members were expressly prohibited from involving themselves in personnel issues. Although Peters frequently consulted with council members about the recruitment and selection process, keeping all members equally informed, he made it clear that he was committed to selecting the best-qualified applicant for the post, whether that be an internal or external applicant.

It was apparent to Peters, however, that it would be difficult for the three internal candidates who applied to be competitive in a field of well-qualified applicants. The combination of underfunded training budgets and an indifferent approach to personnel development under a succession of police chiefs had resulted in, at best, semiqualified internal candidates. Further complicating the process, but making Peters even more resolved to find the most qualified applicant, were his serious concerns about the professional standards of the Adams police department. In recent years, the department had been plagued by problems with missing evidence, shoddy investigative work, allegations of widespread abuse, and several highly questionable incidents involving the use of deadly force.

Applications were solicited nationwide through such resources as the International City/County Management Association (ICMA) and the International Association of Chiefs of Police. More than seventy applications were received. Ultimately, Peters selected six candidates, including all three of the internal candidates, as finalists for the post.

Prior to the recruitment process, Peters had indicated to the council his intention to use an assessment center, facilitated by a professional firm, to evaluate the finalists. Since the assessment center was an unbudgeted item, a supplemental appropriation by the council was needed to fund the effort. Informally, four of the council members indicated their support for the assessment center process; only Mayor Brown was noncommittal.

It was at this point that the union first covertly attempted to influence the selection process in an effort to ensure the selection of an internal candidate. When the appropriation was put on the council's agenda, the union solicited a number of citizens to appear at the council meeting to voice their opposition to an outside firm assessing the candidates' qualifications. Before the council meeting, union representatives privately approached old guard council members to register their objections. While they did not explicitly oppose the recruitment process itself, they strongly protested as wasteful the expenditure needed for the assessment center. The local newspaper, which had been traditionally aligned with the old guard political faction, also blasted the proposal. Although the supplemental appropriation was ultimately approved, the city council reduced the amount to a point well below the lowest quote obtained. Lacking sufficient funding, the assessment center approach had to be abandoned.

The city manager then personally undertook a rigorous review and assessment of each finalist's qualifications and record. After a month of interviews and diligent evaluations, Peters announced his selection: John Wilson, a veteran police commander who had retired from a large metropolitan police force and was currently serving as chief of police in a small city in a neighboring state. Having never served in a police department in which the officers were organized into a union, Wilson himself was not a member of the police union.

The public announcement was received enthusiastically by the newer members of the city council. The old guard council members, the police union, and the local newspaper greeted the announcement with a lukewarm, "wait-and-see" attitude. Mayor Brown did not publicly comment on the selection; he was the only council member who did not attend the public announcement.

Chief Wilson's first few months on the job were relatively quiet, with no significant reaction by the police union. Shortly thereafter, however, disturbing rumors about his personal behavior began to circulate through the community. The rumors were initially vague. It was said that Chief Wilson had a drinking problem. One version had him driving home in an intoxicated condition after an evening at a local private club. Another suggested that he had been forced to retire from the large metropolitan force after twenty-five years of service because of alcohol abuse. These rumors eventually reached Peters.

Peters dismissed the early rumors primarily because he had strong evidence to the contrary. Having personally checked Wilson's background, Peters knew that Wilson had no history of alcohol abuse and that his retirement had been strictly voluntary. He was also aware that Wilson was not a member of the private club where he allegedly was seen in an intoxicated condition. In fact, Peters had been with both Wilson and the fire chief at the time of the supposed indiscretion.

The gossip had also reached the ears of the council members, and Peters quickly reassured them that the allegations had no merit. The old guard members were unconvinced, but the newer members voiced a high degree of comfort that the rumors were, in fact, baseless.

Over the next few weeks, the rumors intensified to a point where Peters reevaluated his previous background review of Chief Wilson. He again found that Wilson's reputation was unblemished in his previous employments and that there was no evidence to support any of the allegations.

Shortly after completing the review, Peters received a visit from Mayor Brown. In a closed-door session, Brown demanded that Peters dismiss Chief Wilson in light of the rumors. Peters explained that his review did not substantiate any of the allegations and, in fact, suggested the contrary. Nevertheless, the mayor held firm to his demand.

Brown pointed out that Peters could dismiss the chief without cause since Wilson was still in his probationary period. Peters conceded that he could do that, but he argued that it would be unethical in his estimation to dismiss any employee based on unsubstantiated, anonymous gossip. To support his contention, Peters cited tenet 11 of the ICMA Code of Ethics, which states the matter very clearly:

Handle all matters of personnel on the basis of merit so that fairness and impartiality govern a member's decisions pertaining to appointments, pay adjustments, promotions, and discipline.

Peters explained that to dismiss Wilson as the mayor demanded would be clearly unethical, and that he, as city manager, would not violate his profession's code of ethics. Brown ended the meeting by heatedly informing the city manager that if he did not dismiss the police chief, it would cost both Peters and Wilson their jobs.

Not long after the meeting between Brown and Peters, the police union issued a press release announcing that it had taken a near-unanimous vote of "no confidence" in Wilson. Accompanying the announcement was a list of "substantiated" allegations of misconduct against the chief. Among them were that he purchased alcoholic beverages while driving a city vehicle, that he allowed his wife to drive a city vehicle, and that he was disrespectful to his officers. Also among the allegations were the previously debunked stories about Wilson's supposed intoxication.

The media, particularly the pro-union local newspaper, pounced on the story. Mayor Brown attempted to call an "emergency" council meeting to have the council formally investigate the allegations. Only after the city attorney informed him that the union's press release did not meet the legal requirements for an emergency meeting did Brown retract the call.

At the next regularly scheduled council meeting, Brown and another old guard council member placed an item on the agenda authorizing the city council to investigate the allegations. At that meeting, Peters read a prepared statement asserting that the allegations were a personnel matter and that, as city manager, he had the sole authority to handle personnel issues. He also called for the union, as well as any other party having any evidence of impropriety on the part of Chief Wilson, to provide the evidence to his office for investigation. Peters's firm stand clearly placed him in open opposition to both the old guard faction of the city council and the police union. Although he realized that this move would clearly damage his relationship with the old guard council members, Peters again turned to the ICMA Code of Ethics, tenet 10, for guidance:

Resist any encroachment on professional responsibilities, believing the member should be free to carry out official policies without interference, and handle each problem without discrimination on the basis of principle and justice.

After clearly stating that they wanted the city council, not the city manager, to investigate Chief Wilson, the police union grudgingly turned their "evidence" over to Peters. The evidence consisted of several pieces of videotape, a statement from a police officer's wife, and statements from union activists and leaders that Wilson did not treat his officers with "professional dignity."

The statements were, essentially, a list of grievances about Wilson's management style. Wilson was attempting to bring about a greater degree of professional discipline in such areas as the use of force, interaction with citizens, and internal professionalism. Examples of the complaints were that the chief had reprimanded the current union president for using vulgar language to a citizen and had implemented a more stringent system for reporting the use of force. Additionally, he had forced two investigators, both of whom were union leaders, to divest their financial interest in a topless bar in a neighboring jurisdiction. In Peters's estimation, none of the complaints was valid. In fact, Wilson was appropriately addressing problems within the department.

The statement from the officer's wife indicated that she witnessed Wilson's wife driving the chief's city vehicle. Upon investigation, it was determined that Wilson and his family were out of town at the time the alleged infraction occurred and that the city vehicle was parked at the police station during that time.

The videotapes proved equally inconclusive. One tape, obtained by union leaders from a convenience store, clearly showed Wilson purchasing a six-pack of beer along with other grocery items. However, it did not show the chief drinking the beer or operating a city vehicle. The other tape, obviously taken from the rear of another vehicle following Wilson's city car, did show Mrs. Wilson accompanying the chief. It was subsequently determined that the chief and his wife were en route to an official function at the time, and city policy allowed for a spouse or guest to accompany the chief under such circumstances.

In short, none of the "evidence" showed anything beyond the fact that Wilson was attempting to correct unprofessional activities among certain police officers, and that the disgruntled officers had responded by covertly obtaining or making videotapes of the chief in an effort to discredit him. The investigation, which the city attorney conducted independently at the direction of the city manager, did not sustain misconduct on the part of the chief of police. Using the same standard that would be applied to allegations lodged against any city employee, Peters ruled that no cause existed to discipline or remove Wilson.

In announcing his findings, Peters made it clear that he would not take action against Chief Wilson, or any city employee, without justifiable cause. The union, local newspaper, and old guard council members immediately branded the investigation a whitewash, and calls for the removal of both Peters and Wilson were made. Within a week, Mayor Brown scheduled an executive session to consider terminating Peters's contract.

After lengthy deliberations in which Peters was not allowed to be present, the city council convened in public session to vote on terminating his contract. The two old guard council members, including Mayor Brown, voted to terminate the contract while the two newer members voted to retain Peters; the fifth member abstained. Without a majority voting to dismiss him, Peters kept his job. Under charter provisions, the abstaining member, a long-tenured member who had developed a strong relationship with Peters, was not required to state publicly his reason for not voting.

Over the ensuing days, pressure from the police union and old guard council members intensified. The union publicly called on the entire council to reconsider their positions "for the good of the community." One council member who voted to support the city manager and chief of police was told that her business would be picketed and boycotted by the police union and its supporters. The other supportive council member was publicly cursed and threatened with political retaliation by a union officer. The confrontation, which occurred in the lobby of city hall, was recorded by a radio news reporter. Yet after the abusive threat was repeatedly aired on news reports, the union not only supported its officer's action, but openly reaffirmed the threat of political retaliation against the council member.

Throughout this period, the council member who had abstained from voting was the object of the most intense union pressure. From repeated threats of political reprisal to the warning that his son's legal practice would be boycotted, the abstaining member was receiving numerous calls and visits from union members and pro-union citizens demanding he change his position and vote to terminate the city manager's contract.

Clearly, the position of both the city manager and the chief of police had been severely eroded by the unrelenting and hostile activity of the police union. What had begun as a whispering campaign to discredit and remove Wilson had turned into controversy that clearly threatened to undermine two of Adams's highest-ranking city officials.

The decision problem

The decision problem that Peters faced in this matter hinged on two pivotal events. The first was when Mayor Brown demanded that he dismiss Chief Wilson without cause. The second was when Peters resisted Brown's attempt to usurp the city manager's authority over what was clearly a personnel matter under the Adams city charter.

Without question, Peters could have terminated Wilson's employment during Wilson's probationary period without cause or explanation, thus ending the controversy with only minimal damage to the city manager's position. However, Peters also knew that reform in the police department was an action item whose time had come. What he could not know for sure was whether yielding to the union on the removal of Wilson would buy him support for other changes in the future or whether this victory would only encourage the union to fight other needed reforms.

Then, too, when the mayor attempted to have the city council investigate the chief of police, Peters could have chosen to stand silent and allow the council to intrude on his personnel authority. Again, he could not be sure whether this course of action would have solidified his support on the council or only encouraged the old guard to attempt further encroachments on his authority.

In either case, Peters could have taken the path of least resistance and caved in to the political pressures being exerted on him. Had he not asserted his principles, he could have removed himself from jeopardy by sacrificing Wilson to the political influence of the police union. The temptation to follow this course was strong, especially since it was becoming increasingly clear that Wilson would be fired anyway; if Peters did not relent and fire him, Peters's successor as city manager surely would.

Peters believed, however, that to fire Wilson would clearly violate the professional code of ethics to which he, Peters, subscribed. Yet he also realized that adhering to strong professional principles and his professional code of ethics might well cost him his job. Even worse, with council members experiencing badly divisive pressures that would make it even harder for them to work as a unit in the future, and with Wilson certain to be fired in any event, there seemed to be no certain benefit for Peters to gain by "falling on his sword" and sacrificing his own job. Furthermore, getting himself fired would most likely mean the end of the effort to bring needed reform to the police department. In short, adherence to ethics in this case might not even be in the short-term best interest of the community.

As Peters reflected on his options, he could identify several possible courses of action. He could

1. Consent to the mayor's demand and fire Wilson. This would relieve the intense political pressure on the council, enable him to keep his job, and, in all likelihood, even gain him the council's support for his effort to professionalize and reform the police department. But to do this, he would have to violate his ethical code.
2. Permit the council, even now, to undertake the investigation. This would undermine his authority as manager, force him to violate his professional

code of ethics, and probably result in Wilson's dismissal for cause. The latter consequence would be most unfair to Wilson.

3. Call for an investigation of the chief by an independent outside agency, such as a state or federal law enforcement agency. The city attorney, however, advised him that this option was not open; such agencies could be asked to investigate matters only when a crime was alleged to occur and no such allegation had been made against Wilson.

4. Appeal the matter over the heads of the council and the union by going directly to the public. Given the newspaper's overt support of the union, however, this path appeared doomed to failure and it would, in any event, pose still more ethical problems. To go over the council's head would require that he act in a manner that could not be expected to "merit the respect and confidence of the elected officials" (tenet 3 of the code).

5. Hold firm to his present position, secure in his knowledge that he was abiding by his code of ethics despite firm evidence that such a path would result in the loss of his job, the dismissal of Chief Wilson, and, almost certainly, the failure of his efforts to professionalize the performance of the police department.

No matter which of the options he chose, the outcome would be a victory for the old guard and a discouraging defeat for the good government aspirations of the council's newer members. Peters had to decide what he was going to do.

Discussion questions

1. If you were in Peters's position, what factors would you have considered in deciding on your course of action? How would you weigh each one?
2. Would you have taken the same position as Peters? Why or why not?
3. Were the ethical grounds for Peters's decisions valid? Why or why not? Would Peters have been justified in dismissing the chief of police based on the allegations filed by the police union? What ramifications might such a decision have had on Peters's ability to manage the city?
4. Is adherence to a professional code of ethics important enough to sacrifice one's job? Why or why not?
5. Under what circumstances should ethical considerations be set aside in order to achieve the best outcome for the community?
6. Leaving aside the question of ethics, what course of action do you think would have brought about the best outcome for the city?

Appendix

ICMA Code of Ethics
with guidelines

1. Be dedicated to the concepts of effective and democratic local government by responsible elected officials and believe that professional general management is essential to the achievement of this objective.

2. Affirm the dignity and worth of the services rendered by government and maintain a constructive, creative, and practical attitude toward local government affairs and a deep sense of social responsibility as a trusted public servant.

Guideline
Advice to Officials of Other Local Governments. When members advise and respond to inquiries from elected or appointed officials of other municipalities, they should inform the administrators of those communities.

3. Be dedicated to the highest ideals of honor and integrity in all public and personal relationships in order that the member may merit the respect and confidence of the elected officials, of other officials and employees, and of the public.

Guidelines
Public Confidence. Members should conduct themselves so as to maintain public confidence in their profession, their local government, and in their performance of the public trust.

Impression of Influence. Members should conduct their official and personal affairs in such a manner as to give the clear impression that they cannot be improperly influenced in the performance of their official duties.

Appointment Commitment. Members who accept an appointment to a position should not fail to report for that position. This does not preclude the possibility of a member considering several offers or seeking several positions at the same time, but once a

bona fide offer of a position has been accepted, that commitment should be honored. Oral acceptance of an employment offer is considered binding unless the employer makes fundamental changes in terms of employment.

Credentials. An application for employment should be complete and accurate as to all pertinent details of education, experience, and personal history. Members should recognize that both omissions and inaccuracies must be avoided.

Professional Respect. Members seeking a management position should show professional respect for persons formerly holding the position or for others who might be applying for the same position. Professional respect does not preclude honest differences of opinion; it does preclude attacking a person's motives or integrity in order to be appointed to a position.

Confidentiality. Members should not discuss or divulge information with anyone about pending or completed ethics cases, except as specifically authorized by the Rules of Procedure for Enforcement of the Code of Ethics.

Seeking Employment. Members should not seek employment for a position having an incumbent administrator who has not resigned or been officially informed that his or her services are to be terminated.

4. Recognize that the chief function of local government at all times is to serve the best interests of all the people.

Guideline
Length of Service. A minimum of two years generally is considered necessary in order to render a professional service to the local government. A short tenure should be the exception rather than a recurring experience. However, under special circumstances, it may be in the best interests of the local government and the mem-

The Code of Ethics reproduced here were adopted by the membership in 1924 and most recently amended in May 1998. The guidelines were adopted by the ICMA Executive Board in 1972 and most recently revised in January 1998.

ber to separate in a shorter time. Examples of such circumstances would include refusal of the appointing authority to honor commitments concerning conditions of employment, a vote of no confidence in the member, or severe personal problems. It is the responsibility of an applicant for a position to ascertain conditions of employment. Inadequately determining terms of employment prior to arrival does not justify premature termination.

5. Submit policy proposals to elected officials; provide them with facts and advice on matters of policy as a basis for making decisions and setting community goals; and uphold and implement municipal policies adopted by elected officials.

Guideline
Conflicting Roles. Members who serve multiple roles—working as both city attorney and city manager for the same community, for example—should avoid participating in matters that create the appearance of a conflict of interest. They should disclose the potential conflict to the governing body so that other opinions may be solicited.

6. Recognize that elected representatives of the people are entitled to the credit for the establishment of municipal policies; responsibility for policy execution rests with the members.

7. Refrain from all political activities which undermine public confidence in professional administrators. Refrain from participation in the election of the members of the employing legislative body.

Guidelines
Elections of the Governing Body. Members should maintain a reputation for serving equally and impartially all members of the governing body of the local government they serve, regardless of party. To this end, they should not engage in active participation in the election campaign on behalf of or in opposition to candidates for the governing body.

Elections of Elected Executives. Members should not engage in the election campaign of any candidate for mayor or elected county executive.

Elections. Members share with their fellow citizens the right and responsibility to exercise their franchise and voice their opinion on public issues. However, in order not to impair their effectiveness on behalf of the local governments they serve, they should not participate in any political activities (including but not limited to fundraising, endorsing candidates, and financial contribu-

tions) for representatives to city, county, special district, school, state, and federal offices.

Elections on the Council-Manager Plan. Members may assist in preparing and presenting materials that explain the council-manager form of government to the public prior to an election on the use of the plan. If assistance is required by another community, members may respond. All activities regarding ballot issues should be conducted within local regulations and in a professional manner.

Presentation of Issues. Members may assist the governing body in presenting issues involved in referenda such as bond issues, annexations, and similar matters.

8. Make it a duty continually to improve the member's professional ability and to develop the competence of associates in the use of management techniques.

Guidelines
Self-Assessment. Each member should assess his or her professional skills and abilities on a periodic basis.

Professional Development. Each member should commit at least 40 hours per year to professional development activities that are based on the practices identified by the members of ICMA.

9. Keep the community informed on local government affairs; encourage communication between the citizens and all local government officers; emphasize friendly and courteous service to the public; and seek to improve the quality and image of public service.

10. Resist any encroachment on professional responsibilities, believing the member should be free to carry out official policies without interference, and handle each problem without discrimination on the basis of principle and justice.

Guideline
Information Sharing. The member should openly share information with the governing body while diligently carrying out the member's responsibilities as set forth in the charter or enabling legislation.

11. Handle all matters of personnel on the basis of merit so that fairness and impartiality govern a member's decisions pertaining to appointments, pay adjustments, promotions, and discipline.

Guideline
Equal Opportunity. Members should develop a positive program that will ensure

meaningful employment opportunities for all segments of the community. All programs, practices, and operations should: (1) provide equality of opportunity in employment for all persons; (2) prohibit discrimination because of race, color, religion, sex, national origin, political affiliation, physical handicaps, age, or marital status; and (3) promote continuing programs of affirmative action at every level within the organization.

It should be the member's personal and professional responsibility to actively recruit and hire minorities and women to serve on professional staffs throughout their organization.

12. Seek no favor; believe that personal aggrandizement or profit secured by confidential information or by misuse of public time is dishonest.

Guidelines
Gifts. Members should not directly or indirectly solicit any gift or accept or receive any gift—whether it be money, services, loan, travel, entertainment, hospitality, promise, or any other form—under the following circumstances: (1) it could reasonably be inferred or expected that the gift was intended to influence them in the performance of their official duties; or (2) the gift was intended to serve as a reward for any official action on their part.

It is important that the prohibition of unsolicited gifts be limited to circumstances related to improper influence. In de minimus situations such as tobacco and meal checks, for example, some modest maximum dollar value should be determined by the member as a guideline. The guideline is not intended to isolate members from normal social practices where gifts among friends, associates, and relatives are appropriate for certain occasions.

Investments in Conflict with Official Duties. Members should not invest or hold any investment, directly or indirectly, in any financial business, commercial, or other private transaction that creates a conflict with their official duties.

In the case of real estate, the potential use of confidential information and knowledge to further a member's personal interest requires special consideration. This guideline recognizes that members' official actions and decisions can be influenced if there is a conflict with personal investments. Purchases and sales which might be interpreted as speculation for quick profit ought to be avoided (see guideline on "Confidential Information").

Because personal investments may prejudice or may appear to influence official actions and decisions, members may, in concert with their governing body, provide for disclosure of such investments prior to accepting their position as local government administrator or prior to any official action by the governing body that may affect such investments.

Personal Relationships. Members should disclose any personal relationship to the governing body in any instance where there could be the appearance of a conflict of interest. For example, if the manager's spouse works for a developer doing business with the local government, that fact should be disclosed.

Confidential Information. Members should not disclose to others, or use to further their personal interest, confidential information acquired by them in the course of their official duties.

Private Employment. Members should not engage in, solicit, negotiate for, or promise to accept private employment, nor should they render services for private interests or conduct a private business when such employment, service, or business creates a conflict with or impairs the proper discharge of their official duties.

Teaching, lecturing, writing, or consulting are typical activities that may not involve conflict of interest or impair the proper discharge of their official duties. Prior notification of the governing body is appropriate in all cases of outside employment.

Representation. Members should not represent any outside interest before any agency, whether public or private, except with the authorization of or at the direction of the appointing authority they serve.

Endorsements. Members should not endorse commercial products or services by agreeing to use their photograph, endorsement, or quotation in paid or other commercial advertisements, whether or not for compensation. Members may, however, agree to the following, provided they do not receive any compensation: (1) books or other publications; (2) professional development or educational services provided by nonprofit membership organizations or recognized educational institutions; (3) products and/or services in which the local government has a direct economic interest.

Members' observations, opinions, and analyses of commercial products used or tested by their local governments are appropriate and useful to the profession when included as part of professional articles and reports.

List of contributors

James M. Banovetz (editor) directed graduate programs in public administration and local government management for thirty-four years. He is professor and director emeritus of the graduate program in public administration at Northern Illinois University and currently is a senior research fellow at the University's Center for Governmental Studies. An honorary member of ICMA since 1978, he also held the Arthur A. Levin chair in urban studies and public service at Cleveland State University from 1991 to 1993. He is an elected fellow of the National Academy of Public Administration, past president of Pi Alpha Alpha, editor of five books in the ICMA Green Books series, and author of the ICMA–NASPAA Guidelines on Local Government Management Education. The founder of the full-time secretariat for the Illinois City Management Association, he holds an M.A.P.A. and a Ph.D. from the University of Minnesota.

Bill R. Adams (Case 6) served as public information officer for a decade, beginning in 1986, with the city of Santee in San Diego County. Prior to that, he worked in news and information in the private sector, primarily covering local political scenes in Washington, D.C., and the San Diego region as a journalist and public affairs specialist. He currently teaches in the San Francisco Bay Area and is an Internet and publication consultant. He earned a bachelor of arts degree from the University of Maryland, College Park, where he studied political science and journalism.

Daniel A. Allen (Case 10) is currently the personnel director/assistant to the city manager of Rock Island, Illinois. He served as village administrator of Dwight, Illinois, from 1992 to 1995. Previously, he held positions with the villages of Palatine, Lake Zurich, and Oak Park, Illinois. He has a bachelor's degree in political science with a concentration in public administration from Augustana College in Rock Island, Illinois, and a master's degree in public administration from Northern Illinois University.

David N. Ammons (Case 15) is an associate professor of public administration at the University of North Carolina's Institute of Government in Chapel Hill. He previously served in various administrative capacities in four municipalities: Fort Worth, Texas; Hurst, Texas; Phoenix, Arizona; and Oak Ridge, Tennessee. His works include six books on local government—most recently, *Municipal Benchmarks: Assessing Local Performance and Establishing Community Standards* (Sage Publications, 1996). He earned his Ph.D. at the University of Oklahoma.

Ronald L. Ballard (Case 6) was, for fifteen years, city manager for Santee, a growing San Diego County municipality. In 1997, he retired as city manager after serving thirty years in local government management. Previously he held positions with several California cities, including that of assistant city manager for National City in San Diego County. He holds a master's degree in public administration from San Diego State University and a bachelor of arts degree from Bethany College, Santa Cruz.

William R. Bridgeo (Cases 1 and 8) is city manager of Augusta, Maine, having recently left his position as city manager of Canandaigua, New York, where he served since 1987. He has served as a local government administrator since 1976. He holds a bachelor's degree in political science from St. Michael's College in Vermont and a master's degree in public administration from the University of Hartford. Bridgeo is the immediate past president of the Municipal Management Association of New York State and a member of the Board of Regents of the ICMA University.

Jacqueline Byrd (Case 7) is president of the Richard Byrd Company, a Minneapolis-based organization serving clients both nationally and internationally. She is currently chair of the Board of Family Services, Inc., and a member of the National Association of Women Business Owners, the Minneapolis Chamber of Commerce, and the Organization Development Network.

Kathryn G. Denhardt (Case 16) is currently a member of the faculty of the School of Urban Affairs and Public Policy at the University of Delaware. She has been doing research and consulting related to outsourcing, competitive contracting, privatization, and governmental downsizing for almost ten years, primarily focusing on the experiences of the United States, Canada, and Australia. Her areas of expertise include the analysis and mitigation of labor and employment issues, cost-benefit analysis of outsourcing decisions, management of public private contractual relationships, and the development of "partnering" approaches. She received her Ph.D. from the University of Kansas and has since worked in the area of public management at several universities. Other research interests include conflict resolution, public participation, and community building. Her work involves the intentional integration of teaching, research, and practice in working directly with governments and communities to understand and solve emerging problems.

John Doe (Cases 5 and 13) is a pseudonym for authors who wish to remain anonymous.

Barry M. Feldman (Case 3) is town manager of West Hartford, Connecticut, having served there since 1985. Prior to that, he served as city manager in Sterling Heights, Michigan; Portsmouth, Ohio; and Lincoln Heights, Ohio. He holds a master's degree in public administration from Pennsylvania State University and is currently completing work on a Ph.D. from the University of Connecticut.

John J. Gargan ("The Case Approach" in the Supplement) is professor of political science at Kent State University in Kent, Ohio. He holds a Ph.D. in political science from Syracuse University, and his major research interests are management capacity building in city government and strategic management.

Harry G. Gerken (Case 20) is executive director of the Southeast Morris County Municipal Utilities Authority. He has also served as city manager in two communities. Educated at Rutgers University, he received a National Endowment for the Humanities Fellowship in 1980 to attend the University of Kansas. Gerken has written a number of articles for local newspapers on local government issues and ethical prob-

lems confronting public officials. He has also taught courses on contemporary ethical problems.

James K. Hartmann (Case 16) is the county administrator for Eagle County, Colorado. He earned his bachelor's and master's degrees in public administration from the University of Central Florida, where he subsequently served as an adjunct instructor in the M.P.A. program. He previously held the positions of assistant to the county administrator and then administrative support division director for Orange County, Florida.

Mary Jane Kuffner Hirt (Case 18) is an assistant professor in the Department of Political Science at Indiana University of Pennsylvania, where she teaches graduate and undergraduate courses in state and local political systems, metropolitan problems, leadership and public accountability, issues in public personnel management, research methods, and public sector financial management, and is coordinator of the department's internship program. Previously, she served as the manager of O'Hara and Forest Hills in Pennsylvania. For the last eight years, she has coordinated a midwinter professional development conference for Pennsylvania municipal managers and administration. She has a master's degree in public administration and a Ph.D. from the University of Pittsburgh's Graduate School of Public and International Affairs.

Kay W. James (Case 8) has been director of development and planning for Canandaigua, New York, since 1986. She has a bachelor of science from Cornell University and a master of public administration degree from the State University of New York College at Brockport.

Mary Theresa Karcz (Case 7) is a senior policy analyst with Ramsey County, Minnesota. She has a master's degree in economics from Syracuse University, with concentrations in public economy and urban and regional economics. Her bachelor's degree in economics is from the University of Illinois in Springfield. She has taught at the University of Wisconsin–Eau Claire, University of Wisconsin–Stout, and Onondaga Community College. She has also been a consultant on several federal training and education-related projects.

M. Lyle Lacy III (Case 15) is town manager of Front Royal, Virginia. He received a bachelor of science degree from Hampden-Sydney College in Virginia and a master of public administration degree from Texas Christian University. During a twenty-five-year career in local government, he has also served as city manager in Alliance, Nebraska; Marietta, Georgia; and Oak Ridge, Tennessee.

Scott D. Lazenby (Case 11) is city manager for the City of Sandy, Oregon. He received his bachelor's degree in physics from Reed College and his master's degree in public management and policy from Carnegie Mellon University. He was previously director of management and budget for the City of Glendale, Arizona, and assistant to the city manager of Vancouver, Washington. He has also taught graduate-level public administration courses.

Jack Manahan (Case 12) is county administrator of Peoria County, Illinois. From 1989 to 1994, he was village manager of Park Forest, Illinois, a Chicago-area suburb. For six years before that, he worked for Johnson County, Kansas, first as assistant director of finance and later as the county's first director of management and budget. He has been a trainer at the Government Finance Officers Association training workshops in governmental budgeting and has taught local government financial management at the college and graduate school levels. He is a former chair of ICMA's Academic Affairs Task Force, and he is on the executive committee of the National Advisory Council on State and Local Budgeting. Manahan holds a bachelor of science degree in education and a master's degree in public administration from the University of Kansas.

Kevin C. McGonegal (Case 9) is a vice president of the Bellevue Realty Company in Wilmington, Delaware. From 1974 to 1987, he was employed by the city of Wilmington in the personnel department and the mayor's office. Positions held included the director of employment and training, deputy budget director, chief labor negotiator, director of the Office of Management and Budget, and chief administrative officer. A graduate of Fairfield University, McGonegal is an instructor for the School of Urban Affairs and Public Policy of the University of Delaware and president of the New Castle County Commercial-Industrial Realty Council.

Tom Mills (Case 19) has been director of executive education at the Fels Center of Government, University of Pennsylvania. A former city official in Philadelphia for twenty-two years, he served the city as deputy managing director, chief deputy court administrator, and first deputy finance director. Mills has also been professor of public administration at Fairleigh Dickinson University (Rutherford campus), a faculty member at Trenton State College and Rider College, and an adjunct professor at Temple University. He is currently a member of the Philadelphia Board of Education. He holds a bachelor of science degree from the Wharton School, a master of business administration from Drexel University, and a master's degree and Ph.D. from the University of Pennsylvania.

John L. Pape (Case 21) is city manager for Bellaire, Texas, and has more than twenty years of municipal government experience. He previously served as city manager of Ada, Oklahoma, and Sonora, Texas. He also served the city of Weslaco, Texas, in several capacities, including assistant city manager, director of economic development, and chief of police. A graduate of the University of Alabama and of the FBI National Academy, Pape is also a certified local government manager. In 1996, he received the Award for Skill in Intergovernmental Relations from ICMA. He has also held numerous leadership and committee positions in ICMA, the National League of Cities, the Texas Municipal League, and the Texas City Management Association. He has authored one book, *Hill Country Chronicles*, as well as numerous articles appearing in such publications as *Texas Town and City* and the *FBI Law Enforcement Bulletin*.

Joe P. Pisciotte (Case 4) is professor of public administration in the Hugo Wall School of Urban and Public Affairs at Wichita State University. From 1993 to 1996, he served as the school's first director. He has also served as director of the Center for Urban Studies at Wichita State University and as professor of government at the University of Illinois, Urbana. While in Illinois, he served as executive director of the Illinois Constitutional Convention, which produced the constitution under which Illinois now operates, and in the governor's cabinet as director of the Illinois Department of Business and Economic Development. He received his Ph.D. from the University of Colorado, Boulder.

Paul M. Plaisted (Case 1), founder and president of Justice Planning and Management Associates, a management consulting and training firm, has spent most of the last twenty years involved in the field of criminal justice. He has served as a line police officer, criminal investigator, police chief, police management consultant, state grants office coordinator, director of a statewide drug enforcement unit, and assistant to the commissioner of the Maine Department of Public Safety. He holds a bachelor's degree in public administration and a master's degree from the Yale School of Management. During his career, he has served on numerous criminal justice boards, commissions, and study committees, and he is currently a member of several professional associations, including the Police Executive Research Forum. Plaisted served as total quality management coordinator for the Maine Department of Public Safety and as a member of the department's Quality Management Council. He is a nationally recognized authority on planning, implementing, and evaluating federal grant-funded programs. He also has extensive experience managing technology-related projects within the public safety arena.

Jeffrey A. Raffel (Case 9) is a professor and director of the School of Urban Affairs and Public Policy at the University of Delaware and former director of the school's M.P.A. program. In 1978 he served as special assistant for intergovernmental relations to Delaware governor Peter DuPoint. He received his bachelor of arts degree in political science from the University of Rochester and his Ph.D. in political science from the Massachusetts Institute of Technology.

Keith A. Schildt (Case 2), the first village administrator of Genoa, Illinois, is now a research associate at Northern Illinois University's Center for Governmental Studies. He is also an instructor in the M.P.A. program at Northern Illinois University and in the university's College of Business. He has provided consulting assistance to numerous public and private sector organizations, concentrating in risk management, safety, and loss control issues. In addition, he previously held various administrative positions in municipal government.

Terry Schutten (Case 7) is county manager for Ramsey County, Minnesota, a position he has held since March 1996. He has been executive director of a major metropolitan county for twelve years. Previous positions include eight years as county administrator for Lehigh County, Pennsylvania; four years as project manager for the National Association of Counties in Washington, D.C.; and two years as executive director of the Central Arizona Association of Governments. He graduated from California State University at San Jose with a

bachelor's degree in social sciences and from the University of Arizona in Tucson with a master's degree in public administration.

Steven A. Sherlock (Case 7) left local government in 1990 to work in both nonprofit and for-profit international work. He is currently president of a nonprofit humanitarian aid organization and a for-profit business development corporation, both of which are working in Southeast Asia.

Glen W. Sparrow (Case 6) is a professor at the School of Public Administration and Urban Studies, San Diego State University. His areas of specialization include state and local management and intergovernmental relations. He has been executive director of the Sacramento and San Francisco Charter Commissions and director of a Comprehensive Employment and Training Act prime sponsor. In addition to teaching, he has provided consulting assistance to cities and counties in California, especially in the areas of incorporation, fiscal impact, and public-private partnerships. In the past decade, he has lectured and consulted at universities in Hong Kong, Canada, Mexico, and Hungary.

Samuel E. Tapson Jr. (Case 17) has served as city administrator for Portage, Wisconsin, since mid 1995. Previously he served as city administrator for Morrison, Illinois, from 1984 to 1995, and for El Paso, Illinois, from 1981 to 1984. Additionally, he served in an administrative staff position with the Des Plaines, Illinois, from 1976 to 1981. He holds a master's degree in public affairs from Northern Illinois University and a bachelor of science degree in psychology from Western Illinois University.

Mary Timney (Case 14) is professor and chair of the Department of Public Administration at California State University in Hayward. She teaches courses in budgeting, administrative ethics, and public administration theory. Prior to completing her Ph.D. at the University of Pittsburgh, she worked in the private sector, was executive director of a nonprofit environmental organization, and worked as a research analyst for a large city government. Her current research focuses on citizen participation and environmental justice.

Susan Von Mosch (Case 7) is a program evaluation specialist for the Minnesota Office of the Legislative Auditor. She previously worked for the Ramsey County Policy and Planning Division. She holds a bachelor's degree in history and political science from the University of Minnesota–Morris and a master's degree in public policy from the University of Minnesota's Humphrey Institute. She has worked as a policy analyst and researcher for several state and local agencies.

Jon A. Walsh (Case 7) is a senior policy analyst with the Ramsey County Public Works Department. He holds a master of arts degree in public administration from Hamline University.

Municipal Management Series

**Managing Local Government:
Cases in Decision Making
Second Edition**

Text type
Times Roman, Trump Mediaeval, Helvetica

Composition
EPS Group, Inc.
Easton, Maryland

Printing and binding
Victor Graphics, Inc.
Baltimore, Maryland